Renewing

the

Dream

Renewing

The Mobility Revolution and the Future of Los Angeles

RIZZOLI Electa

the

Produced in association with Woods Bagot

Edited by James Sanders

Dream

Contents ——————— 1 ———

2 ———————— **3** ——————————————————————

Rendering of The Twist, a proposed interdisciplinary art and placemaking project on Sunset Boulevard, prepared by Woods Bagot's Los Angeles Studio in 2020 in response to a call for ideas from the City of West Hollywood. Located on the site of an existing parking lot, the project offers at a twenty-first-century digital interpretation of the celebrated billboard landscape of the Sunset Strip.

In early 2018, Woods Bagot—the global architecture studio for which I am honored to serve as chief executive officer—began producing a series of programs and studies on the cultural heritage and urban future of Los Angeles, with a special focus on the relationship of mobility, parking, land use, and development. Over the following years, working in association with distinguished cultural and civic partners across Southern California—CoMotion LA, the Los Angeles Chapter of the American Institute of Architects, the Academy of Motion Picture Arts and Sciences, SCI-Arc, the Los Angeles Cleantech Incubator, and the office of the chief design officer of Los Angeles—Woods Bagot and its experience consultancy, ERA-co, held a series of public events and conferences, took part in invited competitions, and produced its own in-depth research efforts and design provocations, many of them exploring the past, present, and future of Los Angeles through the lens of urban mobility.

Recognizing the long-term value of these efforts and seeking to widen and diversify their audience, Woods Bagot has been excited to collaborate with Rizzoli to expand and assemble its studies—along with guest contributions by noted observers and scholars of LA's urban landscape—into this illustrated volume, *Renewing the Dream: The Mobility Revolution and the Future of Los Angeles.* Edited by James Sanders, FAIA—the architect, filmmaker, and author who since 2016 has served as W-B's global design council chair—and produced in large part by the studio's teams in Los Angeles, the W-B and ERA-co research studies and design projects in this book exemplify both the capabilities and skills of our studios as well as our deep commitment to the remarkable city that Woods Bagot is now proud to consider a home.

Founded more than 150 years ago in Australia, Woods Bagot has grown over the decades into an international practice in architecture, design, research, urban systems, data analytics, and strategic consulting. Operating from seventeen studios around the world—in cities across North America, Europe, Asia, Australia, and the Middle East—it has become a recognized leader in more than a dozen sectors, from education and science to transportation and hospitality, from workplace architecture and interiors to retail and mixed-use projects. In recent years, its design projects have helped to define skylines and streetscapes from London to Sydney, from New York to Hong Kong, from San Francisco to Singapore, from Seattle to Dubai. Operating seamlessly across six regions and thus bringing both global and local expertise to its projects, the studio looks not to impose a single, signature style on its design work but instead offers an empathy-driven approach, seeking to build upon the human values of its clients and end users—an approach it calls "people architecture."

In recent years, one of Woods Bagot's fastest-growing sectors has been *cities and places*, recognizing that the studio's larger undertakings often have city-shaping impact, but also that a broad, interdisciplinary understanding of the complex landscape of cities is crucial to the creation of successful urban projects—those which not only satisfy their sponsors and end users but contribute to the appeal and well-being of the larger communities in which they sit.

*Perspective view of the Midfield Satellite Concourse
South at Los Angeles International Airport's Tom Bradley
International Terminal. Designed by Woods Bagot, the
two-story, $1.7 billion structure contains eight gates serving
narrow-body aircraft, replacing an existing regional jet
terminal. Its steel, masonry, and glass exterior features a
series of aluminum "brise-soleil" sunshades, which reduce
solar heat gain in the terminal's interior and serve to screen
views of an adjacent large cargo hangar.*

In this focus on urban opportunities, the core strengths of Woods Bagot's design studios have been reinforced by the wide-ranging capacities and resources of its associated experience consultancy, ERA-co, founded in 2017 and now operating globally from studios in London, New York, and Sydney. While ERA-co's disciplines stretch from user strategy to management consulting to brand experience, one of its most significant areas of expertise is *urban strategy and planning*, to which it brings powerful and innovative tools of data-driven collection, analysis and interpretation. These cutting-edge capabilities have proved critical to the studies that lie at the heart of this book.

In 2017, Woods Bagot made the decision to expand its North American presence—which already included major studios in New York and San Francisco—to the second largest metropolitan region in the United States: Los Angeles. The decision emerged not only from a recognition of the extraordinary opportunities offered by Southern California as an urban market (at $1.6 trillion, its economy would rank independently as thirteenth largest in the world—just shy of the entire continent of Australia), but from the city's status as one of the liveliest and most exciting places on the globe—one whose rich and influential history over the twentieth century has become the springboard for an astonishingly energetic and innovative cultural scene in the first decades of the twenty-first century.

From our studios in the Bradbury Building—itself one of the city's great filmic and architectural landmarks and a keystone of its downtown revitalization—Woods Bagot and ERA-co have been thrilled to participate actively in Los Angeles' diverse and vibrant landscape, through their built commissions and client consultancies as well as through sustained engagement with the city's urban and architectural culture. We are equally thrilled to mark that engagement with this book—whose insight and depth of research represent, we feel, a significant contribution to the ferment of thinking about the intersection of transportation, technology, and urbanism that is stirring in today's Los Angeles—even while advancing the forward edge of that thinking toward the challenges and opportunities of the years to come. Because of the crucial role that Los Angeles has played for nearly a century as a pioneer of influential ways of living in and moving around a city, we believe the work represented in this book will not only strengthen our roots in this extraordinary part of the world, but have resonance all around the globe, helping to reshape the way we envision the future of cities as a whole.

We look forward to further contributing our resources and skills toward enhancing the present and imagining the future of Los Angeles—and cities everywhere.

Top: *A view in 2016 of Interstate 10, one of the 37 limited-access freeways, comprising 650 miles, that serve greater Los Angeles.* Bottom: *An aerial view, taken on January 1, 1957, showing ranks of newly built tract houses in Los Angeles.*

Introduction

The founding idea of this place is infinitude—mile after endless mile of cute houses connected by freeways.... Our whole way of life is built on a series of myths—the myth of endless space, endless fuel, endless water, endless optimism, endless outward reach, and endless free parking.

FARHAD MANJOO, 2019

They still arrive in Los Angeles every day, just as they've done every day for well over a century now: people hoping to make or remake something of themselves. Maybe they're aspiring actors or musicians.... Maybe they're immigrants from El Salvador or Mexico or Korea or Russia or Israel....Maybe they're just Americans who came from other less exciting, less sunny places....But from now on, they'll be coming to a different city. The capital of starting over is starting over.

JEFF TURRENTINE, 2015

LA 3.0

Renewing the Dream is an exploration in words, data, and images of one of the world's most dynamic and influential cities—and a place in the midst of momentous change. That city is Los Angeles, America's second-largest metropolis, whose epic interplay of movement and place over the past century has not only given rise to its own celebrated landscape, but, along the way, reshaped much of the modern world.

In the years after World War II, of course, it was Los Angeles that pioneered a revolutionary new model of urban growth, one that soon swept across the globe to dominate the shape of cities in the second half of the twentieth century: a decentralized, autocentric world of cars, freeways, tract houses, shopping malls, and unlimited parking.

In Southern California itself, this dispersed, low-density way of life grew into something far more resonant than a mere pattern of development: it took on near-mythic status as a crucial wellspring and framework of the "California dream": a powerfully seductive vision built upon an individual family's ability to pursue its destiny within a private suburban homestead, complete with two-car garage, front and backyard, and, often enough, a swimming pool, even while remaining conveniently linked to the rest of modern society—for jobs, school, shopping, entertainment—by way of a miniature, rolling version of its private domain, the family car.

Before the war, other cities in America had built suburbs, usually linked to a dense urban core by rail lines—but it was in Los Angeles, in this postwar era, that the city first *became* a suburb, linked not by rail to a central core but by an immense network of

Top: *Freeway traffic jam, 2008. Consistently ranked as one of the three or four most congested cities in America, Los Angeles offers little room to add new roadways to what is already, by far, the most extensive highway network in the United States. Though major strides have been made over the past half-century in reducing tailpipe emissions— advances pioneered largely by California—traffic-choked freeways filled with gas-powered cars still pose a toxic threat to hundreds of thousands of nearby residents.* Bottom: *Terrifyingly visible to drivers along Interstate 405, the Getty Fire in November 2019 burned for nine days and destroyed 745 acres of northwestern Los Angeles, mostly in the high-income Brentwood area.*

limited-access roadways unlike any seen before, spread evenly across a diffuse landscape of single-family homes and shopping centers—which were themselves oriented almost exclusively to the car.

For half a century, the imaginative allure and relative affordability of this vision brought millions of people—from across the country and then around the world—pouring into Southern California, pushing its expansion across hundreds of square miles of once-agricultural hinterland, and driving up its population until the region had become the second largest in America, after New York.

Of course, as critics noted, LA's seductive place in the imagination could only be sustained by decades of massive and sometimes brutal real-world policies: the clearance of dozens of existing working-class communities (typically for construction of freeways that were themselves disruptive and environmentally damaging), commercial tract development aided by low-cost government-assisted mortgage financing, enormous publicly funded water and utilities systems, and highly restrictive zoning and parking requirements, all of which ensured the untrammeled growth of Southern California's distinctive low-density, car-oriented way of life.

> [Over half a century, Los Angeles'] automotive monoculture spread around the world, from...Caracas to Moscow and, more recently, Beijing and New Delhi. The car reshaped the surface of the planet and poisoned the air above. While the automobile isn't going away, it is losing its primacy. Over the next decade, many of us will find new ways to move.
>
> JOHN ROSSANT AND STEPHEN BAKER, 2019

Since the start of the twenty-first century, however, a new era has begun for this vast, protean metropolis. In ways obvious and not, a new Los Angeles is in the making— a city that might be called *LA 3.0*, to apply the familiar tech locution to the overarching concept of a "third Los Angeles" advanced in 2016 by the architecture critic (and soon-to-be-appointed city chief design officer) Christopher Hawthorne. It is a city that has evolved from the streetcar and boulevard paradigm that defined the pre-World War II era—LA 1.0—but evolved, too, from LA 2.0: the ubiquitous freeway and tract-house landscape of the mid- and late twentieth century. Having largely created the postwar model that still dominates much of the planet, Los Angeles is now pioneering a new, more complex, but potentially no less influential prototype for the future—a more complex, denser, and more diverse kind of place.

As that happens, meanwhile, the postwar "dream" Southern California incubated and promoted for so long is being challenged profoundly, by forces converging from two directions.

On the one hand, the cost of the "dream" has, for many, simply grown too high. As thirteen million people pursue their individual destinies in a single urban region, the collective impact of their sprawling, low-density way of life—still mostly dependent on the automobile—has brought on one grim crisis after another. Ever-growing traffic congestion on freeways—once an annoyance or a punch line—has in the past decade reached a kind of breaking point, strangling day-to-day life across much of the city. The ferocious devotion to single-family homes in many quarters, meanwhile, and the steadfast refusal to consider any kind of denser development, has aggravated the city's appalling deficiency in housing—one that grows worse with every year, and has contributed to the stunning rise in homelessness that is at once a profound civic embarrassment and a heartbreaking human tragedy.

Street scene in Downtown Los Angeles, whose nightlife resurgence over the past decade has been fueled by the widespread adoption of ride-hailing services such as Uber and Lyft. A "growing contingent of urbanites," observed Melena Ryzik in the New York Times in 2014, "have made Ubering...an indispensable part of their day and especially their night life. Untethered from their vehicles, Angelenos are suddenly free to drink, party and walk places. Even as their business models are evolving, these ride-sharing services...have upended the social habits of the area, and rallied its residents to be more peripatetic."

The terrifying wildfires of recent years—fueled by exburban sprawl pushing out into once-remote edges of the region—have brought an almost apocalyptic tinge to a reality that can no longer be ignored or denied: that the model of low-density, suburban-style, freeway-based development—the very way of life Southern California introduced to the world—is increasingly unsustainable in an era of accelerating climate change. "With seemingly the entire state on high alert, literally waiting to see which way the wind would blow," wrote the dispirited California-based columnist Farhad Manjoo as wildfires ripped through large stretches of northern Los Angeles in November 2019, "the idea of the California Dream felt utterly exhausted, ironic, sayable only between air quotes."

From an entirely different direction, meanwhile, has come the other force propelling change: the restless advance of technology, supercharged by leaps in digital innovation and harnessed to transportation as never before, which is transforming LA almost year by year. "In the twenty-first century, Los Angeles has become the epicenter of a mobility revolution that is making, unmaking, and remaking the way we all live and move," the author Greg Lindsay notes in these pages. "The changes can be felt everywhere: in streets and sidewalks, in parking lots and gas stations, above your head and beneath your feet."

> *Arguably, the smartphone is the most fundamental transportation technology of the 21st century.*
>
> HENRY GRABAR, 2019

The tech-enabled mobility revolution has been brewing for years, but the widespread adoption of smartphones—and their geolocation-based apps—has accelerated it with astonishing speed. "No one had an inkling," the transportation expert Samuel Schwartz observes, "that people would change their travel habits so quickly and dramatically. We also have never seen such a rapid change in transportation in our lifetimes."

With startling speed, Uber, Lyft, Revel, and a host of similar ride-hailing and ride-sharing services have been spearheading the shift in the way people move around town. Increasing numbers of younger Angelenos now rely almost exclusively on ride-hailing, as do many adolescents and elderly people, formerly restricted in their ability to travel independently around car-based Los Angeles. The advent of ride-hailing has already transformed the city's nightlife, and is now doing the same to its tourist industry (in recent years the once-jammed car-rental halls at LAX have sometimes grown eerily quiet, as visitors regularly choose the convenience of ride-hailing over a hired automobile).

> *Gadgets in hand, young people are using their electronic powers to reorganize the entire automotive system around their own needs and desires, on their own terms. And who can blame the taste of a new generation? When you discover that hiring a taxi is as easy as ordering a pizza or finding a date, why bother with the hassle of cars? For teens, a car is something to be summoned with a few swipes. The endless search for parking, monthly loan payments, and smelly gas pumps? Leave that to someone else.*
>
> ANTHONY TOWNSEND, 2020

And it's not just Uber and Lyft. Across much of the city, fleets of rented electric scooters now zip tens of thousands of people around the streets (and sometimes sidewalks), while increasing numbers other rely on rented e-bikes, especially those with electric-assist,

LA Metro's new Expo Line at La Cienega, adjacent to the twelve-hundred-unit Cumulus mixed-use development, under construction.

to make the shorter journeys—a few miles or less—that are, in fact, the most common kinds of trips that city dwellers make.

> [D]espite the fervor for things that fly and drive themselves, the transportation ideas currently generating the most excitement are modern twists on old ways of getting around. Electric bikes. Electric scooters. Shared rides. Shared cars. The future of transportation as we experience it—the important and pragmatic challenges that affect our daily lives—could end up looking a lot more like the past.
>
> ALISON GRISWOLD, 2019

Crossing overhead, traveling underground, and running alongside the roads, meanwhile, can be seen another key element of the region's changing mobility: the LA Metro, which is currently expanding its rail network more dramatically than any American city of the last seventy years, including New York. Though skeptics point to annual ridership totals that to date have been—to put it mildly—less than hoped for, and the system (like its counterparts in every city) suffered a serious setback during the Covid-19 pandemic, the transformative impact of the Metro on the densification of the city remains enormous—and will only grow as the system continues its expansion towards the year 2028, when Los Angeles, for the third time in history, will host the Olympic Games.

Hovering over all these other developments, of course, is the largest potential shift of all: the advent of self-driving cars. Though fully autonomous vehicles (AVs) might well represent "the single-most transformative societal change in decades," in the words of transportation expert Mark Rosekind, a cloud of uncertainty continues to shroud everything about their arrival, starting with the date they might be expected to appear—or whether they will ever appear at all. "For a good decade now," the *New York Times* reporter Cade Metz observed in 2022, "a number of companies have been promising that, in just a few years, driverless cars...will hit city streets. Those few years, it seems, are always a few more years."

No less uncertain is the impact that the widespread adoption of self-driving cars would have on the urban landscape, with at least two possible—and wildly different—outcomes sketched in 2019 by the author and critic Anthony Townsend:

> Let's call [one] version of the driverless future self-driving suburbs. This is a vision where we all wake up with an autonomous electric vehicle parked in the garage of our solar-powered, suburban home. It offers us convenient, consumer friendly mobility choreographed by computer. This is the future peddled in one shape or another by Tesla, Google, and GM. Self-driving suburbs are the twentieth century, turbocharged....
>
> The other school of thought shifts our focus from the periphery to the center. Let's call this vision car-lite communes. This is the preferred future of many mayors, architects, and activists. A growing number of companies are buying in, too, mostly those who think the big money in the self-driving revolution will be made selling services like ride-for-hire and delivery instead of vehicles. This strategy is all about exploiting AVs to pack people more closely together instead of spreading them apart—and in so doing, turning cities into green machines that are safe, affordable and healthy for all.

Top: *A visualization of a roadway filled with autonomous vehicles, whose "occupancy zone" LIDAR sensors and onboard computers control the speed and movement of cars and trucks to keep them safely separated from all moving and stationary obstacles.* Bottom: *A visualization of an autonomous rideshare vehicle, summoned by smartphone app.*

Even as all these developments proceed apace, of course, it is worth recalling, as Greg Lindsay writes, that more than six million vehicles fill the streets and roads of today's Southern California. Those vehicles, he notes, have an average life of eleven years, so the private car is going to remain a major presence—if not *the* major presence—in the life of the region for decades to come. But as Lindsay also points out, "the goal of the mobility revolution now underway in Los Angeles is not to eliminate the private automobile":

> *It is to offer a host of alternatives that better suit the variety of trips people make, to better accommodate different populations in the city, to help to usher in a more environmentally responsible and energy-efficient way of life, and, if all goes well, to put a dent in the traffic congestion that in recent decades has slowed movement around the region, at many times and in many places, to an agonizing crawl. It is not the car, but the city's overwhelming reliance on the car, its strangling monoculture, that the leaders of the mobility revolution—public and private alike—hope to see overturned.*

Renewing the Dream began with the simple but powerful observation that hailing an Uber or Lyft, riding a Lime scooter or e-bike, taking the Metro, or (someday) using an autonomous vehicle—for all their obvious differences—share one crucial thing in common: there is no need to park a car. It was this focus on the importance of parking—and the opportunities the mobility revolution held out for reducing the space given over to it—that propelled the research at the core of this book.

Those opportunities still appear obvious to anyone who spends time in the city: the vast acreage devoted to the storage of private cars in endless parking lots along its streets and boulevards and in the parking structures, below or above ground, that accompany almost every residential, commercial, or retail building. These are the product not only of actual demand, but as much—or more—of the highly restrictive, mandated parking minimums (about two spaces per residential unit, and one space for every hundred square feet of commercial use) that have been in force since World War II. (In practice, these requirements mean that parking takes up half as much space—and frequently more than half—as the activity it is serving.)

Perhaps more than any other single factor, these rules have defined the form of the city, firmly determining what can—and, more to the point, what *cannot*—be built. Indeed, as the author and *Renewing the Dream* contributor Frances Anderton has wittily observed, "In Los Angeles, parking drives everything." And it is the potential for change in the realm of parking that remains perhaps the most obvious way in which the new mobility—even simply the advent of ride-hailing—holds out the promise of urban transformation. A quarter century before the arrival of Uber, the architect Doug Suisman presciently (indeed, eerily) imagined its impact on the shape of Southern California. "If Los Angeles imposed a regulation that every car be driven by a chauffeur who never parks it," he wrote back in 1989, "there would be an overnight revolution in the architectural form of the city."

> *This is what the mobility revolution has in store for L.A. It's a real estate story, as it always has been. The value of each piece of land, and the use for it, depends on how people can get there, and where they can go. This was the case in the era of streetcars, and again in the century dominated by the automobile. Once more, changing mobility is poised to reshape life and geography in Southern California.*
>
> JOHN ROSSANT AND STEPHEN BAKER, 2019

In the end, the possibilities for parking are just a few of the manifold ways which new methods of moving around town are redirecting the region onto a profoundly different trajectory from its past. And as in those postwar years, the new model coming into being promises to transform not only Southern California itself, but the modern world it helped usher in.

> Los Angeles...minted the global model for highway-connected sprawl... shaped by thousands of miles of highways, driveways, boulevards, parking lots, and culs-de-sac. This is yesterday's infrastructure. What does it have to do with tomorrow? That's precisely the point. Los Angeles, more than traditional compact cities like San Francisco and Paris, must reinvent itself. The challenges are immense. But the transition, when it comes, will likely be more dramatic—for better or worse —than in most other cities.
>
> JOHN ROSSANT AND STEPHEN BAKER, 2019

Three Ways In

The structure of *Renewing the Dream* reflects its evolution since the project began, in 2018. What started with a study of surface parking spaces in Los Angeles—and of the possibilities for reuse of those spaces—blossomed over the years into a broader look at the relationship of mobility and urban growth. It also came to include contributions by guest observers whose expertise ranges from the history of Los Angeles to advances in transportation and technology. That wide range of materials has been grouped in this book into three major parts, each with its own theme and trajectory, unfolding through its interlinked chapters.

Part 1 of the book, *The Battle of Los Angeles*, introduces in largest terms the relationship of mobility and growth in the region—setting the stage, as it were, for the more focused studies in parts 2 and 3, which explore the ways in which, respectively, the shifting needs and requirements for parking, and the rise of electric vehicles, hold the promise of transformative change.

This survey opens with chapter 1, "Firmness vs. Flow: The Battle of Los Angeles," which frames the changes and conflicts of recent years within the century-long struggle that has shaped Los Angeles—and with it, much of the developed world—since the early twentieth century. In an overview that sweeps from the streetcar culture of the 1920s and '30s, through the postwar suburban landscape, and into the today's push for densification and transit, Frances Anderton traces the rise of the "California dream," and explores how its dedication to motion and flow has long influenced the culture of modern Los Angeles. Taking careful note of the costs of that "dream" on communities that stood in its way, Anderton carries the story into the present by reporting on the hard-fought and sometimes bitter "battle" now being waged across the city: between those who continue to cherish and defend that older, leafy low-rise metropolis, and those who insist it must inevitably give way to a denser, more urban future.

Renewing the Dream's exploration of mobility and urban life is refracted through a different lens in chapter 2, "Sunset Crash," a conversation with Eric Avila, professor of Chicano studies and urban planning at UCLA. Here the emergence of LA's auto-dominated culture is seen through its impact—in human, political, and cultural terms—on the poor and working-class neighborhoods of East Los Angeles, populated largely by Latino residents. Located near the heart of the metropolitan area, these districts sat in the

Top: *Surface parking in Los Angeles, 2020.* Bottom: *Swing Girl, a street mural by Banksy in Downtown Los Angeles.*

Top: *A rendering of the 1.3-mile-long arts corridor Destination Crenshaw, looking south along Crenshaw Boulevard in South Los Angeles.* Bottom: *A view of The Twist, Woods Bagot's placemaking proposal for the Sunset Strip in West Hollywood.*

crosshairs of the vast network of freeways built at a furious pace in the middle decades of the twentieth century. Avila recounts how these working-class communities were disrupted and shadowed (often literally) by the massive new roadways cutting through, but also how they resisted and responded, often forcefully, in political *and* cultural ways.

Chapter 3, "Something New Under the Sun," carries the thread of part 1 from the past and present into the future, through a survey by the author and theorist Greg Lindsay of the various technological and urban advances—many of them pioneered in Southern California—that are upending the way people move around cities. Underlying his inventory of twenty-first-century developments is a consideration of the ways in which these new platforms have demanded a wholesale renegotiation of the relationship of public and private sectors, as not only commercial start-ups but regulatory agencies attempt to navigate the fast-changing landscape of urban mobility.

No book on mobility—especially one with a focus on parking—would be complete without a contribution from Donald Shoup, the legendary planning professor at UCLA who is widely regarded as the world's expert on parking. Chapter 4: "Reclaim the Curb!" carries forward the argument of the previous chapter by proposing a tech-driven solution to the problem of curbside parking, or more accurately, the lack of it: an age-old issue grown worse in recent years thanks the competing demands of Uber and Lyft, Amazon deliveries, bike and e-scooter lanes—not to mention private cars—for the same limited space at the sidewalk edge.

Part 1 concludes with a look at two projects, offering distinct yet complementary ways to reimagine the city's fabric in response to shifts in mobility and technology. The first is represented in chapter 5: "Destination Crenshaw: A Cultural and Transit Corridor Celebrating Black Los Angeles." Here change is being propelled not by tech-based innovation but the other major mobility development of twenty-first century Southern California: the expansion of LA Metro. Learning from the cautionary experience outlined in chapter 2—the disruption of the city's working-class neighborhoods, especially communities of color, by the freeway construction of the 1960s and '70s—Destination Crenshaw proposes a new kind of model, in which regional transit construction becomes the opportunity for community regeneration—in this case through a 1.3-mile-long outdoor arts corridor celebrating the city's contemporary African American culture.

A different kind of cultural and commercial corridor—but no less important to the identity of Los Angeles—is the subject of case study 1 of this book, "The Twist: An Arts and Community Destination on the Sunset Strip," a design proposal prepared by Woods Bagot's Los Angeles Studio in response to a call for ideas from the City of West Hollywood. Located on Sunset Boulevard in the heart of the 1.7-mile-long "Strip," the project combines a future-looking, LED-powered interpretation of the celebrated entertainment billboards of that historic stretch with innovative ideas for urban gathering in the digital age—bringing fully into the twenty-first century one of the great cultural boulevards of Los Angeles.

With the stage now set, part 2 of the volume, *From Parking to Places*, explores the opportunity that first propelled the project as a whole. It opens with chapter 6, "MORE LA: Transforming Parking to Places in Southern California," a research and urban design study carried out by Woods Bagot and ERA-co for a workshop at the second annual CoMotion Los Angeles conference in November 2018. At the time, the MORE LA study was intended as a deliberate provocation, extrapolating from the actual trends taking place in tech-enabled mobility and mass transit to explore, in a visionary yet rigorous way, larger possibilities for reclaiming—for new, more productive purposes—some of the vast acreage of Southern California given over to surface parking lots.

As it turned out, the essential provocation of the MORE LA study—that it might be time for Los Angeles to start rethinking its seven-decade-old predilection for providing endless parking, at all costs—resonated with a rich strain of contemporary urban thinking in Southern California. Three guest contributions in part 2 explore the past, present, and future of parking in Los Angeles—and specifically its relationship to housing and development.

The work of Michael Manville, an associate professor at the Luskin School of Public Affairs at UCLA, immediately stood out—especially as a response to anyone who might respond to MORE LA's provocative approach by arguing that, like it or not, modern Los Angeles could not possibly survive *without* the mandated overabundance of parking that has characterized the city since World War II. Manville's detailed studies of Downtown Los Angeles anatomize the district's remarkable transformation since 1999, when the city passed an "Adaptive Reuse Ordinance," encouraging the conversion of prewar office buildings into residential lofts by (among other things) eliminating LA's strict and inflexible parking requirements. That bold act set off an explosion of residential growth, as Manville explains in conversation in chapter 7, "Downtown Explosion."

Following a similar line of thought, the planner Mark Vallianatos makes the impassioned case for a wider relaxation of the city's traditional parking minimums, far beyond downtown's relatively dense confines. In chapter 8, "The Lost and Future LA," he traces how those parking requirements came into being—a step-by-step evolution fascinating in itself, but also the key to something promising for the future. Before World War II, when less stringent parking restrictions were applicable, a wealth of alternative housing layouts were built in large numbers across Los Angeles, low-rise complexes in various configurations that provided, at most, one off-street parking space per unit, and sometimes no off-street parking at all. All of these models were essentially forbidden when much higher parking requirements were put in place after the war. As Los Angeles searches desperately today for solutions to its chronic housing and homelessness crisis, could some of these older housing types—enabled by reduced parking minimums—provide useful prototypes?

Vallianatos' argument is carried forward in chapter 9, titled (with apologies to Joni Mitchell), "Back to the Garden: The Courtyard Alternative," by this book's editor, James Sanders. Of the variety of prewar alternatives that chapter 8 presents, one in particular—the richly landscaped "courtyard apartment" model of the 1920s and '30s—has carried an unusually powerful allure, evident not only in the continued appeal of surviving complexes but in its place in the popular imagination of Los Angeles, visible in films from *Chinatown* to *La La Land*. Chapter 9 traces how those projects first evolved, explores the architectural and urbanistic sources of their "magic," details exactly why they offer so promising a model for the twenty-first-century city, and then sketches a modern interpretation, laid out along the basic principles of the older courtyard projects—above all their limited provision of off-street parking—but adapted to the needs of contemporary households.

Renewing the Dream was well underway when a new opportunity arose, one aligned neatly with its exploration of twenty-first century mobility and urban growth—especially on opportunities to reclaim land currently devoted to vehicles. As Greg Lindsay points out, the Los Angeles mayor's office has been especially alert to the possibilities offered by the new mobility, and in late 2020, the city's chief design officer Christopher Hawthorne initiated an ideas competition called "Pump to Plug," inviting selected design studios to respond to a reality just over the horizon. The fast-growing adoption of electric vehicles, especially in California—which has banned the sale of gas-powered automobiles after 2035—brings with it a land-use corollary that will transform cities everywhere: the obsolescence of the traditional gas station. There are 550 service stations

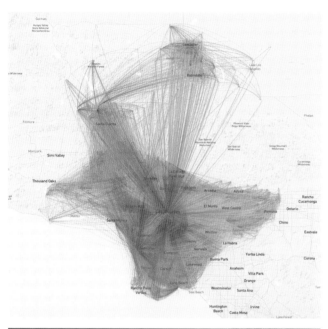

Top: *Data visualization of daily commuting trips in Los Angeles and its surroundings, produced by Woods Bagot and ERA-co for the 2018 study,* MORE LA: From Parking to Places in Southern California. *Bottom: A 1927 courtyard apartment project in Pasadena. Photograph by Julius Shulman.*

in the city of Los Angeles alone, nearly all of them sitting on good-sized plots, usually in high-traffic, high-visibility locations. What becomes of those hundreds of sites when vehicles no longer need them for fuel?

In response to the city's invitation, Woods Bagot and ERA-co tackled the question in two ways, in projects that comprise part 3 of the book, *ReCharge LA*. The first was a citywide data study, prepared by ERA-co and presented in chapter 10: "ReCharge LA Part 1: The Future of the Gas Station." Bringing to bear its advanced machine-learning techniques, the team looked at the *kinds* of sites currently occupied by gas stations— their size, their accessibility to transit and freeways, the character of their communities, and so forth—to create manageable "clusters" of related sites, allowing the team to propose redevelopment scenarios that could be implemented across multiple locations. Their efforts were complemented by Woods Bagot's Los Angeles studio, whose design sketches test the sites' suitability for redevelopment. Once again, the results have been eye-opening, with the reuse of the city's 550 gas-station sites potentially yielding 20,000 dwellings for 40,000 new residents.

The second approach, focused on a single downtown site, is presented as Case Study 2, "ReCharge LA, Part 2: A Prototype EV Station for Downtown Los Angeles," which concludes the book as a whole. Prepared by Woods Bagot's Los Angeles studio, the project explored the architectural opportunities of a prototypical EV station—the launch point for a proposal that draws inspiration from the role of the gas station in Los Angeles' twentieth-century car-based culture—as well as from that car culture itself—and marries it to forward-looking concepts for civic gathering, electronic display, and energy transfer. Not least, the "ReCharge LA" proposal imagines its own transformation over time—as technology evolves, charging times shorten, and new possibilities for urban life emerge—and so carries the past and present of Los Angeles as far as possible into the foreseeable future.

A Kaleidoscopic Portrait

> [If] there's one city in the world that knows anything about reinvention, it's Los Angeles. [On] movie-studio backlot[s]...teams of brilliant production designers...transformed a small patch of Southern California into the antebellum South, first-century Jerusalem, and the Land of Oz. Today there are equally creative, equally dedicated teams of individuals attempting to make Los Angeles into...a better, more sustainable version of itself, one that will be able to meet the formidable water, air, and climate challenges the 21st century is sure to throw its way. With the whole city as their backlot, they're designing the L.A. of the future.
> JEFF TURRENTINE, 2015

Comprising an unusually wide-ranging mix of content—research and data studies, urban design and public art projects, cultural and historical overviews, surveys of current and future technologies—*Renewing the Dream* presents a multifaceted portrait of a great world city at a moment of change: a kaleidoscopic view, as it were, that makes no claims for comprehensiveness, but is rendered instead in glimpses and fragments, a montage-like approach not inappropriate, perhaps, for the world's filmmaking center—or for a place whose complexity, diversity, and sheer size is staggering even by the standards of a global metropolis.

Top: *Electric vehicle charging station, 2021. By 2022, nearly eighty thousand EV charging stations had been installed in California to service the 1.3 million electric vehicles operating in the state. In 2022, EVs accounted for nearly one-fifth of all new vehicle sales in California, a percentage that is expected to double in the next three years.* Bottom: *ReCharge LA, a proposal for an electric charging station and gathering place by Woods Bagot's Los Angeles studio, developed for the "Pump to Plug" ideas competition in 2020, sponsored by Christopher Hawthorne, the city's chief design officer.*

Top: *Production still from* La La Land *(2016), directed by Damien Chazelle.* Bottom: *Micromobility, LA style: Manny Silva, the Compton-based customizer known as "the godfather of lowrider bikes."*

To complement this approach, and to round out its impressionistic portrait of the city, *Renewing the Dream* deploys an equally diverse array of images—archival views and historic maps, interpretive charts and diagrams, contemporary paintings and photographs, film production stills—along with written excerpts, both celebrated and lesser known, from a host of observers over the past century.

This rich panoply of images and texts emerges naturally from a place whose cultural products and scenic landmarks are familiar all around the globe—and have entered the imagination of people everywhere. But beyond its status as one of the world's great cultural capitals, Los Angeles has been a city defined as few others by the formative relationship of its transportation systems and its physical landscape—a relationship so sweeping, even mythic, that it has shaped much of the city's artistic output over the past century.

Here many of those images have been gathered—and put to work—enriching *Renewing the Dream*'s survey of mobility and the built environment. Here are the sweeping (and sometimes heroic) panoramas of the region's freeways by Ansel Adams, Catherine Opie, and Wayne Thiebaud—and the politically charged, distinctly *unheroic* freeway views of Carlos Almaraz and Frank Romero. Here are depictions of the city's quotidian twentieth-century landscape of gas stations, parking lots, and parking meters by Ed Ruscha, Stephen Shore, and the mysterious artist known as Vern Blosum, whose real identity has never been revealed. Here are images of the distinctive kinds of residences—from the "dingbats" of the flats to the estates of the hills—enabled by the city's modern forms of mobility: the lush suburban poolsides of David Hockney, the deadpan apartment facades of James Black and (again) Ed Ruscha, the stark modernist complexes of Julius Shulman.

Here, too, are selections from the rich trove of archival photographs that have documented the region's successive systems of movement, from streetcar lines traversing the sparsely populated canvas of Los Angeles basin in the 1910s to the sinuous, newly opened parkways of the late 1930s. And because, thanks to Hollywood, the growth of Los Angeles has been more tightly intertwined with the movie industry than any other, here are production stills and frame enlargements from celebrated films, rendering in their own memorable way some of the city's most distinctive urban environments, from the 1950s Texaco station of *Back to the Future* (1985) to the freeway musical extravaganza that opens *La La Land* (2016).

Though a volume of this kind can never hope to provide a complete portrait of a city as large and diverse as Los Angeles, the breadth of the subjects, projects and places it looks to explore—from the Sunset Strip to the Crenshaw District, from Inglewood to Boyle Heights to Downtown Los Angeles—offer at least a sketch of the extraordinary richness and complexity of contemporary Los Angeles, even as they point toward a new future for a city whose reach and influence grows stronger with every passing year.

People have stopped visiting Los Angeles. They know if they wait long enough Los Angeles will come to them. So, watch for Los Angeles, appearing shortly in your neighborhood.

DENISE SCOTT BROWN, 1966

1 The Battle

Firmness vs. Flow:
The Battle of Los Angeles
Frances Anderton

The lure of Los Angeles, prewar and postwar. Above: *A late 1930s view of Hollywood Boulevard by night—its skies aglow with the searchlights of movie premieres—captures the glamour and excitement that prewar Hollywood extended to Los Angeles as a whole.* Left: *David Hockney's 1967 painting,* A Bigger Splash, *evokes the dreamy appeal of postwar Southern California: a semi-suburban paradise of detached single-family houses, landscaped backyards, palm trees, and swimming pools, beneath a sky of unchanging, transcendent blue.*

Previous spread: *View of Downtown Los Angeles. Photograph by Ilja Masik.*

Introduction

Many global cities are undergoing rapid change. But perhaps none is undergoing quite the transformation currently underway in Los Angeles. The City of Angels, for generations the apotheosis of the suburban dream, is no longer only building out, but *up*. It is in the midst of a mobility and development revolution—and is at war with itself over what it wants to be.

It is a remarkable turn of events—especially for a city largely shaped for the past seven decades by the owner-occupied single-family home and its handmaiden, the private car. The twinning of the two produced planning decisions, zoning resolutions, and building codes that almost always privileged the automobile over the needs of pedestrians and transit—and, along the way, handed over some two hundred square miles of the metropolitan area to car parking, the extraordinary state of affairs explored in part 2 of this book.

But with the start of the new century came a major shift. For practical as well as lifestyle-based reasons, a new generation of Angelenos started to reject suburban sprawl in favor of urban density and (to a lesser but not insignificant degree) public transit. Hot on the heels of that change came a tech-enabled mobility revolution, bringing ride-sharing, ride-hailing, e-scooters, e-bikes, and a host of other innovations. The results, though still very much in progress, open up provocative questions about the future of a place whose fundamental myth is under serious question—if not open siege.

Rising to a crescendo before the Covid-19 pandemic of 2020–21—and reemerging as the city began its recovery from the profound dislocations of that global catastrophe—this shift has brought forth a profound conflict between two visions of the city's future, one that has taken on the lineaments of a full-fledged battle. It is a battle played out over almost every new multiunit housing block, over new forms of transit and mobility, over proposed changes to zoning—over *any* change, essentially, to the built environment that might undermine the traditional and comfortable use of the car and the pleasant single-family home life that goes with it. It is a battle pitting newcomers against LA natives, young against old. In sum, it is a battle between those that desire an urban lifestyle for Los Angeles, and those who came to the region to get away from all that.

If anything, the struggle has only grown more tangled and complex in the wake of the pandemic, whose impact reverberated in complex and contradictory ways—reducing transit ridership (at least temporarily) for fear of contagion, increasing telecommuting and remote work habits (and thus shifting rush-hour patterns), encouraging bikes, scooters, and other alternative modes of mobility, and even displacing sidewalk parking spaces with outdoor dining "streeteries." No less significant has been the impact of the subsequent upheaval that took place even as people were reeling from the brutal early arrival of Covid: the wave of civil unrest that swept across the country after the shocking, widely viewed killing in May 2020 of a Black man named George Floyd by a Minneapolis police officer. The self-reflection that has come over many disciplines has

The mid-twentieth-century "California dream." Exploding private car ownership in Southern California in the late 1940s and '50s brought with it an explosion of private home building, driven by large-scale tract-house developers who could create almost instant residential communities (such as the city of Lakewood, southeast of Los Angeles, shown under construction in 1950), comprised of thousands of nearly identical freestanding houses, each sitting on its own private lot.

deeply affected urban planning, which must grapple with the profound and abiding role of racism in the shaping of modern Los Angeles. Well into the 1960s and in some cases beyond, the practice of "redlining," racially restrictive covenants, and government-imposed patterns of freeway construction combined to functionally segregate Los Angeles (as Eric Avila elaborates in chapter 2). Many mid-century transportation and development projects are now understood to have harmed or even decimated communities of color, while enabling white homeownership and flight to the suburbs.

Indeed, it is difficult to grasp fully the current struggle over the future of Los Angeles without understanding its deep-seated origins—birthed in a century-old dream of domesticity and open mobility, haunted by the shadow of pervasive racism, intensified by the recent push to denser development, and poised uneasily in the wake of a pandemic that has challenged all previous assumptions about city life.

A Castle of One's Own

> *The houses and the automobiles are equal figments of a great dream, the dream of the urban homestead, the dream of a good life outside the squalors of the European type of city, and thus a dream that runs back not only into the Victorian railway suburbs of earlier cities, but also to the country-house culture of the fathers of the U.S. Constitution...Los Angeles cradles and embodies the most potent current version of the great bourgeois vision of the good life in a tamed countryside.*
>
> REYNER BANHAM, 1971

It is well over a century since Angelenos first began leaving packed cities or rural towns to live in a new kind of environment that lay somewhere between the two, where the spread of the single-family home meshed with seemingly infinite mobility—in a basin of topographic splendor—to create a distinct pattern of land use, lifestyle, and identity. "Coastal Southern California wasn't urbanized through the piecemeal subdivision of freeholder farms, as was much of the East Coast and Midwest, but through the planned development of miles-square tracts of ranchland originating in Mexican land grants," the author and Los Angeles native D. J. Waldie observed in 2020:

> When passed . . . into the hands of . . . capitalists in the 1870s, the pattern of Southern California development was set: a large tract of land...would be improved as a unit and sold as acreage for farms and orchards and further broken down in the twentieth century into house lots. . . . Developers in Los Angeles made fortunes by convincing buyers that they had acquired a whole landscape by owning just an eighth of an acre.

In the early twentieth century, land all across the Los Angeles basin, and beyond, was platted and subdivided into endless lots, then filled mostly with single-family homes, costumed in a mind-boggling variety of historical styles, and fitted out with generous yards and driveways. And people came in droves.

"[A] million and a half people moved to greater Los Angeles in the decade 1920–30 alone," writes the landscape historian Wade Graham in his 2016 book, *Dream Cities: Seven Urban Ideas That Shape the World*, "and most of them came, at least in part, because they believed the promises that every man and woman could have a castle of their own." That "castle," he says, took its cues first from the romantic architecture of

Largely ignored or dismissed by architectural critics, the single-family houses of Southern California have caught the eye of artists such as Robert Ginder, whose 1980s photorealist depictions of the modest bungalows of Compton—the South Los Angeles neighborhood in which he was raised—are transfigured by arched framing and gold-leaf skies to recall Italian devotional paintings of the fourteenth century.

Firmness vs. Flow: The Battle of Los Angeles

Footpaths and Roadways, pre-1860

Railroads

Pacific Electric Railway

Automotive Highways

Freeways

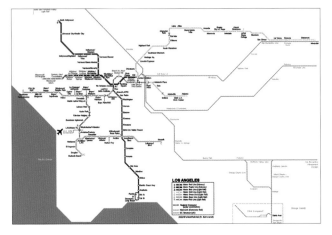

eclectic designers like Bertram Goodhue and then from the fantasy movie sets that filled the studio lots of early-twentieth-century Los Angeles.

Getting to these "castles," however, usually required a car.

By 1930, Graham notes, "the region had 800,000 cars (two for every three people); then it had millions. Today, Los Angeles County has ten million people, one part of a five-county supercity of more than *eighteen* million sprawling across much of Southern California, transported by nearly that many cars. It is the largest urbanized area in the United States, known to specialists as a 'conurbation'—a city at regional scale, but an 'urb' made up mostly of suburbia."

All of this was not strictly "a romantic suburbia, by any means," Graham points out. But although "there are endless gradations in types of buildings and streets," he observes, "the widespread Garden City ideal produced strict rules limiting building heights and neighborhood density." This set Los Angeles on a path to the current struggle between defenders of single-family neighborhoods—who have dominated residential zoning—and developers of more homes.

Los Angeles's pattern of growth may have been amplified by the car, but it began with the train. As the English architecture historian (and LA transplant) Reyner Banham pointed out in his classic 1971 book, *Los Angeles: The Architecture of Four Ecologies*, the city's distinctive pattern of growth—its vast suburban dream, available to millions— was in fact made possible by successive layers of transportation systems, diverse in character but united in their intent to render, he said, "almost every piece of land in the Los Angeles basin conveniently accessible and thus profitably exploitable." Suburbia first arrived in the late nineteenth century by way of a railroad system spread "with as little difficulty as toy trains on the living room carpet," Banham writes, "and later the Pacific Electric interurban lines, and later still the freeways."

> The uniquely even, thin and homogeneous spread of development that has been able to absorb the monuments of the freeway system without serious strain (so far, at least) owes its origins to earlier modes of transportation and the patterns of land development that went with them. The freeway system is the third or fourth transportation diagram drawn on a map that is a deep palimpsest of earlier methods of moving about the basin.
>
> REYNER BANHAM, 1971

In 1940, the first freeway—a high-speed automobile roadway separated from surface streets, pioneered by Germany's 1930s autobahns and by Robert Moses's 1920s parkways on Long Island—was launched in Southern California with the Arroyo Seco Parkway (now Pasadena or 110 Freeway) connecting Pasadena and Downtown Los Angeles. By the time a half century of freeway construction neared its end in the Southland with the opening of 105 Freeway in 1993, these concrete structures—stunning in their engineering and design, sometimes brutal in their social and urban impact—had brought on an almost unimaginable reorganization of the landscape of Southern California.

Tying the region together more firmly than ever before, the network of postwar freeways made vast tracts of low-cost land accessible to middle-class families, especially on its once-agricultural fringes—Orange County to the south, the San Fernando and San Gabriel valleys to the north, the "Inland Empire" around San Bernardino to the east. In those sprawling areas, homes were sold, largely to white families, with the help of federal housing loans and the GI Bill.

Opposite: *The sprawling character of Los Angeles, widely regarded as a product of the automobile, was in fact largely established by older layers of transportation. For decades before the auto became ubiquitous in the 1950s, the Pacific Electric (Red Car) and Los Angeles (Yellow Car) interurban streetcar systems—which at their peak covered the region with an astonishing 1,675 miles of track, tracing the outlines of much of modern Southern California—encouraged the city's distinctive dispersed, low-density patterns of settlement. David Brodsly's 1981 comparative maps reveal what Reyner Banham called the "palimpsest" of transportation systems in Southern California—today extended by a new layer, all but unimaginable when those maps first appeared: the expansive network of the Los Angeles Metro (bottom), as completed by the time of the Summer Olympics in 2028.*

Above: *Los Angeles's earliest freeways— such as the richly landscaped Arroyo Seco Parkway, which opened in 1940—offered thrilling possibilities for an architecture of movement, to be experienced not from the traditional fixed vantage of a pedestrian but the ever-shifting viewpoint of a car traveling fifty miles per hour or more.*

Firmness vs. Flow: The Battle of Los Angeles

The postwar freeway system and tract-house development together brought forth one of the most striking and best-known urban landscapes in the world: the Los Angeles metropolitan region, home to more than thirteen million people across five counties and 4,800 square miles, whose seemingly endless stretches of private homes were given shape by a network of massive concrete roadways.

Top: *A 250-foot-wide swath of houses and streets is leveled to make way for a Los Angeles freeway, 1961.*
Right: *The home of a Black family being demolished for the construction of the Harbor Freeway southwest of downtown, 1948. In all, the homes of more than a quarter of a million Los Angeles residents were destroyed to make way for the freeways, and the communities of hundreds of thousands more were sliced in two by the new roads.*

But the building of the freeways had enormous social and human costs, falling most heavily on poor and working-class communities—often those of color. Running east-west across the middle of the Los Angeles basin, Interstate 10 created a sharp dividing line between the northern, more affluent parts of the basin and the poorer, predominantly Black communities to the south. The 405, running north-south, created a schism between the westernmost beach towns along the Pacific Ocean and everything east. The 110, the 10, the 101 and the 5 freeways encircled Downtown Los Angeles like a latter-day moat, making it a citadel of sorts where for decades few people lived except the poor and indigent, who congregated in the Skid Row blocks of the city's historic downtown. Many of the freeways and their towering interchanges scythed right through the city's older neighborhoods, perhaps most famously in the politically powerless Mexican American community of Boyle Heights. They split communities asunder, showering them with pollution, and causing public health problems—asthma, cancer, and heart disease—that would plague their populations for generations. As the technology historian Paul Josephson observes, "The poor disproportionally bear the costs of automobility."

The freeways also intensified the formation of a cityscape that increasingly spurned pedestrians. Civic buildings and shopping centers turned their backs on the street, entered instead from rear parking lots (like the 1929 Bullocks Wilshire or the 1940 May Company department stores), or garages (like later postwar shopping malls). Houses, offices, and cultural buildings were planned according to the needs of parking. Side-walks were narrowed or even removed to widen pavement and were deprived of the

Ed Ruscha's 1967 series, Thirtyfour Parking Lots in Los Angeles—an aerial photographic portrait of Los Angeles widely admired for its sheer graphic power—neatly captures the physical evolution of the city across the mid-twentieth century. The original 1940 May Company department store (top), designed by Albert C. Martin, places its parking lot at the rear of its Art Moderne building—which, fronting the sidewalk with show windows, activates and defines Wilshire Boulevard in traditional urban fashion (even if many of its customers entered by the back door). By contrast, the May Company building of the 1960s (bottom) is set back far from the street and surrounded entirely by parking, leaving the surrounding sidewalks devoid of spatial definition, or any interest at all for pedestrians.

Dennis Keeley, Blue Bus *(2016), from his photographic series,* Freeway: A Survey of the Quotidian Landscape.

Renewing the Dream

Firmness vs. Flow: The Battle of Los Angeles

trappings of inviting, walkable streets: benches, shade structures, and trees. Walkers or bus-riders were reduced to lower-caste citizens.

Firmness to Flow

Whatever glass and steel monuments may be built downtown, the essence of Los Angeles, its true identifying characteristic, is mobility. Freedom of movement has long given life a special flavor there, liberated the individual to enjoy the sun and space that his environment so abundantly offered, but the manifold advantages of a great metropolitan area within its grasp.

RICHARD AUSTIN SMITH, 1965

It was the mobility afforded by the car and expanded by the freeway that—for better or worse—made modern Los Angeles the unique place it had become by the late 1960s and early '70s. By the middle of the twentieth century, "flow" had become the city's defining trait, awing visiting planners and journalists and inspiring painters, singers, filmmakers, writers. In 1964, the British novelist John Fowles, touring the city, wrote almost rhapsodically of "the great flow of power up and down the freeways, easy and controlled and fast—everywhere this characteristic American mode of moving, a sort of jet age tempo."

[T]he language of design, architecture, and urbanism in Los Angeles is the language of movement. Mobility outweighs monumentality there to a unique degree...and the city will never be fully understood by those who cannot move fluently through its diffuse urban texture, cannot go with the flow of its unprecedented life.

REYNER BANHAM, 1971

Los Angeles moves or it isn't Los Angeles anymore.

D. J. WALDIE, 2021

In his 1981 book *L.A. Freeway: An Appreciative Essay*, David Brodsly observes that the freeways were immensely successful in allowing postwar Los Angeles to surge in population and prominence and dramatically expand its prewar reputation as "the first major city that was not quite a city." Indeed, he argues, the freeway can be said to have saved the mid-twentieth-century city. "When Los Angeles began drowning in the popularity of the garden-city vision," he writes, "the freeway was offered as a lifeline. The L.A. freeway makes manifest in concrete the city's determination to keep its dream alive." He describes the freeway as the "cathedral of its time and place" that—when not jammed bumper to bumper—offers the driver a meditative, almost spiritual experience:

The freeway itself did not revolutionize transportation in Los Angeles; it was an extension of the automobile, the radically new form of transportation which did revolutionize urban development. The freeway system was in fact a conservative force, promising the metropolis the clear and coherent structure it had lacked since the decline of the urban railways. Earlier modes of transportation created a multicentered way of life served by widespread patterns of movement, but development of the freeway system is...the formalization of that process...[The] freeways were really more a product than a cause of the prevalent urban

Above: *Catherine Opie, Untitled #27, from the* Freeway *series, 1994–95. Best known for her portraiture and studio images, the photographer Catherine Opie has also sought to capture the monumentality of Southern California's freeways—which, she observed in 2018, were "literally an iconic landscape as much as Egypt is in relationship to the pyramids."*

Following page: *Production still from* La La Land *(2016), directed by Damien Chazelle. Shot over a period of two days on a closed-off section of interchange between Interstates 105 and 110, the film's spectacular opening sequence— in which hundreds of frustrated motorists, locked in a rush-hour standstill, leap out of their vehicles to stage an exuberant music-and-dance number—rested in its very premise on the worldwide notoriety of Los Angeles's traffic jams. Photograph by Dale Robinette.*

33

Firmness vs. Flow: The Battle of Los Angeles

Renewing the Dream

form. They were consciously conceived and executed to serve a long-established pattern of decentralized, low-density development.

DAVID BRODSLY, 1981

The automobile "managed to reverse the millennial primacy of architecture over movement. Firmness gave way to flow," declared the architect Doug Suisman in his 1989 examination of the city's distinctive linear urbanity, *Los Angeles Boulevard: Eight X-Rays of the Body Public.* The automobile made Los Angeles into the familiar endless carpet of low-rise buildings, across five counties, punctuated by higher rise downtown areas— what Suisman calls "the vast, polynucleated metropolis of our day."

But even by the time Brodsly wrote his "appreciative" essay in 1981, many Angelenos were getting sick of daily driving. It was becoming clear that the push for growth encouraged by the freeways had, in a sense, worked all too well, bringing more people, more commuters—and more traffic. The greater the number of people using freeways, the less "free" they became, and instead started to be known around the world primarily for smog, gridlock, and endless commutes. "By the last few decades of the twentieth century," the writer Jeff Turrentine observes, "the city itself seemed stuck in an existential traffic jam of its own devising."

> *Like countless others before us, we had been lured to Los Angeles by a mythic sales pitch depicting sunny skies, palm trees, ocean breezes, new creative opportunities, and the freedom to stretch one's legs and move about. But quickly we would come to appreciate an inescapable irony: the pitch had proved too effective. So many had heard it and heeded it over the years that Los Angeles had become a standing-room-only Shangri-la. We were free to move about, all right—on traffic-clogged roads that made the "freedom" of driving feel more like indentured servitude.*
>
> JEFF TURRENTINE, 2015

> *[O]ur freeway system, the five-hundred-mile armature for...Autopia, once a wonder for its scope and scale, has stalled, with less than thirty miles of new interstate roadway built in the last twenty years. By comparison, with recent Asian, or even Canadian, infrastructural improvements, California's once bold eight-lanes and cloverleaves look haggard and Lilliputian.*
>
> JOE DAY, 2009

In the 1980s, the city's leadership at last started a serious push for the return of mass transit, and in 1990 the Blue Line opened, the first in a sprawling network of light-rail and subways across the Southland. In 2016 voters approved a massive transportation spending package called Measure M, which dramatically accelerated transit funding and development.

> *Notwithstanding its ongoing love affair with the automobile, LA is in a public-transit frenzy. In Mid-Wilshire, crews were clogging up the westbound side of the boulevard around La Brea, readying the D Line extension for its anticipated debut a scant eighteen months from now. Downtown, the Regional Connector is slated for completion next year, giving Angelenos a one-seat train ride from East LA to*

35

Firmness vs. Flow: The Battle of Los Angeles

In recent years, the monthly Sunday festival CicLAvia has drawn hundreds of thousands of cyclists to tour streets that are closed for the day to vehicular traffic.

The arrival of the Metro was only one sign of a desire for a more pedestrian-friendly lifestyle. Pop-up farmers markets started to appear in Los Angeles parking lots as early as the 1980s. In 2010 came the first CicLAvia, bringing thousands of cyclists to closed-off streets, which helped create the impetus for a network of bicycle lanes that is gradually unfurling across the region. Community activists and planners pushed for more shared public spaces in neighborhoods underserved by parkland, and in 2012 proudly cut the ribbon on Grand Park, on a stretch of land between the Music Center and City Hall that had been rendered inaccessible by the redevelopment of Bunker Hill and the construction of a parking structure underneath. In 2019, the City of Los Angeles even appointed its first city forest officer, dedicated to planting ninety thousand trees on the city's thoroughfares to provide the shade and cooling necessary for walkable streets.

"Now nearly every change in LA streets is made in favor of the user who is not in a private car: the pedestrian, the cyclist, a commuter on a bus or train in LA," observed Christopher Hawthorne, the *Los Angeles Times* architecture critic (and later the city's chief design officer), in his 2014 introduction to the twenty-fifth anniversary edition of Suisman's *Los Angeles Boulevard*. "This change is part of a major shift in the way Los Angeles thinks of itself," he continued. "The city of the single-family residence is barely building stand-alone houses any longer; in recent years between 95 percent and 98 percent of the new residential units constructed in LA. have been condominiums or apartments."

These residential units are being built by developers who are primarily building not on open tracts of land but on "infill" sites—shoehorning multistory, mixed-use mid-rise buildings, and sometimes high-rise towers, into the densifying downtowns of many of Los Angeles County's eighty-eight cities, at transit intersections and on arterial boulevards.

The LA dream, in other words, has morphed from the "castle of one's own" with a bucolic backyard to a rental unit or condo with decks or shared terraces for enjoying the sunshine. If the ultimate in residential leisure in the 1950s was the backyard swimming pool, today it might be the shared rooftop pool with a fabulous view of the megalopolis.

As the explosion of single-family house construction in the 1950s was driven by a revolution in transportation—cheap cars, cheap gas, fast new freeways, and free parking—so too these newer changes in domestic architecture have been underpinned, in a less causal way, by a mobility revolution of their own, pioneered as before in Southern California, and propelled, as Greg Lindsay details in chapter 3, by a panoply of mobility innovations, encompassing the private and public sector, techies and tinkerers, dreamers and hucksters.

If some of the more futuristic of these mobility concepts have so far had only minimal effect on the city's development landscape, the impact of others, as Lindsay points out, has been very real—and has been amplified by the multidecade build-out of

Among the more provocative of alternative transportation approaches in Southern California is a proposed gondola connector between Union Station and Dodger Stadium in Downtown Los Angeles, 2022, allowing baseball fans to avoid traffic and parking problems by easily reaching the stadium through Metro and train connections.

A series of high-rise "transit-oriented developments" rise next door to a new Yellow Line station at Pico Boulevard. The dramatic expansion of the LA Metro over the past decades has already begun to transform the shape of Los Angeles, not only through its direct passenger volume (which to date has fallen well short of optimistic projections) but through its impact on new construction, which clearly points to a denser, more urban version of the low-rise city.

the region's now-sprawling Metro system, which has already changed the face of much of the city, encouraging densification along dozens of boulevards and other streets. Ironically, the system's greatest impact may come less from its actual ridership than the increase in allowable density—and decrease in parking requirements—for hundreds of sites near its stations. These have already encouraged numerous clusters of mid- and high-rise development projects, creating not only formidable skylines but the kinds of imposing urban canyons once associated with New York and Chicago.

Not that Angelenos in such dwellings are ready to give up on the car altogether. Despite their proximity to mass transit, most new luxury apartment or condominium towers provide private parking in multistory stacks built aboveground, known as parking podiums. Just because people chose to live in a swank apartment or condo in Downtown Los Angeles or Hollywood doesn't mean they intend to get around exclusively—or even mostly—by public transit. So the city has produced a bizarre new building type: a tower sitting atop a six- or seven-story garage. The wide roof of the parking podium often serves as an outdoor communal space—a garden in the air—for the tower's residents.

After more than two decades of construction, this dramatic densification of the city has grown to a degree that surprises and startles newcomers—and frightens and infuriates older homeowners. And so the great battle is joined.

"NIMBY" vs. "YIMBY"

Aerial view of suburban houses in Lakewood, 2020. Despite the surge in new multifamily construction—which now constitutes more than two-thirds of the new units approved each year by Los Angeles—74 percent of the residential land in the city remains zoned exclusively for single-family houses.

[M]any of the most stubborn cliches and stereotypes about L.A. and Southern California are crumbling or being held up for new scrutiny. Increasingly the city and region are taking real, measurable and often controversial steps to move past the building blocks of postwar Los Angeles, including the private car, the freeway, the single-family house and the lawn. [T]he city is no longer pushing out at the edges but folding back on itself, doubling back, looking to develop more intensely the sections it developed lightly before—or even overlooked entirely in its race to grow at the periphery.

CHRISTOPHER HAWTHORNE, 2016

Any place housing fifteen million people is nothing if not a metropolis. But many of Los Angeles's citizens still resist metropolitan life. They

Renewing the Dream

didn't buy into it fifty years ago—when center cities were genuinely unpleasant—and they don't want to buy into it today.

JOSH STEPHENS, 2020

Comfortably settled in their suburban enclaves, Los Angeles homeowners long ago formed themselves into hundreds of powerful "neighborhood associations" which, by the late twentieth century, were fiercely turning back all attempts to densify single-family areas, usually in the name of preserving what they termed "neighborhood character"—a stance known by the now-familiar nickname, NIMBY ("Not in My Backyard"). In the 1970s and '80s voters fought for the downzoning of neighborhoods, causing many multifamily neighborhoods to be reclassified as single-family, and lowering density limits in those areas that remained zoned for multifamily use. In 1986 they went further, passing a measure called "Proposition U" to drastically restrict commercial and office construction on major boulevards. The intent may have been to slow the construction of large-scale office buildings, but the result was severe constraints on *any* development that might incorporate housing, such as mid-rise apartments over shops. Together, the downzoning measures resulted in a stunning reduction of LA's overall population capacity, from ten million to four million. Even at the time, the *Los Angeles Times* urged a "No" vote on the Prop U measure, calling it "the most extensive one-shot effort to limit future development in the city's history." But few cared what the *LA Times* thought: the measure passed two to one. "[Los Angeles] homeowners wield shockingly disproportionate degrees of political power compared to renters," observed the urban critic Josh Stephens in 2020:

> *Politicians appeal to homeowners of detached homes...for a few major reasons. Stability: they'll be there to vote, year in and year out. Engagement: homeowners know who their public officials are. Unity: homeowners define their interests, and often vote as blocs, because of homeowners' associations. Wealth: duh. Meanwhile, renters are transient, politically naive, disparate, and often poor.*

In the twenty-first century, however, the tide began to change. A new generation of Angelenos, faced with increasingly astronomical rents, joined with builders in an

An accessory dwelling unit (ADU) in Southern California, inserted into a suburban garage. Thanks to changes in state and local legislation, the number of ADUs in Los Angeles has exploded, more than doubling in the four years after 2017, and in 2022 accounting for nearly a quarter of all new housing permits in the city. In addition to generating valuable income as rental properties, ADUs can provide families with an inexpensive home for a teenager or young adult, or a "granny flat" for an aging relative. "They are particularly useful in giving older homeowners the ability to downsize and age in place," notes Christopher Hawthorne, "without leaving their neighborhood and losing important family and community bonds." In the face of fierce opposition in many low-rise neighborhoods to larger projects, ADUs have proved a politically palatable way to increase the city's overall residential density, one lot at a time.

Firmness vs. Flow: The Battle of Los Angeles

emergent YIMBY ("*Yes* in My Backyard") movement to encourage new residential development, and, presumably, bring down the price of housing. But their efforts to support the construction of multifamily residential buildings in downtown Santa Monica, Venice, Koreatown, and Hollywood met a wall of resistance in two 2016 ballot measures: "LV" in Santa Monica and "S" in Los Angeles.

These ballot measures were precipitated by ferocious neighborhood struggles over specific projects. Among them were several developments involving "star" architects: mixed-used towers designed by Rem Koolhaas, Frank Gehry, and Stanley Saitowitz in Hollywood and Santa Monica. No matter their architectural pedigree, each proved a lightning rod for media controversy and community resistance. The projects have spent years in litigation, gradually being reduced in scale and ambition.

In the end, both the "LV" and "S" measures failed to pass, suggesting the future lies with the pro-growthers. But in Santa Monica, at least, the victory was short-lived. In 2020, voters threw out the pro-growth council and managed to kill the Koolhaas project, while slowing development in the beach city's downtown.

Moreover the "slow-growthers" still have enough clout at the homeowner-association level to contest any project that, in their view, threatens their neighborhoods. One project, an effort by two nonprofit development groups to build 140 units of desperately needed affordable housing in Venice by the renowned architect Eric Owen Moss, has been tied up for more than eight years.

Back in 1971, Reyner Banham described Los Angeles as having "room to swing the proverbial cat," and blessedly unlike "older cities back east—New York, Boston, London, Paris—where warring pressure groups cannot get out of one another's hair because they are pressed together in a sacred labyrinth of cultural monuments and real estate values."

That was then. Now Angelenos have discovered their history, too. Whether driven by a genuine affection for the faux-Tudor, Spanish, French château, ranch, and other architectural styles of LA's older residential neighborhoods or simply opposition to more density or outsiders, "conservation" has consumed many single-family residential neighborhoods, from upscale Beverly Hills to historic Leimert Park in South LA. They are forming restrictive "historic preservation overlay zones" that might save a beloved neighborhood from outsize mega-mansions or oversized apartment buildings—but conveniently manage also to thwart new construction of reasonably scaled housing.

The picture is complicated by the fact that much new development is proceeding in communities that were themselves once victim to redlining and urban renewal, like South LA and Boyle Heights. Sensitivities are high. New growth tends to be market rate because the cost of land makes it impossible for developers to build affordable housing, causing gentrification and displacement. As a result, working-class renters fearful of losing rent-controlled apartments have formed odd-bedfellow coalitions with affluent slow-growthers from upscale neighborhoods.

Unable to force change at a local level, housing activists took the fight to the California state capitol in Sacramento. In 2017, they pushed through a law permitting the construction of accessory dwelling units, or ADUs, nicknamed "granny flats," along with JADUs, or Junior ADUs, meaning a second unit attached to the existing house. This has brought about an impressive surge in construction of small, secondary dwellings in the backyards of single-family homes. Having successfully opened a crack in the door to allow more density in low-rise neighborhoods, activists went further, led by California state senator Scott Wiener, who introduced his incendiary "SB 50" legislation, a proposed statewide law that would override local zoning laws and *mandate* upzoning in economic hot spots and sites near transit stations.

Santa Monica Station of the Expo Line with new apartment construction in the background, 2016. Connecting downtown, the USC campus, South Los Angeles, and Culver City to the beaches of Santa Monica and Venice, the Expo line, which opened in 2012, provided the fabled "train to the sea" that had been promised Angelenos for generations, and has proved particularly popular with teenagers and college students, who no longer need a car to reach the ocean. It has also become a magnet for new large-scale residential development adjacent to its stations.

This proved a step too far even for the fifteen members of the Los Angeles City Council—most of whom claimed to want to see more transit-oriented development—and they all urged their Sacramento colleagues to oppose it. The bill failed, and then failed again in 2020—although by a closer vote—when Wiener presented it with new qualifications. The city's politicians weren't quite ready to relinquish one of the few powerful tools they have at their disposal—local control over development—and LA homeowners, along with opponents of gentrification, backed them to the hilt. Finally, in 2021, less-aggressive versions of the bills, now called SB 9 and SB 10, were passed by the State Senate and signed into law by governor Gavin Newsom, newly empowered by a landslide in a recall election. The measures permit the addition of two to four dwellings on a single-family lot; close to transit, up to ten units are allowable. The bill will bring what advocates call "gentle density" to single-family neighborhoods for the first time in decades and represents a small revolution in a state so long resistant to any intrusion on the garden-city dream. Many homeowner associations, needless to say, have bitterly fought all of these propositions.

The ambivalence about the changes coming to Los Angeles is felt even by those pushing for them. Many Angelenos have voted with their tax dollars for increased public transportation, but they still support a car-based Los Angeles in their personal choices.

Firmness vs. Flow: The Battle of Los Angeles

New tract houses under construction at the Porter Ranch development, in the northwest corner of the San Fernando Valley, 2017.

It has not escaped notice that only a handful of the architects, planners, and elected officials advocating for density actually *live* in a rental or condo multifamily building close to transit. The majority make their homes, like so many other Angelenos, in single-family houses—and drive their cars to work and back every day.

Other than the popular Metrolink commuter train that delivers people to the outlying exurbs and the even more popular Expo Line, carrying flocks of beachgoers to the Santa Monica shore, ridership on trains had been flat, and on buses was dropping, even before the impact of the 2020 pandemic. (Meanwhile, car use has been going up, notwithstanding growing traffic paralysis on many roads.) Transit boosters, however, argue that once the Metro network is built out, by the end of the 2020s—in time for the 2028 Olympic Games—ridership will rise dramatically.

> *Another Los Angeles—potentially better than the twentieth-century city—is being invented that may critically question and democratically reform the city's distorted power relationships.*
>
> D. J. WALDIE, 2021

All assumptions about the future, of course, were put into question by the arrival of Covid-19 in the spring of 2020. If some of the most dramatic effects of the pandemic proved transitory, others, including the explosive rise in remote working, may prove far more lasting. Perhaps the largest by-product of Covid for the "battle for Los Angeles" is the question mark it raises around the future salability of a dense, urban lifestyle. Even before the pandemic, many millennial-age Angelenos—despite being vocal advocates for densification—were already indicating with their feet their disaffection with the high cost of housing and other growing challenges of Los Angeles. The 2018 census showed that almost 100,000 people left Los Angeles County, the biggest net loss in the country (gains came mostly in births), meaning Los Angeles is experiencing out-migration. A follow-up survey in early 2019 found that millennials made up the majority—63 percent—of those looking to transplant.

And where were these young people moving? To outlying, cheaper areas of the Southern California region, like Riverside, in San Bernardino County, fifty miles to the east—or out of state entirely, to places they could afford the very product that attracted Angelenos in the first place: the single-family home, doubtless reached by a car. It turns out LA-style high-rise and mid-rise residential living appeals largely to young (primarily single) people, and empty-nesters. For both groups this can often last less than a decade. When people form a family, many want to build equity, or yearn for space and land, and so the house and backyard—or "castle"—seems once again desirable. And yet the wave of condo development rolls on, and with every passing year, Los Angeles grows denser and more urban. Only time will tell how the great battle over the city's future plays out.

Los Angeles helped birth, incarnate, mythologize, and export the "city that was not quite a city." In recent years, it has been struggling to take on the attributes of a traditional metropolis. It has been doing so not out of a sense of the infinitely possible that formed Los Angeles but rather out of recognition of constraints. This is in some ways a sign of maturity, reflecting an understanding that resources have limits and that humanity is not well served when it defers entirely to the car.

If it is unlikely that the original, sun-kissed LA Dream is expiring any time soon, neither are the forces pushing the city into denser and more urban directions going away. It is now up to inspired developers, transit builders, financiers, and architects to give form and image to the new LA dream, cars and parking optional.

2

Sunset Crash
A Conversation with Eric Avila

As Frances Anderton observes, the history of mobility in Los Angeles is not only charged with endless promise and epic innovations but has been fraught with human tragedy—especially for the city's less-privileged inhabitants, very often people of color, who found themselves on the receiving end of the sweeping urban transformations. In his books and essays, UCLA professor Eric Avila has sought to explain the underlying forces driving the planning, funding, and construction of the freeway system of the mid-twentieth century, to understand their relationship to other large-scale changes—urban renewal, slum clearance, and the rise of a modernist vision of the city—that were transforming Southern California in those same decades, and to document the social, political, and cultural impact of the city's shifting means of mobility on its most marginalized citizens. As an outgrowth of this exploration, he has examined the extraordinary cultural reaction of Los Angeles artists—white, Black, and Latino—to the new systems of transportation, and especially to a generation of Chicano artists, centered around the East Los Angeles neighborhood of Boyle Heights, who responded creatively and politically to the massive and often brutal impositions on their communities in the last third of the twentieth century.

James Sanders   *Something that emerges in your books—and something many of us have been aware of since Reyner Banham's 1971 book,* Los Angeles: The Architecture of Four Ecologies—*is that the automobile was not quite as formative in the shaping of Los Angeles as is commonly imagined; that the city's distinctive low-density, decentralized landscape began to emerge long before the automobile became dominant. Before the arrival of the freeways, in fact, Los Angeles was built around the largest streetcar system in the world. How would you describe that earlier, streetcar-based city?*

Ansel Adams, Freeway Interchange, Los Angeles, 1967.

Eric Avila   I would say that the streetcar created a kind of urban paradox in the early decades of the twentieth century. On the one hand, streetcars obviously promoted decentralization and suburban sprawl—even before the introduction of the freeway and the mass adoption of the automobile. And that was largely through the process by which streetcar development was tied to real estate development and land speculation. People like Henry Huntington [the powerful owner of the Pacific Electric system] would build streetcar lines to distant tracts of land on the periphery of the settled urbanized area. And there he would build housing tracts—subdivisions—and coordinate that effort with the extension of streetcar lines. So in many ways these prototypical suburban communities took shape through the foresight and conception of builders and developers and wealthy landowners like Huntington.

On the other hand, the streetcar also worked to *centralize* Los Angeles. Downtown Los Angeles became [a genuine] "downtown" and kind of reached the apex of its devel-

Streetcar traveling down Santa Monica Boulevard, at the Sawtelle district of Los Angeles, ca. 1910.

opment in the 1920s and '30s. And that was tied to a streetcar system that fed into the downtown core. And there were in fact two streetcar systems. One was the Red Car [the Pacific Electric], the more famous and better known, a regional interurban system that connected widely separated communities across Riverside County, Los Angeles County, Orange County, and Ventura County. But downtown had its own streetcar system, the Yellow Car [the Los Angeles Railway], and that promoted the centralization of business, of industry, of commerce, and of consumption. And that was tied to the downtown core. So two things were going on: the decentralized suburban [trajectory] that Los Angeles became famous for, one that is often mistaken for the automobile and the freeway. But on the other hand, the bolstering of a centralized downtown core in the 1920s and '30s.

JS *A constant of Los Angeles, and a major theme of this book, is the intimate and complex relationship of mobility and urban development. In the prewar era, what was the relationship of the streetcar to the kinds of communities that emerged as an outgrowth of its construction? Specifically, what were the economic consequences of the streetcar system, especially for that era's working people and people of color?*

EA I think you have to remember that in the early decades of the twentieth century, community formation in Los Angeles was a highly segregated process, divided by race and class. Many of the early suburban developments, places that are among the more famous suburban communities of the Southern California region, places like Beverly Hills or Pasadena or Palos Verdes, were—the word they used at the time was "protected"—by deed restrictions, restrictive governance, homeowners' associations, zoning. And a lot of suburban communities followed that pattern of "whites-only" through various public policies and private practices. So this meant that working-class people of color really had few options in terms of settlement—and residential settlement in particular. And the two communities that stood out from this at the time were Boyle Heights and Watts.

Boyle Heights in the early twentieth century was a racially and ethnically diverse working-class neighborhood. And Watts took shape in a similar pattern in the 1910s and '20s. And that was because a lot of racial, ethnic, and religious groups were not able to access suburban neighborhoods that were restricted to white Protestant Americans. And the streetcar was essential to the development of Watts and Boyle Heights. The streetcar sustained access to jobs taking shape in other parts of Southern California, in Orange County, for example, and in the San Gabriel Valley or the San Fernando Valley—the largely agricultural sector of the economy—but also in the burgeoning industrial and manufacturing sector of the economy that took shape in the 1930s.

Watts, for instance, was a classic example of a racially and ethnically diverse working-class community that was directly tied to streetcar development because Watts was home to what was known as the Watts Station. And that was a rail station that connected all these different lines that ran all over Southern California—from Orange County to the San Fernando Valley, from Santa Monica to the San Gabriel Valley. And most of them went through downtown. So people who lived in Watts—and this was true of Boyle Heights as well—relied upon the streetcar for access to jobs as well as access to sites of leisure and recreation and consumption…at least those that were not racially restricted for white-use only.

JS *With its massive concrete viaducts and overpasses, the freeway system sometimes feels like it was built around the time of the pyramids—as if it's always been there—but in fact there was a very conscious and deliberate choice, not all that long ago, to construct what you call "the largest public works program in the history of Los Angeles." How was the freeway system conceived and promoted? Who was behind it? What were its stated goals, and what were its unstated goals?*

EA Well, the modern freeway system that defines twentieth-century Los Angeles really was born in 1956 with the National Interstate and Defense Highway Act that Congress unanimously passed during the Eisenhower administration. Eisenhower was a Republican, and both Republicans and Democrats in Congress overwhelmingly supported a national highway project to connect cities to each other but also to connect neighborhoods and communities *within* cities. So the national highway system was built both as an interurban and an *intra*urban system. And Eisenhower was a military man; this was after World War II, but [America] was still in the midst of the Cold War—the war in Korea, the war in Vietnam—and highways were [seen as] essential to the defense effort because a lot of that defense effort was channeled toward the Pacific Coast, and Los Angeles received the lion's share of federal expenditures for highway construction. So that's how I would explain the origins of LA's modern highway system that we love and hate today [laughs].

JS *Although to be clear, they had already built some of the freeways by 1956, such as Arroyo Seco and the Hollywood freeways.*

EA Yes, sure, there is a "prehistory" to the modern highway system of the Eisenhower era. Going back to the late 1930s, the Arroyo Seco freeway was the prototype of what

Arroyo Seco Parkway, 1944.

became the modern freeway system. But I think of that as a different generation of highway building. The Arroyo Seco was built at the behest of powerful political and economic leaders tied to Downtown Los Angeles, many of whom lived in the wealthy suburb of Pasadena. So those businessmen wanted a modern highway to connect those two communities through the historic Arroyo Seco riverbed. That highway was built in the mold of the "parkway" concept that had been designed and planned in New York, like the Hutchinson River Parkway. There was a different set of goals: not just to connect a wealthy suburb to a downtown core but to promote a kind of leisurely, recreational ideal of automobile mobility. That was a powerful and influential mode of urban planning at the introduction of the automobile age—this ideal of integrating nature into the city. And the automobile could be that kind of linkage between nature and urbanization.

Fast-forward to the 1950s, with rapid population growth in Southern California, rapid industrialization, plus the outlay of hundreds of millions if not billions of federal dollars towards a national highway infrastructure, and that kind of parkway-oriented,

Renewing the Dream

pleasure-driven "nature-and-city" relationship was quickly abandoned for a much more technologically efficient and rapid means of building an integrated highway network that dispensed with all the frills of tree plantings and landscaping and curvatures and that was about straight concrete lines from point A to point B.

JS *Virtually from the start, it seems there was an understanding that in addition to being a new kind of high-speed transportation system, the freeways would be an instrument of slum clearance and urban renewal. How did this second agenda, so to speak, arise and play out?*

EA You have to think about the context of the American city in the mid-twentieth century, and the rise of a decentralized military-industrial complex that took shape through coordinated and calculated federal, state, and local policies, [which] directly affected the means by which modern highways were built—particularly after 1956 and

Working-class homes in Los Angeles being destroyed for freeway construction, 1959.

Sunset Crash

*Construction of Interstate 10 (the Santa Monica Freeway),
seen from Hoover Street, leveling a 300-foot-wide swath
through African American communities southwest of
Downtown Los Angeles, 1961.*

Renewing the Dream

Wayne Thiebaud, Heavy Traffic, *1988.*

Sunset Crash

the Interstate highway program. So while the federal government was coordinating plans for highway construction, at the same time it was also coordinating plans for slum clearance, urban renewal, and public housing. And I think highway construction is part and parcel of those larger policies and programs that were intended to redesign and reinvent American cities in the mid-twentieth century. Part of that goal, according to New Deal programs, was to clear cities of the working-class and immigrant slums that were rooted to the turn of the century, or even back to the late nineteenth century, with the great waves of immigration from southern and eastern Europe. And to follow the kind of modernist ideals of city design and city planning that were largely born formally in Europe in the early twentieth century.

And the experience of World War II in Europe certainly played a role in creating a template for how to rebuild cities in the aftermath of devastation and destruction. American urban planners learned a lot about how to use bulldozers and wrecking balls to rid the cities of the old slums and to impose a new model of order upon the metropolis, to erase the old, late-nineteenth-century vestiges of disorder, which were largely recognized through the persistence of slum housing and immigrant neighborhoods. The problem, I think, is the way that race was directly tied to ideas about slums and blight, and how racial communities and ethnic communities became the target for not just public housing programs, but also urban renewal and slum-clearance programs as well. And I think you'll find in most American cities in the 1940s and '50s, a lot of the men who were implementing federal plans for urban renewal and slum clearance were also the same men who coordinated highway construction programs and procedures.

These men shared the ideals, the perceptions, the values, and the assumptions that—the first word that came to my mind was "afflicted"—the planning community of the mid-twentieth century, though one might think of a more benign word to use. And I think most urban historians of the twentieth century would agree that redlining also had an influential role in kind of providing a template or a foundation for understanding the problems with American cities that needed to be "fixed," and [the practice of] redlining usually defined those problems in terms of race and poverty. So highway construction was coordinated with urban renewal and slum clearance and the wrecking balls and bulldozers that were sicced on the landscape of American inner cities. They were used not only to build corporate plazas and highway interchanges and modern freeways and skyscrapers and parks but also targeted the vestiges of racial and ethnic poverty in the city.

JS *According to reports of the time from the Division of Highways quoted in your books, some individuals and communities located in the path of new freeways seemed prepared to give up their properties in the name of progress—and eminent domain payments from the government—but in many other places, there was a great political challenge to the proposed roads. I wonder if you could speak about the different political responses to freeway planning and construction in at that time.*

EA   There were protests all over Los Angeles against the imposition of freeways through residential neighborhoods. In Boyle Heights, going back to the early 1950s, there were organized protests, what we might call traditional expressions of political protest: packing committee hearings before the Division of Highways, circulating petitions, circulating flyers, knocking on doors, asking residents to sign petitions, to oppose the construction of the 101, the 10, the 5, the 60, and the 710 freeways. I think those expressions of political protest are a reflection of the original racial and ethnic diversity and working-class character of Boyle Heights, which really experienced its heyday in the 1920s and '30s. So there were protests against the incursion of five

Carlos Almaraz, Sunset Crash, *1982.*

freeways in Boyle Heights, but to no avail. On the other hand, you could go to Beverly Hills where there was a proposal to build a highway along Santa Monica Boulevard, but the people of Beverly Hills in the early 1960s staged similar expressions of political protests, petitions, and packing committee hearings—and they won. So there is no freeway in Beverly Hills; the plan for the Beverly Hills freeway was canceled. And I think that says a lot about the unequal distribution of political power and economic wealth in the Los Angeles region.

JS *The freeways brought with them not only a new way to get around the region but novel kinds of urban experiences for those who drove on them. How would you characterize those new experiences, in terms of the individual driver but also on ways of seeing—or not seeing—the larger city?*

EA I think of the freeway as part of a whole host of new cultural experiences, cultural spaces, and cultural institutions that were born during the era of mass suburbanization in the United States, underwritten, of course, by federal policies dating back to the 1930s, the Home Owners' Loan Corporation and Federal Housing Administration and GI Bill of Rights: freeways, theme parks, shopping malls, television, suburban tract-housing developments. These all reflected a new socio-spatial order that was born in the age of mass suburbanization. And the reason I think they are *suburban* and not *urban* is because they marked a very clear and conscious departure from older models of urban experience that took shape in the late nineteenth and early twentieth centuries. To me, the paragon of that older model of urban experience could be a space like Coney Island in New York. It could also be the streetcar or the subway. It could be the sidewalks and busy streets in Times Square. These were spaces that brought diverse strangers together and promoted the anonymity and congestion and crowds of modern urban life.

This new suburban order that took shape after World War II was dedicated to a kind of segmentation of the urban public. And it's segmentation by race and class. It also included a clear rejection of that bustle of crowds that traditionally defined the experience of urban modernity and urban life. In the same way that shopping malls insulate consumers from the streets of the city, the same way that Disneyland was built to kind of create this insular, self-contained universe of pleasure and attraction, the same way that

Carlos Almaraz, Longo Crash, *1982.*

Sunset Crash

Frank Romero, Harbor Freeway, 2010.

the television promoted a retreat from the movie theater and other [communal] institutions of modern urban life, so the freeway separated drivers from the bustle of the city. It atomized drivers moving autonomously through the city—not only within the contained space of the automobile but also within the contained space of the freeway itself, which usually ran either above or below the surface of daily urban life in the city.

JS *By the 1980s and beyond, the LA freeway system brought forth a remarkable range of cultural responses, especially in painting and photography. What drew artists to the subject of the freeway, and how did they respond in various ways?*

EA There's no question that for an entire generation of American artists, the freeway has been a source of creative inspiration: these strange, imposing, but also heavily used and essential features of the postwar city. These structures are inspiring from a creative perspective in the same way that other aspects of urban design and infrastructure have inspired artists across millennia; that there's nothing new or surprising about that to me, I totally understand that. What I found to be interesting [in Los Angeles] is the Chicano generation of artists who *weren't* inspired by the freeway. I really don't think they could have cared less about the freeway. They *were* inspired by depicting their community. And it so happened that their community was plagued—was riddled—with freeways, largely because of the racial underpinnings of highway construction and other federal programs in the mid-twentieth century.

So when I think of [artists like] Ansel Adams or Wayne Thiebaud, or James Doolin or Catherine Opie, these people set out to say: the freeway is a fascinating monument. And I want to capture it and render it to either heighten its alienating qualities or to marvel at its design. But it *wasn't* about: I'm going to go back to my community and paint my community and write about my community and celebrate my community in all of its beauty and hideousness. Those are two very, very different things. And if you think about the history of urban policy and you think about the history of highway construction and the way that it was tied to redlining and slum clearance, you have to consider the racial dimensions of that discrepancy.

WB *Could you sketch for us, going back to the late 1950s, what was it like to see those bulldozers show up in an area like Boyle Heights, and the impact it would have had on life in those communities, which were already shifting substantially to a Chicano population?*

EA It's interesting, because there's an entire generation of Mexican American artists and writers who grew up in Boyle Heights. Many of them were the children or grand-children of Mexican immigrants born and raised in Boyle Heights in the 1940s and '50s who became very involved with the politics of the Chicano movement in the 1970s. And an important part that political movement was creative work like art and literature and muralism. And this generation of young Chicano activists who came of age in the '70s turned their creative focus upon the problems and possibilities of living in a community defined by race and poverty, and their creative works are, for me, the best resource for understanding what Boyle Heights was like in the age of the freeway.

So you could go to the paintings of Frank Romero or Carlos Almaraz or the muralism of Judy Baca or the novels of Helena Maria Viramontes to get a very graphic sense of the tremendous upheaval that these people witnessed as children, as teenagers, as young political activists, in the 1960s and '70s—and, you know, Boyle Heights after 1956 literally witnessed an invasion of bulldozers and wrecking balls coming in, tearing up the landscape, destroying homes, destroying communities, in order to build five intersecting freeways and the freeway interchanges that consumed massive amounts of land. Based on my reading, that's how people experienced highway construction in Boyle Heights— which, as we said, was tied to urban renewal and slum clearance and, going back to redlining documents of the 1930s, was very clearly defined as a slum because of its racial and ethnic poverty.

JS *Chicano artists certainly seemed to view and represent the freeways distinctively in their work. In the paintings of Frank Romero and David Botello, the massive raised overpasses and viaducts—typically seen from beneath—appear less as inspiring works of engineering than intrusions on the city's landscape. Carlos Almaraz's intense, graphic paintings of freeway crashes and explosions, meanwhile, seem to connect to a long thread of apocalyptic imagery woven into the culture of Southern California, from Joan Didion's essays on the Watts Riots to "the Burning of Los Angeles" theme in Nathanael West's 1939 novel,* The Day of the Locust. *Why did these Chicano artists choose to render the freeway as they did? What do we learn from their powerful images?*

EA With regards to Carlos Almaraz, there's a very simple answer, I think, to under-standing his fixation on the freeway. When I was doing research in the Smithsonian Archives of American Art, there's a transcription of an interview with Almaraz, and he talks about living in Boyle Heights and Echo Park in close proximity to freeways and routinely hearing or seeing car crashes on the freeway. That just became a fact of his daily life. What gets a little more complex is when you realize that Almaraz died of AIDS in 1989. And in the years before he died, in the early 1980s, he began to paint these haunting, violent, but also beautiful images of destruction on the freeway. They could be a metaphor for his own sense of destruction. As a historian, I can't really venture beyond the written evidence that is accessible to me, but I think that is something worth considering. But like Botello and Romero, he was simply painting the ugliness and the beauty of the community that he was raised in, which became a barrio—in no small part because of things like highway construction—during the 1960s and '70s. For Botello and Romero it was all about: I'm going to tackle the barrio as the subject of art because no white artists in this country would ever come here to paint this neighborhood, they just don't care about it.

That's why Ed Ruscha took a U-turn in Downtown Los Angeles when he was doing *Every Building on the Sunset Strip*. He only went so far and when he got to downtown, he took a U-turn and went back to the West Side. No [outside] artist was going to go into East LA, but it so happened that there was this entire generation of artists who saw beauty in their neighborhood that was ravaged by highway construction. That suffered from many forms of inequality and oppression based on the racial and socioeconomic character of the neighborhood. And for them, that was a political act, to take up the barrio as the focus of their work.

And my challenge to my colleagues in the field of urban history and urban planning is to recognize this body of work as a form of knowledge. It's not just a pretty picture. It's not just art, it's not just peripheral to the political and economic struggle of people living under the conditions of inequality in the city; these paintings, these novels, these murals, these images constitute a form of knowledge that is equally as important as the data urban planners in the California Division of Highways compiled in the 1940s and '50s in order to determine routing selection for federal and state highways. But we don't know how to walk that bridge between what we think of as politics on the one hand and what we think of as culture on the other. And as long as we're unable to cross that bridge, I won't be optimistic about equitable solutions to the chasms and divides that have been built into the fabric of American cities.

JS   In Folklore of the Freeway *you include a 1984 painting by Frank Romero called* Pink Landscape, *showing one of the earliest aboveground Metro lines, commissioned to celebrate the opening of a new transit line. As the half-century era of the freeway's overwhelming dominance has given way to new kinds of mobility in the twenty-first century, how do you see the city's relationship between mobility and urban development evolving?*

EA   Well, I see it as evolving. I think beginning in the 1970s with the foresight of mayors like Tom Bradley, who realized that the automobile and the freeway as a way of life was not sustainable. Especially after 1973 with the energy crisis and the oil boycott by OPEC nations and high gas prices and lines at gas stations; this was a real crisis for Americans who believed that automobiles and the freeways were here forever, that this was the future. That came to an abrupt end in the 1970s, and in Los Angeles Tom Bradley planted the seeds for the beginnings of a new generation of mass transit, a combination of heavy and light-rail. During his terms as mayor of Los Angeles in the 1970s and '80s, Bradley was able to get the ball rolling on the beginnings of LA Metro, which began as that one line, the Purple Line, from Downtown Los Angeles into Hollywood, that opened in 1993.

That marked the beginning of a new age of mass transit. And I think that subsequent forms of community protests in East Los Angeles and in Southeast and South Los Angeles, with a focus on transit inequality and environmental racism, dovetailed with the opening and expansion of the Metro in the 1990s and beyond. So it is a new age, I think, a new era of mass transit, even as we struggle to adapt to the challenges that the automobile and the freeway continue to pose in the region.

Frank Romero, Metro Blue Line Commemorative Poster,
1990.

JS *The situation in Los Angeles—as in New York—is exceedingly charged today with
a problem that many other older American cities would love to have: that they have
become attractive to too many people of means. Lots of people—especially young people—want to live in the big "superstar" cities and of course that brings many good things
with it, but it also brings enormous issues in terms of rising rents and lack of affordable
housing and other things. And I think it's obvious to everybody that there's a major crisis
in Los Angeles, and in Southern California as a whole, in housing its people. How might
that evolve as we go forward; is there any hope?*

EA Great question. This is far outside my own expertise, but I am encouraged by the
search for new solutions. And I am encouraged by the role that community activists are
playing in kind of heightening the urgency of this search for new solutions. I'm fasci-
nated by the politics of anti-gentrification in East Los Angeles and South Los Angeles.
And I'm pleased that people are beginning to understand the negative consequences
of gentrification and the toll that it takes on what's left of LA's working-class communities. The middle class has been decimated, and Los Angeles, like most [successful]
American cities, has become polarized between the haves and the have-nots. But I
think that mass transit entails the possibility of a more just society—as long as there
are active policies in place and measures taken to minimize the inequities intended
within gentrification, housing, construction, environmental justice, and a whole list of
concerns that community activists are bringing to our attention. Certainly.

An autonomous delivery robot, produced by Serve Robotics, navigating streets and sidewalks on its own to carry out a food delivery on the streets of Los Angeles, 2020. The robot features a childlike, vaguely anthropomorphic appearance of the vehicle—a deliberate design feature intended to make the robot seem friendlier and more familiar to dogs and pedestrians.

3 — Something New Under the Sun: The Mobility Revolution in Southern California
Greg Lindsay

Save Our Sidewalks

> *The story of Los Angeles, like that of most cities, is a tale of changing mobility.*
>
> JOHN ROSSANT AND STEPHEN BAKER, 2019

One night in September 2017, electric scooters mysteriously began turning up on the sidewalks, bike paths, and boardwalks of Santa Monica, California, a compact ocean-front city on the west side of greater Los Angeles. The unmarked vehicles belonged to Bird, a local start-up renting them by the minute via a smartphone app. Though the scooters were placed in public outdoor spaces, Bird chose not to seek approval from—nor even inform—any city or county officials before scattering their devices around town, a decision inspired, presumably, by Uber's policy of "permissionless innovation": transgress first, seek forgiveness after. ("After," in this case, meaning months or even years later, once a stream of revenue had begun to flow in, a substantial customer base had been established, and high-powered lobbyists could be brought in to influence government officials and agencies.) Sure enough, the little two-wheeled devices—which could be picked up and left almost anywhere and were easy and intuitive to use—immediately began to catch on with residents and visitors alike, and within months thousands of them could be found strewn all over the sidewalks. Despite a popular backlash and the threat of bans, a sizable piece of public space had been colonized, overnight, by a new and privately operated form of transportation.

Unlike previous start-ups, Bird tossed a bone to cities in the form of "Save Our Sidewalks" (SOS), a pledge to contribute $1 per scooter per day toward building dedicated bicycle and scooter lanes. Like a toy version of the fabled 1940s General Motors streetcar conspiracy—in which, it has long been claimed, the giant automaker deliberately acquired and dismantled Los Angeles's aging but still-popular electric streetcar lines to encourage a switch to gas-powered buses and cars—Bird openly dared public officials to transfer street lanes and curbside parking away from its competitor: automobiles.

The company quietly sank the SOS program in early 2019, claiming cities misspent the funds. By then, however, Bird had logged more than 100 million rides in 120 cities and become the first start-up to be valued at $2 billion in less than a year of existence. Just as Uber and Lyft had demonstrated how a combination of new technology and deep-pocketed investors could upend the taxi business and strong-arm regulators, Bird's tactics hinted at how the next wave of mobility companies would seek to remake the urban fabric itself.

Whether or not Bird or any of its competitors endures in its current form, the emergence of dockless scooters, electric-assist bicycles, and other modes of "micromobility" represent the first significant new category of vehicles to appear on the streets of Los Angeles in more than a century. Unlike passenger-carrying drones or fully autonomous

The fast-growing popularity of dockless shared vehicles such as Bird and Lime in many Los Angeles communities— including Santa Monica (above)—has brought with it an unsightly corollary (above, right): dozens of e-scooters strewn casually by their previous users along city sidewalks and other public open spaces, infuriating residents and officials.

vehicles—technologies already a decade or more in the making, yet still mostly speculative—the rise of micromobility vehicles has been astonishingly brief and very real. Analysts for scooters and their like giddily point to adoption rates higher and faster than ride-hailing automobiles, while noting that two-fifths of all car trips cover less than four miles (a distance easily covered on two wheels rather than four). Or in other words, a world ripe for the picking.

Even if their promise to transform cities is never fully realized, electric scooters hint at a radically different model for urban mobility. Instead of piloting your own large vehicle from driveway to freeway to a parking space at an office or shopping mall you may never set foot in again, imagine riding an electric-assist bicycle to an all-day café-cum-courtyard work space a few minutes away—all booked seamlessly through an app and paid for with a tap. The scooter might even come to you; Spin, Segway-Ninebot, and others are developing semiautonomous versions capable of delivering themselves, making it possible to summon one to your door.

And that represents just one of the dozens of possible transportation scenarios being energetically pursued in Los Angeles at this moment. Their sheer variety—in their scale, in the technologies they employ, in the nature of their sponsors, even in their very domains of motion (not just the surface of the city, but above and below it)—is remarkable. But for all their differences (and as Bird's rollout demonstrates), they present a common, profound challenge to the status quo of urban movement: entangling the public and private spheres in ways not seen in a century or more.

It used to be so simple. For much of the past century, the dividing line in America between private and public transportation was clear, stable, and all but immutable. It was in many ways a rivalry, to be sure—one in which, decade after decade, the private automobile seemed increasingly victorious. Most Americans owned a car—many suburban households owned two or three—which they used to travel almost everywhere. To enable the movement of those private vehicles, city and state governments built, maintained, and regulated the public thoroughfares on which those cars traveled, along with plenty of curbside and other parking spaces to store them when not in motion. States and municipalities also—and often reluctantly—provided public transportation: buses that used the same streets and roads as cars and, in larger urban centers, rail and metro lines to move people within and between cities. Until fairly recently, more accommodation was made each year for cars and less for public transit. New highways and freeways were constructed, and existing roads widened, to speed the flow of traffic, and more parking spaces were provided, on-street and off. Public transportation agencies, meanwhile, were ever more starved for funds and often forced to reduce service. Over time, fewer people tended to use transit, and those that did were increasingly marginalized. It was an obvious—and perhaps unfair—contest, but one whose boundaries were well-defined, well established, and essentially fixed.

No longer. In the past decade, the explosion of new kinds of mobility has begun to change everything about this long-standing arrangement—blurring and intertwining those once-firm lines of demarcation between public and private. The most obvious symbol of the change, of course, has been the unbundling of the large, lumbering, all-purpose automobile into a profusion of new modes of travel—often smaller, more agile, and tailored to different purposes or distances. Even more revolutionary, if less visible, are the startling innovations in digital technology—above all the emergence of smartphone-enabled apps—that allow for all kinds of vehicles, from the newfangled electric devices of Bird and Lime to the fleets of conventional sedans and SUVs operated by Uber and Lyft, to be seamlessly rented on demand, rather than owned or leased. It has been the widespread acceptance of the *sharing* of vehicles, even more than new kinds of vehicles themselves, that in many ways represents the most radical leap for the vast majority of Americans—Southern Californians above all—who have long regarded the ownership of a private automobile not only as an inalienable right but as an extension of one's personal identity.

> Arguably, the smartphone is the most fundamental transportation technology of the twenty-first century. It is our constant companion… [and] has changed the way we travel. It also connects travelers to new information, to nearby vehicles, and perhaps most importantly, to anyone going their way.
>
> HENRY GRABAR, 2019

And yet even these striking shifts in the way we live now may not represent the most potent or transformative impact of the new mobility revolution being pioneered in Los Angeles. The story of Bird's unexpected appearance in Santa Monica—from the visible change it brought to the city's streets and sidewalks to the unseen but no less profound challenge it posed to the agencies whose mission it is to regulate those streets and sidewalks—foretells a remarkable renegotiation of the relationship of private companies and public officials that have long governed and given shape to the modern city.

Just as railroad lines, then streetcar networks, and then automobiles (and the great freeway network built for them) successively reshaped the physical and socioeconomic landscape of Los Angeles, a new generation of technologies—nearly all of them underpinned by the digital revolution that has transformed every aspect of contemporary life—now promises to remake the region once again, in ways that we can just now begin to glimpse.

The Kitchen

> I want everyone to come here and try stuff. I want LA to be the kitchen where all this is cooked.
>
> ERIC GARCETTI, MAYOR OF LOS ANGELES, 2018

It was hardly a coincidence that Bird chose Santa Monica to launch its new service—nor that the start-up was located in Los Angeles in the first place. By the late 2010s, the sprawling West Coast metropolis had become the world's cauldron of innovation in urban mobility.

In some ways this was surprising. No city, after all, has been more closely identified with the reigning mode of twentieth-century transportation—the private automobile—that all these newer innovations, one way or another, are bent on superseding. Los Angeles also presents a unique—and uniquely challenging—regulatory landscape for any would-be mobility entrepreneur. Unlike the relatively unified structure of most American cities, LA's political map is a bewildering patchwork of eighty-eight different jurisdictions—not only the City of Los Angeles itself, where power is divided between the mayor and a fifteen-seat city council, but dozens of smaller independent cities like Culver City, Beverly Hills, Bel-Air, West Hollywood, Inglewood, and, yes, Santa Monica, each with its own strong-willed mayor and council. As if that were not complicated enough, there are also scores of "unincorporated" districts—many of them right in the middle of town—which are legally not part of *any* city and are instead operated by Los Angeles County (governed by still another five-member council). Even a short-distance vehicle might cross three or four municipal boundaries on a typical trip. Who's in charge?

Yet these obvious drawbacks have been more than outweighed, in recent years, by the region's outstanding assets. First, of course, is LA's famously sun-washed, temperate

Map of metropolitan Los Angeles, 2020, comprising five counties, eighty-eight independently incorporated cities, and large unincorporated areas of Los Angeles County and its adjacent counties.

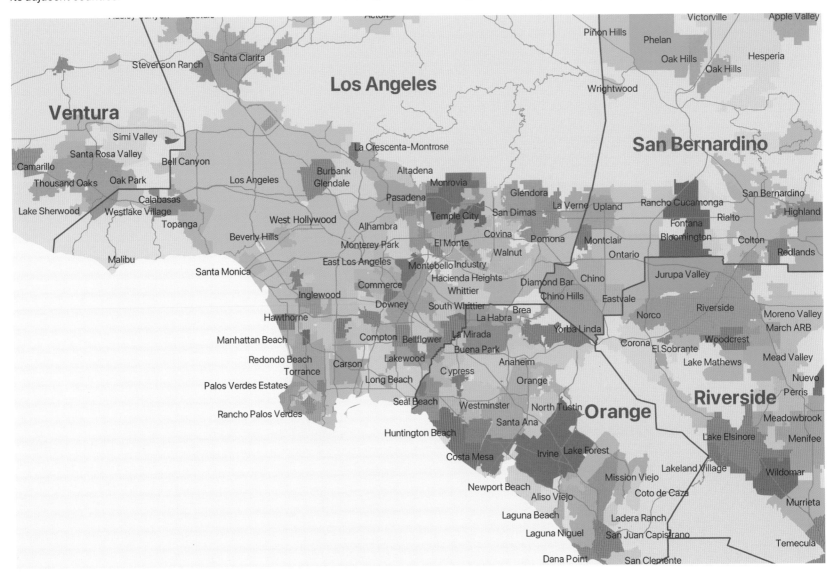

Renewing the Dream

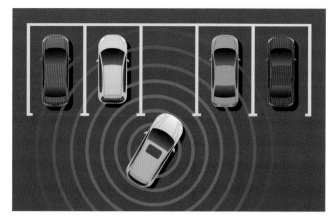

Unlike private cars, which require a parking space at both their point of origin and their destination, shared autonomous EVs—summoned by smartphone app much like today's Uber or Lyft (bottom), and retiring overnight to a remote charging area, where they would park themselves (top)—would likely require no parking accommodation within the city.

climate, which makes open-air devices like dockless scooters and electric-assist bikes an attractive and realistic alternative to fully enclosed, climate-controlled vehicles. Then there is Southern California's long heritage of leadership in aerospace technology and its large pool of engineering talent, whose expertise in lightweight structures and innovative materials has proved readily transferable to the design and fabrication of these new, highly efficient contrivances (as well as more ambitious proposals to move people above and below the city's surface). Widespan, ground-level work spaces for start-ups are relatively easy to locate within the sprawling industrial reaches of the region, and multiple sources of venture capital are not far at hand, especially with Silicon Valley just a few hundred miles to the north.

Beyond these worldly advantages, furthermore, lies a larger energizing reality: the very scale and seeming intractability of its traffic crisis—for decades an aching fact of life for the city—makes Los Angeles exceptionally open to exploring alternative ways to move around. Even as they oversee the largest public-transit construction effort in America in eighty years, LA's leaders have thrown out a welcome mat to all comers in private mobility. "My goal, and the goal of this city," then-Mayor Eric Garcetti declared in no uncertain terms in 2018, "is to be transportation capital of the world."

By then, he was well on his way to getting his wish. "For electric bus manufacturers, designers of flying machines, ride-sharing app-developers, tunneling companies—for mobility entrepreneurs of every stripe and color—LA present[s] an immense and ravenous market for miles," write the urbanists John Rossant and Stephen Baker. "The coming transition is bound to transform the economy, the cityscape, and life itself in this sun-soaked expanse of California." Responding to the city's enormous market opportunities as well as its mayoral "invitation," a head-spinning array of new transportation concepts, proposals, and inventions have begun development across Southern California. Some are tiny, some are huge. Some are already well in use, others still in prototype, and yet others reside only, for now, in the dreamlike realm of digital renderings.

At one end of the spectrum are "micro" solutions, ranging from the diminutive Bird scooter to slightly larger electric-assist bicycles to a new breed of small but enclosed two-seat, electric hybrids such as the Arcimoto—intended to fill, in the words of its inventor, Mark Frohnmayer, the "enormous [market] space between the motorcycle and the car" and well-suited, its promoters claim, to the vast majority of short-range trips that city dwellers actually make in their full-sized autos. (So short they can be parked sideways, like a Vespa or a Harley, these lightweight, three-wheeled vehicles take up a third of the space, at most, of a conventional automobile—though few if any models have yet to catch on with the general public.)

At the scale of the full-sized automobile, of course, there are the countless prototypes under development—by tech companies, auto manufacturers, and other major players—for fully autonomous electric vehicles, which will not only drive their occupants around town, but, as a crucial corollary, make their own way to parking spaces and charging stations (likely located in remote, less-expensive quarters of the city) when not in use.

Not least of the questions about the future of self-driving cars is whether the familiar model of individual vehicle ownership, or an on-demand model using shared vehicles (essentially similar to Uber or Lyft, without the drivers), will ultimately make more economic and technological sense. "Right now most companies working on self-driving cars are working on them as the prelude to a self-driving-car service," the journalist Alexis C. Madrigal writes. "So you wouldn't own your car; you'd just get rides from a fleet of robo-cars maintained by Waymo or Uber or Lyft." In both cases—but especially the service-oriented model—there will be almost nothing left of today's pressing need for vehicles to be stored in proximity to the people they serve—that is, in centrally located parking lots and garages.

Of course, the question of whether the widespread public adoption of such fully autonomous vehicles will come five years from now, or fifteen, or twenty-five—or *ever*—is one that elicits widely differing responses, to put it politely. Many skeptics point to the still-abiding truth spoken by transportation expert Jameson Wetmore in 2003: "that automated driving has been "'only twenty years away' for sixty years." After more than a decade of intense activity and over $100 billion in private and public investment, early optimism has given way in many quarters to sober realism. "Long term, I think we will have autonomous vehicles that you and I can buy," the Gartner market researcher Mike Ramsey says. "But we're going to be old."

In the meanwhile, there are the handful of truly ambitious—if almost entirely speculative—"macro" solutions proposed for Los Angeles, which call on major engineering breakthroughs to move large numbers of people under the earth or in the sky. Uber Elevate, an aerial division of the rideshare giant since acquired by Joby Aviation, initially conceived—and commissioned design concepts for—a series of raised landing pads scattered around the city, from which hundreds of unmanned passenger-carrying drones ("electric Vertical Take Off and Landing" devices, or eVTOLs) would whisk thousands of well-to-do Angelenos from one end of the region to the other, following the air-space corridors above existing freeways. Whether Los Angeles should be following the lead of São Paulo—home to the world's highest number of helicopters per capita, along with truly staggering inequality and traffic—is rarely discussed.

The mind-boggling technical, environmental, and regulatory obstacles to aerial flyways are rivaled only by its subterranean rival: the tunnel initiative promoted by the Boring Company, the dryly named start-up founded by the omnipresent tech entrepreneur Elon Musk. Dismissive of unmanned drones in the sky (sooner or later, he suggests, one of them will "drop a hubcap and guillotine someone"), Musk is certain the answer to LA's traffic problem lies in the other direction: a network of underground tunnels laced beneath the region, in which individual vehicles are carried on high-speed electric "skates" to vertical access points all over town, where elevator-like lifts carry each auto to and from street level.

Despite the science-fiction-like aura of the concept, Musk's company has succeeded, by all accounts, in achieving significant advances in the traditional boring process—substantially bringing down the cost-per-mile of underground construction—and has built a full-scale, 1.14-mile-long test tunnel under Hawthorne, in southwestern Los Angeles. But given Musk's assessment of transit—"It sucks....It's a pain in the ass....

A visualization of the seductive if still-elusive dream of the fully autonomous vehicle, allowing drivers to use laptops for work, email, or games during their daily commute.

A proposed "SkyPark" airport for eVTOLs for central Los Angeles, designed by Mithun|Hodgetts + Fung in 2019 for Uber Elevate, lifts its landing surface onto a steel-mesh roof structure strong enough to sustain the load of flying vehicles and passengers, while porous enough to allow a measure of sunlight to penetrate to a covered public park beneath, two acres in size.

And there's like a bunch of random strangers, one of who might be a serial killer"—it's again unclear why ordinary Angelenos should root for private tunnels explicitly designed to separate the rich from everyone else. "The degree of contempt autonomists hold for public transit," the author Anthony Townsend notes, "is shocking." The technology writer Paris Marx goes even further, arguing in 2022 that "these technologies are likely to reinforce the trends of growing tech billionaire wealth and these billionaires' desires to close themselves off from the rest of society":

> Recall that the first of Musk's proposed tunnels was designed to make it easier for him to get to and from work without getting stuck in traffic with everyone else. Rather than a network of tunnels for the masses, such a system could be redeployed as one designed by and for the wealthy, inaccessible to the public and connecting only the places that the rich frequent: their gated communities, private airport terminals, and other exclusive areas of the city.

In some ways resembling a reimagined subway system, in others a modern iteration of the postwar car-and-freeway model, Musk's ambitious concept, like nearly every other urban mobility proposal now being floated—above, below, or on the surface—represents a further blurring of the lines between private and public movement and space and, in order to be commercially implemented, will require entire new structures of regulation and oversight. It is striking, however, that nearly all of these proposals and schemes share the Los Angeles region as their incubator and testing ground.

View of a 1.14-mile-long segment of test tunnel constructed by the Boring Company beneath Hawthorne, California.

Thanks to its intrinsic advantages of climate, market, and scale, as well its local government's enthusiasm, Los Angeles has found itself, for better or worse, on the front line of a worldwide struggle over the shape of the future city, one pitting private, self-proclaimed "disrupters"—tech entrepreneurs and start-ups with their eye set firmly on profitability and market share—against public agencies and administrators who must briskly evolve their tactics and vision in order to protect the interests of the larger public, and who, in the end, retain enormous power over how and by whom the public space of the city is used. The outcome of this conflict will not only determine how Angelenos move through the Southland but also help to define the face of the region itself.

The ramifications of this struggle have only been magnified by the Covid-19 pandemic, which as of this writing has killed well over a million Americans, including more than thirty-two thousand in Los Angeles County alone. In the first months of lockdown in 2020, sharing took a back seat to isolation as Angelenos swiftly went back to their own cars. Within months, driving in the city returned to pre-pandemic levels while the number of Uber trips globally fell by half. To compensate, Uber pivoted to the delivery side of its operations, which is now bigger than its ride-hailing business. It is poised to grow bigger still after a series of acquisitions including Cornershop (groceries), Postmates (meals), and Drizly (liquor), surging ahead of competitors DoorDash and Grubhub in terms of market capitalization now that investors demand profits instead of growth.

As thousands of small businesses shuttered amidst the early pandemic fallout, storefronts were rapidly replaced by "micro-fulfillment," "ghost kitchens," and "dark stores" accessible only by app and hidden from view. Parking spaces may well disappear in a city filled with Ubers, self-driving scooters, autonomous shuttles, and delivery robots, but will they take much of the streetscape with it?

Walled Gardens

The larger story of this unfolding struggle over the city's future begins with a blunt reality: with more than 6.4 million vehicles on the streets and freeways of today's Southern California, the private car is in no danger of disappearing anytime soon. The average vehicle life in the region is eleven years, so even if Angelenos were somehow never to replace any automobile they currently own (an unlikely scenario, to say the least), there would still be plenty of cars on the road a decade from now.

But the goal of the mobility revolution now underway in Los Angeles is not to eliminate the private automobile entirely. It is to offer a host of alternatives that better suit the variety of trips people make, to better accommodate different populations in the city, to help to usher in a more environmentally responsible and energy-efficient way of life, and, if all goes well, to put a dent in the traffic congestion that in recent decades has slowed movement around the region, at many times and in many places, to an agonizing crawl. It is not the car, but the city's overwhelming *reliance* on the car, its strangling monoculture, that the leaders of the mobility revolution—public and private alike—hope to see overturned.

But how? An obvious if traditional answer is the development of a major rapid-transit system, crisscrossing the region with a mesh of rail lines, like those found in most of the world's great cities. To a degree that would have evinced astonishment in anyone who knew the car-based Los Angeles of 1990, Angelenos have pushed ahead in the years since with the construction of an ambitious rail network—then doubled down on Election Day 2016 by voting with their wallets for Measure M, a Los Angeles County sales tax increase passed by an overwhelming 72 percent of voters, designed to generate an

Construction of new tunnel and station for the Los Angeles Metro, 2018.

estimated $120 billion for massively expanded rail, rapid bus, and bicycle lanes over the next four decades. A shorter-term milestone is 2028, when the city will be hosting the Summer Olympics for the third time in its history. By then, Los Angeles expects to have completed twenty-eight major transit projects, including literally doubling the size of the Metro system. No American city has seen anything like it since the eve of World War II, when the completion of the Independent (IND) line in 1940 capped four decades of furious subway construction in New York.

It remains a stubborn fact, however, that to date many of those same voters have shown considerably less interest in taking public transit themselves. A 2019 poll conducted by UCLA's Michael Manville suggests the old *Onion* parody headline might be on to something: "98 Percent of U.S. Commuters Favor Public Transportation For Others." The actual numbers were less lopsided, of course, but it is still the case that in a non-pandemic year only about 7 percent of the population of Southern California uses public transportation. (The pandemic cut that figure in half, though ridership began rising again swiftly as the viral threat receded.) Supporters of Measure M effectively wanted their neighbors to ride the train or bus so they could drive to work unimpeded. A half-cent sales tax increase was a small price to pay for less congested freeways.

Even as new lines continued to open, ridership on LA Metro's new rail lines grew only slightly over the past five years. The far larger ridership on the LA County's *buses*, meanwhile, fell 19 percent in that same period, as the economic boom—and historically low-interest loans for first-time auto buyers—siphoned tens of thousands of working people from buses to newly affordable new or used cars. Metro officials vowed to go back to basics, with redesigned and updated bus routes and more frequent service.

Previous spread: *The Expo Line passes a mixed-use development called Cumulus, under construction, 2020. Located adjacent to the line's La Cienega station, the development contains over 1,200 apartments and fifty thousand square feet of retail, located in two structures, including a thirty-one-story tower.*

Others suggested taking a longer view, especially in light of the immense amount of apartment, office, and retail construction now underway adjacent to Metro stations (a real estate formula suddenly challenged in 2020–21 by "Covid flight" to more spacious housing, permanent work-from-anywhere policies, and same-day e-commerce, but which, like transit ridership, seems to be reasserting itself in the pandemic crisis' aftermath). At some point, it is safe to assume, a significant number of Angelenos, like their counterparts in New York or Chicago, may well find it easier and more appealing to walk a block or two from their high-rise apartment to a Metro station than crawl for hours through heavy traffic.

Still others have argued that "there's an app for that"—or at least there should be—and that buses and trains should act more like Uber. Or be run by Uber itself. In truth, the dramatic rise and pervasive adoption of Uber, Lyft, and their ride-hailing rivals in the mid-2010s shocked and awed veteran transportation planners. "No one had an inkling, including me, that people would change their travel habits so quickly and dramatically," the noted traffic engineer "Gridlock Sam" Schwartz recently confessed. In the space of a few years, Uber and Lyft overturned the traditional status markers of California car culture, with driving one's own vehicle taking a back seat, for many, to being driven by someone else.

Despite their hardball tactics in establishing and expanding their services, both companies assiduously asserted themselves as allies to cities in "the war on cars." Seizing on the observation by UCLA's Donald Shoup that the average automobile is parked 95 percent of the time, they insisted the unparalleled convenience of their roaming fleets would eventually supplant private ownership and redound to the city's benefit (not least, as argued elsewhere in part 2 of this book, by liberating the vast acreage of surface space now dedicated to parking).

But as has become clear through the research of academics, transportation officials, and even the companies themselves, ride-hailing succeeded in reducing the need for parking by injecting hundreds of millions of new vehicle miles traveled (VMT) into American city streets. Just as venture capital subsidized their artificially low fares, so many residents paid the price for their constant motion. Uber and Lyft drivers, according to the companies' own data, comprised 2.6 percent of pre-pandemic traffic in Los Angeles County, a formidable number indeed. Congestion has risen accordingly. And not coincidentally, bus speeds have fallen in tandem, sometimes to a crawl, producing a vicious circle in which transit's supposed allies contribute to the wave of frustrated riders abandoning transit.

Given this disheartening situation, one might be tempted to fight fire with fire. Responding to ride-hailing's instant gratification, transit advocates have countered with "mobility-as-a-service" (MaaS). In this vision, a single smartphone app combining route-finding, booking, and payment across multiple modes of travel would extend both public and private services, while retaining a large measure of public control over the movement of people. Fares would be replaced by monthly all-you-can-travel subscriptions (similar to smartphones' data plans), in hopes of convincing customers to get on the train, or back onto the bus. In this vision, old-school transit operators will be recast as "*mobility integrators*," Anthony Townsend writes, "expanding into the business of MaaS while continuing to operate trains and buses. This would gradually expand the role of government from simply building and running trains and buses to orchestrating the flow of mobility data and mobility-service transactions."

Linking fixed transit lines to the go-anywhere flexibility of the new mobility modes would seem to solve the long-standing "last mile" dilemma that has bedeviled the region's transportation planners for years: unlike denser Eastern cities where a high percentage of people live in walking distance of metro stations, people in low-density Los Angeles often

Renewing the Dream

Mobility-as-a-Service apps bring a city's entire transportation system, public and private, to a smartphone screen, including constantly updated real-time data on departure and arrival times and route changes.

live too far from a station to conveniently walk. How should they traverse that last mile? A cheap, readily available electric scooter, electric-assist bike, or Uber ride might be just the answer. Indeed, Phillip Washington, the former head of LA Metro, has proposed an organic analogy for this hybrid, with the Metro's rail and bus lines as the system's sturdy trunks and branches, and scooters, bikes, and hailed vehicles as fine-grained tendrils, spreading just about everywhere (see page 117).

Although MaaS platforms have launched in a handful of overseas cities—including Berlin, Helsinki, and Singapore—perhaps the biggest proponents of the idea in the United States, ironically enough, are Uber and Lyft. The former began to pivot with the arrival in 2017 of a new CEO, Dara Khosrowshahi. "I want to run the bus systems for a city," he declared in his first public remarks. I want you to be able to take an Uber and get into the subway...[then] get out and have an Uber waiting for you." Setting aside the fact that its pilot projects connecting commuters to transit have not shown much success, there's a lot to unpack in that statement. Uber, of course, has no intention of running buses on behalf of cities, but is already happy to sell bus tickets through its app in Denver and London, with more cities on the way. Khosrowshahi has since expanded his aim for Uber to become nothing less than "the operating system for your everyday life."

When scooters and e-bikes arrived on the scene, meanwhile, early data suggested they would cannibalize short ride-hailing trips. Uber promptly acquired Jump bike—an on-demand electric-assist smart bicycle service—while Lyft, not to be caught short, bought Motivate, which operates public bikeshare systems in New York, Chicago, and elsewhere. The latter deal included exclusive rights to host docking stations on public property and the public right of way—potentially invaluable real estate for future mobility offerings. In short order, Lyft added bicycle stations and bus stops to its own app, and the company's cofounder, John Zimmer, began talking up "transportation-as-a-service."

Their dueling efforts to vertically integrate ride-hailing, micro-mobility, and public transport did not go unnoticed. Transit advocates warned of the two companies retreating behind privately controlled "walled gardens," precluding open competition in favor of a local monopoly—at least a duopoly.

All through the rapid rise of ridesharing, back in the mid-2010s, public officials had begged, threatened, or cajoled start-ups to share the data necessary for understanding the scope and scale of their operations—to no avail. But although they were essentially flying blind and stripped of regulatory powers by state lawmakers, the officials at the Los Angeles Department of Transportation (LADOT) had vowed to be better prepared when the "Next Big Thing" appeared. It was just then that Bird arrived.

E-scooter corral and dedicated two-wheel vehicle lane in San Diego, 2020. Adapting swiftly to the challenges and opportunities of micromobility, many Southern California cities have provided street space for both the movement and storage of shared vehicles.

Code Is the New Concrete

While the Internet engendered its own virtual worlds on screens, mobility takes place in the physical realm we inhabit, much of it in our shared space. It involves roads and bike lanes, and machines that can hurtle down sidewalks and bang into us. It has to be managed. So from the get-go there's a clear role for government.

JOHN ROSSANT AND STEPHEN BAKER, 2019

When Bird e-scooters began flocking to the sidewalks of Santa Monica, the region's transportation officials worried they were about to be overwhelmed yet again, as they had been when ride-hailing came out of nowhere. This time, however, LADOT was ready. For months, its staff had worked with software engineers and counterparts from around the country to create the Mobility Data Specification (MDS), an open standard for receiving data on the status of a vehicle—where it is, what it's doing, and when a trip begins and ends. Originally designed for the perpetually imminent arrival of self-driving cars, it was immediately re-tasked to deal with the clear and present danger.

MDS also allowed regulators to *send* instructions as well. Is a bike lane closed? Have your app route around it. Did someone throw your scooter into the canals of Venice Beach? Please retrieve it. Did you promise to serve low-income neighborhoods as part of your operating permit? Then redeploy more of your vehicles there. And so on.

A public agency writing its own software standards was unprecedented—but very likely necessary, in the twenty-first century, to retain any semblance of control over the public realm. "We plan the streets, and we design them—but we also regulate and operate them," noted Seleta Reynolds, then general manager of LADOT (and an energetic advocate of a transit-driven future for Southern California) who commissioned MDS. "Code is the new concrete."

Santa Monica became the first city to make MDS a prerequisite for Bird and other scooter companies when the code went live in the spring of 2018. (Within months, Los Angeles, San Jose, Seattle, Austin, and seventy other cities had followed suit.) These cities were not afraid to use their newly expanded power. In July 2019, Santa Monica rebuked Bird for exceeding the number of vehicles allowed by its permit, citing "data anomalies" registered by the MDS. Consequences were swift, with Bird being instructed to downsize its fleet, while Jump and Lyft received a bump in theirs.

As one might expect, cities wielding MDS did not endear themselves to all operators. Uber and others cried foul, citing privacy concerns. Raw data could be de-anonymized, they argued, allowing LADOT to trace individuals' movements and share that information with law enforcement, among others. Supporters bridled at the apparent hypocrisy. The debate moved first to the California legislature, then to the courts. At heart, the issue is: who owns the data emanating from private vehicles on public streets—the company, the customer, or the city?

If MDS was the first tool to make all of Los Angeles machine-readable, it surely won't be the last. A company named Coord—a spin-off of the Google-subsidiary Sidewalk Labs—is on a mission to inventory every stretch of curb in fifteen cities, starting with Los Angeles. Its ambition: to create "a world in which every square foot is priced," in the words of CEO Stephen Smyth. This "asphalt marketplace" would use the concept of dynamic pricing (see chapter 4) to allocate and reallocate curb space and lane space in real time, according to cities' wishes.

Other start-ups, with names like Humn.ai and ClearRoad, envision similar approaches to freeway tolling. Even the Los Angeles County Metropolitan Transportation

Authority has begun exploring the mechanics of implementing congestion pricing in Southern California. What began as a struggle over data is quickly becoming a battle to control the profits of an increasingly contested public realm. "This isn't just going to become a fee," says Townsend. "It's going to become a market for access, because you can turn city streets into a giant ATM."

One way or another, agencies like LADOT are determined to stay ahead of the situation. If they fail to assert their presence in this brave new world, they realize, the urban mobility of the twenty-first-century city will be defined by tech entrepreneurs—driven almost entirely by their own financial goals and mandates—rather than the needs of the thirteen million inhabitants of greater Los Angeles. "We could repeat the mistake we made a century ago," Reynolds says. "We adjusted the city around the technology, instead of the other way around."

Crossing the Lines

Several of the tantalizing opportunities outlined in *Renewing the Dream*—especially those to reimagine new uses for the endless miles of parking and gas stations scattered across Southern California—arise from the overarching reality of the twentieth-century city: the widespread appropriation of the city's public space for use by the private automobile. Indeed, the size of the city's existing parking inventory and the number of service stations (see chapters 5 and 11) can be considered a clear sign of victory in the private car's triumph over every other kind of urban mobility across the second half of the twentieth century. But the clear lines of that epic battle are now starting to fade, as the generation of advanced, digitally enabled devices and systems now arriving inevitably complicates and confuses that once-simple landscape. Together, they point to a future for urban mobility, which, among other features, will almost certainly include an intricate and meshed interweaving of public and private interests, in ways that continue to evolve year by year—if not month by month.

The possibility of liberating miles of excess surface parking and obsolete gas stations will be just two parts of this new and complex landscape—one whose larger consequences, as they unfold in the coming years, may well be as profound as the earlier revolutions that brought forth the city we know today. For now, we can merely glimpse the lineaments of the ways in which this newest transportation paradigm will remake, once again, the great capital of mobility that is modern Los Angeles.

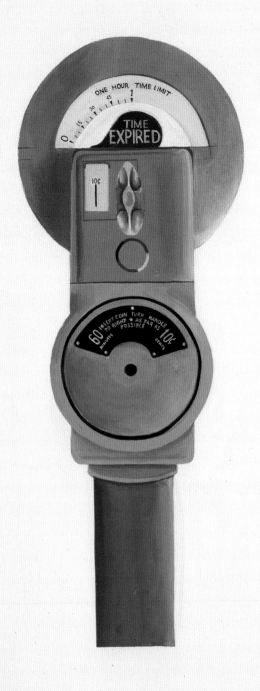

TIME EXPIRED

Reclaim the Curb!
Donald Shoup

Parked cars have colonized city streets for so long that they seem to own the curb lanes, but new travel demands are now competing for time at the curb. Amazon wants loading zones; Uber and Lyft need curb space to pick up and drop off passengers. Transit riders want dedicated bus lanes, cyclists want bike lanes, and pedestrians want wider sidewalks. "What everyone wants," the economist Thomas Sowell observes, "adds up to more than there is."

How can cities manage the curb lane properly? Not with current parking policies, it would seem. For example, a recent study of Uber and Lyft vehicles on Santa Monica Boulevard in West Hollywood found that because only 5 percent of the curb space had been reserved for loading, 41 percent of rideshare vehicles were forced to double-park in an active traffic lane to load or unload passengers—a condition both inconvenient and dangerous. Rideshare vehicles that had stopped in traffic for pickups or drop-offs were double-parked for thirty-seven minutes per hour, delaying all traffic on the street.

Another recent study compared a rental bike station on one side of Broadway in New York with parking spaces occupying the same curb length on the other side of the street. During an hour, two hundred people arrived at or departed from the bike station, while only eleven arrived at or departed from the parking spaces. If we measure productivity by the number of people served, the bike station was eighteen times more productive than the parking spaces.

Converting curb parking spaces to bike stations and ride-hailing loading zones might serve more people and improve the traffic flow, but the shift is problematic for two reasons. First, it is hard to measure the productivity of alternative curb uses. Second, cities lose meter revenue when converting curb parking to other uses. But cities can address both issues by charging the right prices for *all* users of the curb lane.

The only way to know whether the price of parking is right is to look at the results. The right price will leave one or two open curb spaces on every block (to allow convenient access for anyone who wants or needs to park immediately), but most spaces will be occupied (to provide convenient parking for customers of the adjacent stores or other uses). This is the "Goldilocks" principle of parking prices—not too high, not too low, but just right (it's also known as the "85 percent solution"). Planners cannot reliably predict the right price for parking on every block at every time of day, but they can use a simple trial-and-error process to adjust prices in response to occupancy rates. The right price for curb parking resembles the US Supreme Court's definition of pornography: you know it when you see it. With Goldilocks pricing (not too high, not too low), drivers never have to search for an open space.

The notion of dynamic pricing for curb parking was once merely theoretical because changing the prices frequently on a traditional mechanical parking meter was impractical. But technology has now simplified the task. Employing digitally enabled and wirelessly connected parking meters, Los Angeles, San Francisco, Boston, and other cities have begun to set curb parking prices variably in order to leave one or two spaces on every block open at all times, so finding a curb space is no longer like winning the lottery.

Time Expired, by Vern Blosum, 1962. One of a series of realist paintings of everyday objects (including parking meters), Time Expired *was produced under the pseudonym "Vern Blosum" by a Southern California abstract artist whose true identity remains a mystery to this day. Intended at the time as a light-hearted mockery of Pop Art's fascination with commonplace items—such as Andy Warhol's Campbell soup cans—the Blosum paintings have since come to be recognized as significant and serious artworks in themselves.*

Because the demand for curb space varies throughout the day and the supply is fixed, prices must vary to balance supply and demand. Dynamic prices can ensure that parking spaces are both well used *and* readily available.

If curb prices stay fixed all day, parking occupancy will usually be too high or too low, and rarely right. But the "right" results can be surprising. During the first two years after San Francisco began varying curb prices to manage parking demand, prices *declined* sharply in the morning and increased only in the midday and afternoon. On many blocks, the price fell to $0.25 an hour in the morning from the previous price of $2 an hour all day.

Motorists may argue that curb parking spaces are "priceless," but anything is priceless until it is put up for sale. For example, market prices will reveal where it makes sense to shift some spaces from privately owned cars to higher-paying shared cars (like Zipcar). Consider a block in a dense neighborhood with five hundred residents and twenty curb spaces. Twenty cars shared by five hundred people will serve many more residents than twenty privately owned cars can.

Market prices for the curb will also show where shifting land from parking to dedicated bike or bus lanes will increase curb productivity. If the market price of parking is low, bike and bus lanes will cost little in lost meter revenue compared to the time and money savings on safer bikes and faster, more reliable bus service.

How much land can be converted from curb parking to more productive uses? Laid end to end, New York City's three million on-street parking spaces would stretch almost halfway around the earth and cover about seventeen square miles of land, thirteen times the size of Central Park. The parking subsidy is astronomical because 97 percent of New York's on-street parking is free. If New York's on-street spaces earned only $5.50 a day (the price of a round trip on public transit in New York), the total revenue would amount to more than $6 billion a year.

The case is similar in San Francisco. Laid end to end, the city's 275,000 curb parking spaces would stretch longer than California's coastline. Combined into one piece of land, all this curb parking would cover Golden Gate Park, yet 90 percent of San Francisco's curb spaces are free.

Los Angeles County has 3.6 million curbside parking spaces, 20 percent more than New York City and 13 times higher than San Francisco. Los Angeles County has 18.6 million on- and off-street parking spaces, which amount to about 200 square miles or 14 percent of the county's incorporated land area. The area devoted to parking is 40 percent greater than the 140 square miles of roads and highways in the county. As a result, greater Los Angeles is thirteen million people connected by a traffic jam.

Because delivery trucks and rideshare vehicles spend such short times at the curb, converting only a few long-term parking spaces to short-time loading zones should satisfy the delivery demand on most blocks. Delivery drivers will save valuable time because they can park quickly in legal curb spaces, without getting tickets for double parking. Better loading zones can make the whole transportation system more productive.

Cities can charge delivery vehicles for parking by the minute, with prices set to produce reliable availability. Many trucks and rideshare vehicles paying a high price per minute for short parking sessions can yield far more revenue than a few cars paying a low price per hour for much longer sessions. Delivery companies need legal and reliable curb parking and are willing to pay for it (parking fines are not deductible as business expenses). Charging for time at the curb will also produce a copious data stream showing how drivers use the curb, how long, and how often.

Transparent, data-based pricing rules can depoliticize parking. If demand dictates prices, politicians will not be able to raise prices to gain revenue or reduce them to please voters. Prices will go up and down because the goal is to optimize curb occupancy, not

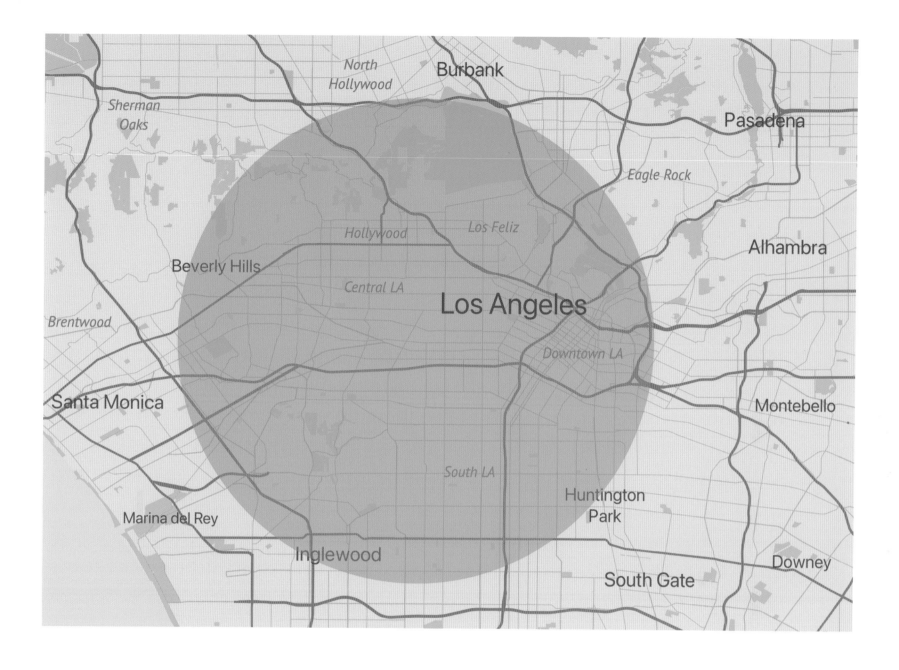

The total amount of space dedicated to parking in Southern California—more than two hundred square miles—is represented by the circle at the center of the map (compare with map on page 111).

Reclaim the Curb!

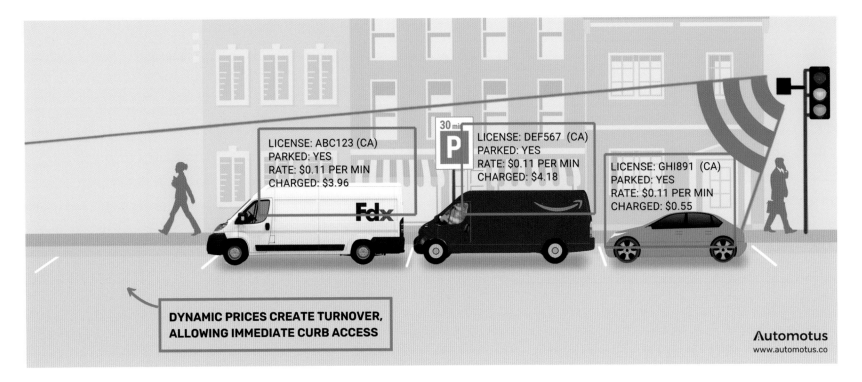

LICENSE: ABC123 (CA)
PARKED: YES
RATE: $0.11 PER MIN
CHARGED: $3.96

LICENSE: DEF567 (CA)
PARKED: YES
RATE: $0.11 PER MIN
CHARGED: $4.18

LICENSE: GHI891 (CA)
PARKED: YES
RATE: $0.11 PER MIN
CHARGED: $0.55

**DYNAMIC PRICES CREATE TURNOVER,
ALLOWING IMMEDIATE CURB ACCESS**

Λutomotus
www.automotus.co

The Automotus system is one of several now in operation that enables dynamic pricing of curbside parking and waiting space.

maximize revenue. Prices provide essential information, and markets can perform some functions that planners simply cannot.

To gain the necessary political support for the market prices, some cities (including Boston, Houston, Pasadena, Pittsburgh, and San Diego) dedicate their meter revenue to paying for added public services on the metered streets. Everyone who lives or works in one of these "Parking Benefit Districts" can see their meter money at work cleaning sidewalks, removing graffiti, and planting street trees. If the meter revenue pays for public services that residents and local business owners want but will not get unless drivers pay for curb parking, demand-based parking prices make political sense.

Consider a thought experiment: which would you prefer in your neighborhood? Priced curb parking with clean and safe sidewalks, or free curb parking that's hard to find? If you park off-street or do not own a car, you would probably prefer paid curb parking with clean, safe sidewalks.

Drivers generally don't want to pay for curb parking, but Parking Benefit Districts can convince residents they want to charge for it. The curb lane can benefit everyone, not just drivers who park for free on the street. Cities shouldn't subsidize curb parking unless they want more cars, congestion, and pollution and don't have any better use for the money.

The raw pragmatism of bribing residents to charge for curb parking might make Machiavelli blush. Nevertheless, Parking Benefit Districts can create an upward spiral in a neighborhood's public life. Parking meters pay for public services that will increase the neighborhood's appeal, which will increase the demand for curb parking, which will increase the meter prices, which will further increase the revenue for public services. This upward spiral may be slow but rent from the curb lane will eventually provide stable revenue for neighborhood public services.

Paying for parking should be like paying for gasoline. Drivers expect to buy as much gas as they want at any filling station, although they may complain about high prices. Similarly, drivers should be able to park on any block, although they may complain about the prices. There is one hugely important difference between paying for gasoline and paying for parking. When you pay for gasoline, the money disappears, often overseas.

When you pay for curb parking, the money remains in your locality, paying to clean the sidewalk you alight on, plant street trees you walk under, and provide added security for both you and your car. Returning meter revenue to the metered districts can increase both the parkers' willingness to pay for curb parking and the community's eagerness to charge for it.

More affluent Parking Benefit Districts will probably generate higher parking revenue. To ensure equality in spending for public services among all the districts, a city can use what in public finance is called "power equalization." Regardless of the curb revenue earned in each district, the city can distribute the revenue equally (per curb space or resident) among all districts. With paid curb parking and power equalization, revenue for public services will flow from affluent neighborhoods with high curb prices into poor neighborhoods with low curb prices.

Cities can also give parking discounts for low-income drivers, just as they give discounts on electricity and water bills for low-income residents. Cities can also use some of the curb parking revenue to provide an equivalent benefit, such as transit passes, to low-income people who cannot afford a car.

Crowded curb parking turns out to be a great opportunity disguised as an insoluble problem. If cities price the curb properly, drivers will use it appropriately. The necessary technology already exists, so future progress must come from better public policies. To manage the curb fairly and efficiently, cities should let prices guide the planning.

View of Sankofa Park, at the north end of Destination Crenshaw, showing Kehinde Wiley's monumental bronze sculpture of an African woman on horseback. "I wanted to expand this question of a struggle for representation," Wiley has observed, "and [the] struggle for human rights and for visible signs of dignity, which is essentially what sculptural monuments are—what we as a collective society stand behind, what we gather around and consider to be our high watermarks as a society."

Renewing the Dream

5 — Destination Crenshaw: A Cultural and Transit Corridor Celebrating Black Los Angeles

Francesca Birks and James Sanders

A Historic Project

Destination Crenshaw is a historic project for Los Angeles and the world. The stamp we will make on Crenshaw Boulevard with more than 100 unique art installations, ten African American-themed pocket parks, and culturally minded street and landscaping improvements will be a living reflection of Black LA and the creativity that pours out of our community.

MARQUEECE HARRIS-DAWSON, 2020

In May 2011, the Los Angeles Metropolitan Transportation Authority announced its decision to proceed with the construction of a new $2 billion, 8.5-mile light-rail line connecting the system's existing Expo Line to Los Angeles International Airport (LAX), the city's primary aviation facility and the second busiest air-travel hub in the United States.

The decision made sense—certainly at the citywide and regional scale—and it was welcomed in many quarters. Linking directly to the interiors of the airport's nine terminals by way of an "Airport Metro Connector," the new transit line would provide a convenient new way for LAX's eighty-eight million annual passengers—as well as its fifty-thousand employees—to travel to and from the airport, allowing Los Angeles to join most major cities in the world in having a rail link to its major air hub.

But for those communities along the route of the new line, specifically the Crenshaw district, a largely Black area of South Los Angeles, news of the announcement sparked a wave of apprehension and even anger—and for obvious reasons. Though the environmental effects of a light-rail line would obviously be far less destructive than those of a freeway, the Crenshaw/LAX proposal—a major transportation route, imposed by distant regionwide authority on a marginalized community, essentially cutting the district in two—inevitably summoned the not-so-remote memories, and still-abiding realities, of the profoundly damaging impact of Los Angeles's freeways on Black and Latino neighborhoods in the 1960s and '70s, especially in East and South Los Angeles (see chapter 2).

Misgivings only grew when Metro's plans revealed that a twelve-block stretch of the new line running through the Crenshaw District would be placed *at grade*, with tracks and cars running down a center strip of the area's main north-south artery, Crenshaw Boulevard. LA Metro said the decision was financial—a savings of $1.5 billion—and that ridership studies at the time did not justify the additional expense of an underground or raised alignment—but as the community couldn't help but notice, Crenshaw/LAX would be nearly the only Metro line along a major commercial boulevard in Los Angeles to be placed at grade. Wilshire, Sunset, Hollywood, Ventura—all of these boulevards enjoyed transit service placed belowground or, occasionally, above street level.

And there was another concern. Gentrification was already impacting many former working-class areas of Los Angeles and was certain soon to affect the Crenshaw

One of the early developments of the Crenshaw district, Crenshaw Villa, under construction, 1938.

area—with or without the new train—but, as one man said, "the train would put it on steroids." Located miles away from the nearest freeway, the district had been largely disconnected from economically advantaged parts of Los Angeles. But the new line's arrival would bring the area within twenty or thirty minutes of much of the rest of the city—and as local residents knew all too well, the past decades had demonstrated that the addition of a Metro station sent a district's rents rising an average of 30 percent faster the neighborhoods surrounding it. "So you had people who were already on edge economically," a local leader observed, "and you're going to put in this thing that's just going to make that worse."

For all its social and economic challenges, the Crenshaw district had long carried special meaning and resonance for the city's African American residents. The largest and most densely populated Black community in America west of Chicago, the area—named for its developer, the banker George L. Crenshaw—arose around World War I as one of the first planned suburbs in the United States and a strictly white enclave. After 1948, when the Supreme Court struck down the blatantly racist rules that had forbidden people of color from purchasing or renting its houses, the area enjoyed a vogue with successful Japanese Americans, followed by middle-class and working Black families, whose blue-collar jobs in the city's then-thriving industrial plants often allowed them to purchase one of the district's modest but tidy single-family homes. (To this day, even after the economic and social dislocations of recent decades, the Crenshaw district enjoys some of the highest rates of Black home ownership in Southern California.)

Like many poor and working-class communities in Los Angeles and other American cities, the Crenshaw district was double pummeled in the 1970s and '80s by deindustrialization and the arrival of crack cocaine, which wrenched apart the district's physical and social landscape. Though major strides have since been made in reducing the street crime and gang violence associated with the crack epidemic, the problems of industrial flight—and an endemic lack of employment opportunities—remain very real, along with the dramatic rise of an issue besetting all of Los Angeles, homelessness.

Along the way, however, something else was brewing in the Crenshaw area and its surrounding districts: a stunning artistic renaissance. From the historically Black communities of South Los Angeles a new generation of artists, musicians, and filmmakers were exerting an influence on every corner of American culture, from pop music to Hollywood films to museum installations. There was the rapper and songwriter Kendrick Lamar, whose 2017 album *DAMN* would go on to receive a Pulitzer Prize. The actress and comedian Issa Rae, writing, directing, and producing the groundbreaking HBO series *Insecure* and *Awkward Black Girl*. The filmmaker Ava DuVernay, directing and writing feature films and dramatic series such as *Selma* and *When They See Us*. The abstract artist Mark Bradford, creating immense public artworks for LAX, the Hirshhorn, and the US Embassy in London. And, not least, the figurative painter Kehinde Wiley, whose landmark works include the official portrait of President Barack Obama and *A Portrait of a Young Gentleman*, occupying pride of place at the Henry Huntington Art Museum in Pasadena opposite its original inspiration, Thomas Gainsborough's iconic *The Blue Boy*.

It was this last movement—the emergence of the Crenshaw district and neighboring areas as the epicenter of an explosion of Black artistic creativity, recognized all around the world—that would offer the key to a very different future for the proposed transit corridor, one that would not sunder and damage the surrounding community but seek to unite and strengthen it.

Destination Crenshaw

By 2015, as the Crenshaw/LAX line entered its final phase of design—and a few sections near the airport actually began construction—antagonism and hostility to the project was reaching a crescendo. It was at that tense juncture that a newly elected Los Angeles councilmember Marqueece Harris-Dawson—representing not only the Crenshaw community but the entire Eighth District, an area of 250,000 people encompassing Hyde Park, Baldwin Hills, View Heights, Vermont Knolls, and other primarily Black and Latino communities across a vast swath of South Los Angeles—came onto the scene. Rather than attempting, uselessly, to fight the project, Councilmember Harris-Dawson urged the community to attempt something more daring: to reshape it to meet their needs. Gathering the ideas and inspiration of local business owners, artists, community members, and activists, a new vision of the LAX/Crenshaw line began to form.

Aerial view of the Crenshaw/LAX Line, running at grade down the center of Crenshaw Boulevard, looking south, 2022. The recently completed SoFi sports and entertainment stadium, located in Inglewood, is visible in the distance.

> Up until now Crenshaw's really been the kind place that, as the young people say, "if you know, you know." If you know where to go, you can see amazing things. If you're just driving down the street as a tourist, you won't know what's happening. And so we said let's build around it. And they came up with the idea of building an open-air people's museum, so that when you drive by, you see the best of our art, you see our story, and you see the hopes and dreams of our folks.
>
> MARQUEECE HARRIS-DAWSON, 2022

From the work of a major Black artist like Lauren Halsey—whose signature hieroglyphic pieces about South Los Angeles could be viewed in the galleries of the Wilshire District, but not in South Los Angeles itself—to the popular fashion-forward streetwear and footwear driven by the area's hip-hop culture but requiring a visit outside the district to purchase—the need and vision for the project, Harris-Dawson recalled, became clear. "Let's bring everybody home. Let's create a space that everybody's going to be coming through anyway, where all of that's available and on display."

That inspiration came, in part, from an unlikely source. Reading the *Los Angeles Times* one day, Harris-Dawson was struck by a story about an effort by business and community leaders in Beverly Hills to have their extension of the LA Metro travel not above or below grade, but *at* ground level. Who would want a train line at grade, he wondered?

> And they said, look, we're Beverly Hills. If a train's going to come through, we want you to see what we have so you'll get off the train and spend money. Cause we have a lot of nice stuff. I mean, it's Beverly Hills, right? And I was like, oh my goodness, why haven't we thought of this? We have a lot of nice stuff. People sing about our stuff. People make movies about our stuff. People develop fantasies around our stuff. Why wouldn't we take advantage of all the eyeballs that are going be in our neighborhood coming from LAX. By this time we were knew we had a good chance to get the Olympics in 2028, so the whole world coming out of LAX has to go down Crenshaw Boulevard.
>
> MARQUEECE HARRIS-DAWSON, 2022

"It evolved organically," one official later recalled, "not a single 'a-ha' moment, but the result of lots of community input."

Seeking to build a design team that would itself showcase the diverse creative energies of the city, the project selected the Black architects Gabrielle Bullock, FAIA, and Zena Howard, FAIA, principals at Perkins & Will who had recently worked on the National Museum of African American History and Culture in Washington, DC, and the landscape architecture firm Studio-MLA, headed by the El Salvador-born Mía Lehrer, FASLA.

As the effort took shape, it looked to satisfy multiple goals. At the most obvious level, it would enhance the Crenshaw district with amenities and attractions drawing not only local residents but people from all around Los Angeles as well as domestic and international visitors—expanding the community's economic base and reinforcing its status as a creative incubator. The project, as Lehrer notes, would also achieve several urbanistic and environmental missions, serving to "create viewing opportunities . . . mitigate storm runoff water . . . and alleviate the urban heat island effect contributing to the sustainability of the Crenshaw neighborhood."

At the largest level, finally, the project would celebrate the historic, cultural, and civic contributions of Black citizens to America's second largest city.

A Linear Outdoor Museum

By 2019, years of community consultation had given rise to an innovative concept. The new Metro transit line had been transformed from a utilitarian transportation corridor into the vibrant urban armature: a twelve-block-long array of rotating and permanent art installations, with eleven new pocket parks and a variety of programs and exhibitions, all tied together by a new, richly landscaped streetscape—a "linear outdoor museum," in the words of one design reporter, that "unlike traditional museums . . . won't be bound by walls or ceilings."

As its designers recognized, Crenshaw Boulevard is the first residential district encountered by passengers—an estimated 5.9 million annually—coming into the city from LAX. Viewed through the windows of Metro's train cars, Destination Crenshaw would not only showcase the community to visitors from around the world but do double-duty as a gateway to the city as a whole. This exposure would also provide a kind of advertisement for the project itself, as visitors intrigued by the large-scale artwork and landscape amenities glimpsed from the train might well decide to return to the area during their stay.

Responding to the intrinsically linear nature of the transit line's right-of-way, Destination Crenshaw's installations and amenities are laid out as a kind of necklace of four distinct (yet interrelated) thematic zones, unfolding in a kind of linear "narrative" for residents and visitors walking or driving along the length of the corridor. Each themed zone responds to the specific context of its location, and each provides the visitor with an experience celebrating a different aspect of the neighborhood's heritage and of African American culture and history. "Destination Crenshaw...honors not just the neighborhood as a creative hub, but also Black L.A.'s impact on popular culture and social change," observes Zena Howard. Our role . . . is to translate . . . the very real, very significant voices and energy of Black L.A."

Togetherness: Located on the north end of the project around an existing triangular plaza at Forty-sixth Street, the *Togetherness* zone honors the resilience of Black culture, borne of ancestral heritage and modern necessity. Centered on Sankofa Park, a new public space south of historic Leimert Park, this section encourages gathering by showcasing artwork, exhibitions, and programming at various scales. Rising from the sidewalk level in a series of switchback ramps, the park culminates in an elevated overlook

Top: *The upper level of Sankofa Park, at the north end of Destination Crenshaw, which rises from the sidewalk in a series of switchback ramps and culminates in an elevated overlook offering panoramic views to the north of the skyline of Downtown Los Angeles and the Hollywood sign, and, to the south, of the nine-block stretch of Destination Crenshaw itself, allowing residents and visitors to situate the project and its community within the larger geography of the city.* Center: *A view of a landscaped sitting area of Sankofa Park, featuring an artwork by Maren Hassinger,* An Object of Curiosity, Radiating Love, *a six-foot-diameter "interactive orb" that, surrounded by motion-sensor LED lights, glows pink as visitors approach.* Bottom: *A view of 54ᵗʰ East Park, featuring a thirty-six-foot-tall burnished stainless steel sculpture called* Columns, *by the artist Melvin Edwards. In addition to serving as a highly visible landmark and orientation marker for the project, the vertical composition "represents how our stories build upon one another," Edwards observes, "how we stand on the shoulders of those who came before us, and how our collective engagement in our community becomes the very structure of its success."*

A view of Charles Dickson's large stainless steel sculpture, Car Culture, *features three elongated figures inspired by West African Senufo ritual objects, capped by a fiber-optic wired "crown" of car fronts and ends and a fanciful engine, recalling auto dealerships and body shops that once stretched much of the length of Crenshaw Boulevard, along with the lowrider culture that still thrives in gatherings in nearby Leimert Park and elsewhere across South and East Los Angeles. "Cars are a fundamental component of Crenshaw street life," notes the artist, "that brings together innovation, creativity and the unbounded joy of gathering."*

offering panoramic views of Downtown Los Angeles's skyline and the Hollywood sign, and, to the south, of the twelve-block stretch of Destination Crenshaw itself, thus firmly situating the Crenshaw community—and South Los Angeles—among the city's world-famous landmarks.

Dreams: Located at Fiftieth Street, the *Dreams* zone marks the realm of unbounded aspiration. Here the oldest artwork in the district, the "Great Wall of Crenshaw," will be restored and enhanced with an adjacent parklet, interpretive signage, shade structures, and landscaping. Created in the early 2000s by the graffiti collective Rocking the Nation, the eight-hundred-foot-long mural retells key moments of Black American history through portraits ranging from the abolitionists Harriet Tubman and Frederick Douglass and the musicians Dizzy Gillespie and Jimi Hendrix to the activists Malcolm X and the Reverend Martin Luther King Jr.

Firsts: Located at the crossroads of Crenshaw Boulevard and 54th Street, the *Firsts* zone celebrates stories of the significant moments and innovations—stretching from the local to the international stage—that have transformed Black Los Angeles over the past half century. Several pocket parks in this area activate the south corners of the intersection, which will be anchored by a new headquarters building for City Council District 8.

Improvisation: Marking the southern end of Destination Crenshaw at the corner of Slauson Avenue, the *Improvisation* zone celebrates the significance of improvisation in Black culture and community. In addition to small art installations, this zone is home to the Crenshaw Monument, a landmark for the entire area and a major point of arrival to the district from southern parts of the city.

Destination Crenshaw's four activity zones are unified by an overarching theme—*Grow Where You're Planted*—inspired by the African giant star grass. "Known to thrive in inhospitable environments" Gabrielle Bullock observes, "the grass reminds us of the history and resiliency of Black LA, whose deep community roots have strengthened over the decades despite facing years of root shock."

> *Used by slave traders as bedding in their ships, the grass thrives in alien lands despite inhospitable conditions. Today, it remains a profoundly resonant reminder of African American history, the patterns of global dispersion, and Black resilience in the face of violence and racism.*
>
> DESTINATION CRENSHAW, 2020

Funding and Operation

For all of its imaginative concepts, Destination Crenshaw would have remained a dream had it not been for the substantial financing secured for its construction and operation. It is arguably the willingness of government and philanthropies to fund the Crenshaw project that marks the true evolution of Los Angeles from the freeway era of the 1950s and '60s, when scarcely any thought—much less aid—was given to those communities damaged or destroyed by the clearance for and construction of massive regional roadways.

LA Metro itself proved to be one of the project's largest supporters, in two ways: by substantially underwriting the effort financially, and by donating land needed to construct the extension but not needed for the completed line. "They recognized that they wanted the train to be something the community embraced and felt like they had a stake in," Harris-Dawson notes, "something that presented an opportunity rather than

Renewing the Dream

Diagram of the four theme and activity zones of the Destination Crenshaw project.

something that was imposed upon them against their will." Significant funding was also received from the City of Los Angeles, the County of Los Angeles, and the State of California, whose departments followed LA Metro's lead. Declaring that "Destination Crenshaw is a jobs plan and a small-business rescue plan, all in one," Karen Bass, then a U.S. Congresswoman and now mayor of Los Angeles, has arranged for a total of $4.4 million in federal support.

That public funding was supplemented by private support from foundations and individuals. The Getty Foundation, a longtime force in the Los Angeles cultural and philanthropic landscape, invested $3 million to cover the commissioning, fabrication, and conservation of the first group of artworks, along with funds for an apprenticeship program for local residents in public arts and art conservation. The Ballmer Group, Weingart Foundation, McGrath Abrams Family Foundation, and Issa Rae also came in with significant gifts.

Destination Crenshaw is operated on an ongoing basis by is a not-for-profit organization based in the district, whose responsibilities include maintenance and repair, events programming, the commissioning of new artwork, and the continued expansion of the project, so that the initiative will continue to serve the community in the years and decades to come.

A Homecoming

> *Los Angeles continues to set the standard for design and construction that strengthens our communities, and celebrates cultural and social change. Projects like Destination Crenshaw are important because they work with communities to plan and design their shared future.*
> KAREN BASS, MAYOR OF LOS ANGELES, 2022

Given the fraught circumstances that had given rise to the Crenshaw effort in the first place, it was crucial that the leadership demonstrate the project's significant community benefits: major investment in jobs, workforce development, public art commissions, neighborhood beautification and the stabilization and enhancement of the district as a whole. The grim twentieth-century heritage of Black communities being damaged or displaced by large-scale transportation projects would be transformed into a twenty-first century model in which a regional transit improvement becomes the generator of local economic and cultural revitalization.

That model called for support of retail stores and other businesses on and around Crenshaw Boulevard. It offers restorative design solutions for the community through improvements to the public realm. And it creates an engine of cultural advancement by engaging both emerging and established Black artists, who have been commissioned to create large-scale artworks.

> *[For Sankofa Park, Maren] Hassinger is creating a pink fiberglass sphere and planting motion-sensor LED lights around it to make the sculpture seem alive or alert. Nearby will be [Charles] Dickson's large stainless-steel sculpture of three Senufo ritual figures under a canopy of cars, celebrating the dealerships that used to line Crenshaw and the lowrider culture still alive today. The artist's plan is to hire local auto body shops to paint the cars different colors.*
>
> JORI FINKEL, *NEW YORK TIMES*, 2021

In fall 2021, the Los Angeles Cultural Affairs Commission approved Destination Crenshaw's first seven permanent public art projects. The commissions, mostly sculpture, feature the work of Black artists with strong links to Los Angeles, including Charles Dickson, Melvin Edwards, Maren Hassinger, Artis Lane, Alison Saar, Kehinde Wiley, and Brenna Youngblood.

Four of the initial seven artworks are being installed at Sankofa Park at the corridor's northern end, the project's major gathering place. Among the most prominent of these is a large bronze sculpture by the celebrated Los Angeles artist Kehinde Wiley, presenting a twenty-first-century African woman seated on horseback—a contemporary response to the heroic military monuments of the Confederacy, now being removed or reconsidered in many Southern cities and towns. For the world-renowned Wiley, who was born and raised on Crenshaw and Jefferson Boulevards, the project "is essentially a homecoming...I think it's really important that I spent so much of my time working all over the world and having the work be seen and appreciated by publics near and far, but it's particularly poignant to have it in my own home community."

In itself, this first phase represents the most extensive public commissioning of Black art in American history but is only the start of the project's stated goal of including at least one hundred sculptures, murals, and other works by 2027—establishing what Jason Foster, the group's president and COO, calls "the largest public art exhibition by Black artists in this country." Other observers have compared the effort to the projects of the New Deal, when, in response to poverty and hardship, the government took the lead in creating ambitious public works that were at once functional and worked to beautify and elevate their communities.

In leveraging a major transportation project to coalesce and support an economically challenged community rather than divide and destabilize it, Destination Crenshaw offers cities everywhere a vibrant and suggestive model of how imaginatively conceived and executed transportation projects can reverse a once-tragic heritage and instead become a force for community engagement, cultural celebration, and positive social change.

> *Let's create something using the investment of Metro as its basis . . . and that's what we're doing. Obviously, as a resident of this community, I reject violently the notion that because I'm Black, if I like nice things, I have to go live in a predominantly white neighborhood. And that doesn't take anything away from the legitimate concern that people have about gentrification. But I think the way you deal with that concern is by going on offense, rather than constantly playing defense.*
>
> MARQUEECE HARRIS-DAWSON, 2022

Aerial view of Destination Crenshaw, looking south from the multilevel lookout of Sankofa Park.

Destination Crenshaw

The Twist:
An Arts and Community
Destination on the Sunset Strip
Matt Ducharme and
Woods Bagot Los Angeles Studio

PROJECT TEAM
Matt Ducharme
Rick Gunter
Christiana Kyrillou
Ryan Lee
Kent Wu

Rendering of The Twist, showing crowds gathered to view an evening art installation.

The billboard landscape of the Sunset Strip, Los Angeles, 2014.

Just beyond Crescent Heights Boulevard, where the...tower of the Chateau Marmont looms up against the hills, Sunset Boulevard alchemizes into the fabled Sunset Strip. Here...the boulevard becomes twisty and sensual, the Hollywood hills nudging down against it on one side, an intoxicating panorama of city lights spread out below it on the other. The street's energy becomes louder, its lore thicker and more varied, as a blur of nightclubs, hotels, restaurants, boutiques, and those famous outsized billboards pass by.

AMY DAWES, 2002

Introduction

Developed by Woods Bagot's Los Angeles Studio in 2020 in response to a call for ideas from the City of West Hollywood, The Twist is an interdisciplinary art and placemaking project, transforming an existing parking lot on the iconic Sunset Strip into an "experiential community hub" that can accommodate a wide range of activations and events. Conceived as a catalyst for urban life and activity, the novel concept merges an expressive shape, state-of-the-art technology, and flexible programming to create a destination that seamlessly merges the physical gathering of people and the virtual space of modern digital display.

At the project's heart is an LED-paneled structure—essentially an outdoor art installation in itself—that joins two adjacent digital billboards into a single, spectacular, full-color, ever-changing display system, one whose screens can be programmed independently to showcase artwork and promotional content or be synchronized as part of a commissioned multimedia experience. Shaped by way of an emblematic *twist*, this central display and its flanking double-sided billboards embrace a ground-level area that can accommodate a variety of cultural and program offerings relevant to the city's present and emerging lifestyles, and its diverse needs and audiences.

In its design and concept, The Twist reinterprets in contemporary terms the heritage and vibrancy of the Sunset Strip—especially the constellation of billboards that, for nearly three-quarters of a century, have made it one of the best-known and most captivating places in the world. A twenty-first-century amplification of what one observer calls the Sunset Strip's "Technicolor history," The Twist is intended not only as a celebration of this rich urban legacy, but a source of civic pride for the City of West Hollywood and an emblem of its reputation today as a cultural vanguard for Los Angeles.

More than simply a billboard, The Twist is an immersive urban environment that activates pedestrian experience, highlights events and programs unique to the local culture, transforms an ordinary parking lot into a site for a multiple activities and spontaneous interactions and, in its design and concept, embodies the distinctive mix of cultural creativity, commercial promotion, dazzling imagery, and, not least, auto-oriented mobility, for which Los Angeles has become known around the globe.

> *The amazing billboards [of the Strip] are now the most visible and often the most exciting art forms in Los Angeles....cleverly sited and beautifully painted glorifications of the momentarily famous.*
> CHARLES MOORE, PETER CAMPBELL, AND
> REGULA BECKER, 1984

The Strip and The Twist

There are few experiences more quintessentially "LA" than cruising along the bends and straights of the Sunset Strip, the legendary 1.7-mile-long stretch of Sunset Boulevard between Beverly Hills and Los Angeles, attempting to keep one's eyes on the road while looking in awe at the freestanding billboards that line each side of the thoroughfare.

For much of the twentieth century, this length of the boulevard was still unincorporated county land, legally outside the jurisdiction of the cities of Los Angeles or Beverly Hills and thus scarcely regulated by any municipal authority: the ideal home for a series of legendary hotels, bars, and stylish nightclubs—Ciro's, the Mocambo, Café Trocadero—that were able to sidestep Los Angeles' still-puritanical nightlife laws and stay open into the small hours. Building on that glamorous reputation, in the 1950s this same loosely regulated stretch became home to a spectacular assemblage of freestanding billboards and—a bit later—giant "tall-wall" murals fitted onto the sides of buildings. In the 1960s and '70s, as the city's music industry rose to prominence, major record labels joined the fray, and the faces and names of movie stars and directors were supplemented by those of rock-and-roll legends, pop divas, and, more recently, hip-hop idols.

Over the decades, these outsized promotional images have come to play a key role in the commercial and cultural ecology of the city's entertainment business and, as the preferred place for studios and networks to preview and build excitement for their latest projects, embodying as nothing else Hollywood's strange mix of global reach and clubby, hyperlocal character. "For decades [the billboards] have taken the temperature of the boulevard,"

the writer Amy Dawes notes, "and been a kind of insider's code aimed at agents and producers shuttling to and from their Sunset Strip offices, telegraphing that this star is making a comeback...this record company is betting the bank on this new band...this cable network goes all the way to promote its original series. Along the way, they entertain tourists, distract motorists, and have become as much a part of the landscape as the Hollywood sign." The Sunset Strip might have been "vain, brittle, superficial, hollow even," observed the great California historian Kevin Starr, but it was "urban, nevertheless, and resonating with the magic of place."

> *Unique, indelible pieces of the skyline—proclamations that this is no ordinary zone, but a place where life is lived in the fast lane, where youth, style, fame, and the entertainment industry are top priorities—the oversized billboards hoist the ego and id of career-crazed Hollywood into the sky for all to see.*
> AMY DAWES, 2002

Today, perhaps only New York's Times Square rivals Sunset Boulevard as a spectacular outdoor showcase of American popular culture, but unlike the largely pedestrian orientation of Manhattan's great urban crossroads, the Sunset Strip—a place properly experienced only in motion—offers a unique monument to the vehicular mobility that has long defined its surrounding city.

For the Woods Bagot design team, rooting The Twist within the auto-oriented urbanism of Los Angeles meant drawing deeply on that urbanism's origins, beginning with the notion of a building serving as a large, three-dimensional "sign," exemplified by the oldest extant McDonald's, an early 1950s structure in the Los Angeles suburb of Downey, California, its lighted tilted roof and iconic double arches rising above an otherwise boxy and modest hamburger stand—a classic example of what the architects Robert Venturi, Denise Scott Brown, and Steven Izenour, in their 1972 landmark book *Learning from Las Vegas*, described as a "decorated shed."

Focused on the Las Vegas strip, but obviously relevant to Southern California as well, Venturi, Scott Brown, and Izenour's seminal work was amplified at nearly the same time by the groundbreaking analysis of LA's "Autopia" in Reyner Banham's 1971 *Los Angeles: The Architecture of Four Ecologies*. Together, the two books introduced the radical notion (for the time) of an automobile-oriented urbanism, whose structures were designed

Top: *The oldest extant double-arched McDonald's, dating to 1953, in Downey, California.* Bottom: *A drawing from Learning from Las Vegas (1972), by Robert Venturi, Denise Scott Brown, and Steven Izenour, illustrating their concept of a "decorated shed": a simple functional building whose "architectural" identity relies on a detached, overscaled signlike element.*

Top: *The LA-based rock group, The Doors, pose in 1967 in front of their own oversized promotional billboard on the Sunset Strip (top), which by the late 1960s had become as crucial to the music industry as it had been for Hollywood (bottom). "The most coveted status symbol in the music business," the architect Charles Moore and his colleagues observed, is "not a platinum record but a personal salute on the Strip."*

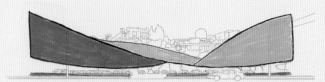

Top: *Initial concept sketch of The Twist.* Bottom: *Aerial view showing the project concept: a band of continuous electronic panels—two advertising displays at each end oriented to Sunset Boulevard and a central section devoted to cultural programming—wrapping around the parking lot, which becomes a flexible gathering space during evenings and weekends.*

Top: *Aerial view of the project site on Sunset Boulevard in West Hollywood, between North Olive Drive and La Cienega.* Bottom: *Nighttime view of the lighted billboards of the Sunset Strip, September 2018.*

Renewing the Dream

to be grasped from the windshield of a vehicle speeding at forty miles per hour, rather than by a gently ambling pedestrian, as nearly all architecture had been experienced since time immemorial.

In Los Angeles, of course, the evolution of automobile-oriented, large-scale signage was carried a crucial step further, becoming not merely a means of drawing attention to a fast-food restaurant or a gambling casino or resort (as in Las Vegas), but to serve as an integral component of the media-driven culture of the late twentieth century. The stylishly art-directed billboards along the Sunset Strip—impressive enough simply as giant objects unfolding in space and time—took on far greater cultural significance as the ever-changing, larger-than-life touchstones of the universe of American mass entertainment that, by the 1970s, had come largely to center on Southern California. "To deprive the city of them," Banham declared, "would be like depriving San Gimignano of its towers or the City of London of its Wren steeples."

In 1984, the once-open lands of the Sunset Strip became part of a newly incorporated municipality, the City of West Hollywood. Though modest in population—just over 35,500 residents in 2020—the city has swiftly become a global presence in the worlds of design, entertainment, fashion, and nightlife, home to everything from the Pacific Design Center—the iconic "Blue Whale" by architect Cesar Pelli—and the surrounding West Hollywood Design District, to the world-famous nightspots, comedy clubs, and hotels of the Sunset Strip itself. Production companies, independent film studios, talent and management agencies, tech companies, chic boutiques, and elegant restaurants all make their home within its concentrated boundaries, which comprise a total area of less than two square miles. "The Sunset Strip," one contemporary observer notes, "is an entity unto itself—a scene that belongs not so much to the neighborhood as to the world."

As the self-described "custodian" of the world-famous billboard legacy of the Sunset Strip, the City of West Hollywood has sought to ensure that the vibrant character of the boulevard remains fully contemporary in spirit and style, even while respecting its unique historic mix of culture and commerce, now nearly a century old. In 2019 it adopted the Sunset Arts & Advertising Program, which it described as a "comprehensive process to address the future of billboards on the Sunset Strip... and a groundbreaking effort to reimagine the world's premier locations for outdoor advertising." As part of that program, it invited outdoor media companies and architecture firms to present innovative concepts and designs for selected billboard sites along the boulevard. For its proposal, Woods Bagot selected a prominent site on the northern side of the street, between Queens Road and La Cienega Boulevard, currently occupied by a parking lot.

In developing its response to the city's call for ideas, the Woods Bagot Los Angeles Studio recognized from the very start that, as one designer put it, "this 'billboard,' in a sense, needed to be anything but." Expanding their proposal far beyond the single billboard suggested by the sponsors, they instead proposed a major destination—a genuine urban *place*—that would reflect and indeed intensify the iconic character of the existing Sunset Strip. Combining three-dimensional and two-dimensional components, The Twist comprises a 20,000-square-foot open space—occupied by parked cars during weekday hours but turned over to a wide variety of uses and activities in the evenings and on weekends—sheltered by a sinuous, twisting series of digital screens, whose ever-changing displays and presentations transfigure the central gathering area into a twenty-first-century hybrid of real and virtual space.

To be sure, The Twist includes elements that recall traditional Sunset Strip billboards. A pair of large, double-sided LED displays at either end of the project—carefully angled to catch the eye of passing motorists (and the growing group of pedestrians who stroll on the boulevard's sidewalks, especially by night)—act as digital "portals" for the project. During the day, these four large digital screens can provide substantial advertising revenue—thus supporting the business model of the overall project—but can also be used during evenings and weekends to reinforce and expand The Twist's unique multimedia opportunities. Or, potentially, both—a typical evening might see the two outside-facing screens continue to present revenue-generating displays for new films, episodic series, or music projects, while the two inner-facing screens become part of the artistic and cultural offerings of The Twist's central gathering space.

Though they might appear at first glance as separated roadside screens, the two double-sided billboards at the project's ends are actually part of single continuous structure, linked to each other by the curling, ribbonlike LED element that gives the project its name: The Twist. Uniting the digital panels on either side, this central display is nothing less than an art installation in itself, one that offers the opportunity to present cultural offerings at all times of day, seven days a week. At times, The Twist's central screen can serve as a stand-alone cultural display, with the flanking screens showcasing other programming or commercial promotions; at other times it can be synchronized so that all three screens present a single, spectacular, panoramic experience. At all times it provides a fluid, continuous, ever-changing element that transforms The Twist from a group of discrete rectangles into a sinuous, unified design.

But The Twist does far more than that. In wrapping a sizable ground-level area in state-of-the-art LED screens, it creates a new kind of immersive environment that reimagines the relationship between physical and digital space, even as it seeks to make intimate and engaging the traditionally distant relationship between the Strip's large-scale elevated displays and its life at sidewalk level.

The floor of this space, currently used as an open-air parking lot, will remain so during daylight hours in the workweek, though its surface will be repaved and restriped and additional spaces added as a result. (The front edge of the lot will be framed by natural plantings to provide comfortable and safe separation between sidewalk and parking spaces.) The project also calls for the installation of several fast-charging EV stations in the lot—one of the features, along with its exploration of large-scale electronic screens, that relates this project to the ReCharge LA project, prepared by Woods Bagot's Los Angeles Studio for the "Pump to Plug" study sponsored by the chief design officer of the City of Los Angeles in 2020 and featured in this book as case study 2.

Cradled within the surrounding immersive displays, this space offers endless possibilities for the interaction of urban programming and digital art. The Twist could present a contemporary art showcase one week, and a local cultural heritage festival the next—with the imagery and visuals coordinated in creative and imaginative ways at both. On weekday evenings The Twist could become a drive-in movie theater showing the premiere of the latest film by an independent studio or producer. On weekends it could host a pop-up market fundraiser for a local non-profit group benefiting the community, or a food-truck night, or a livestreamed musical performance or sporting event. Flowing seamlessly between physical gathering and state-of-the-art video-driven imagery, the space would inevitably be in high demand by companies and brands—from a new clothing or footwear line to an NFT entrepreneur—seeking innovative ways of reaching and engaging new audiences, providing another source of commercial revenue to cross-subsidize its cultural and community initiatives.

Energy Efficiency and Environmental Sustainability

In the twenty-first century, large-scale digital billboards—with their high-intensity light output—inevitably raise concerns about energy use and environmental sustainability. The Twist addresses those concerns through an innovative, environmentally responsible approach that can actually serve to educate the public about contemporary sustainability.

Taking advantage of the southern orientation of the site, the component LED strips that comprise The Twist's displays are fabricated with embedded solar panels, collecting energy throughout the day and resulting in one of the first energy-*generating* billboards of its kind—enough energy, in fact, to entirely power its own digital content and operation, making the project as a whole net-positive.

The project also offers an opportunity to promote a connection to the natural environment through biophilia. The entry to the site is filled with natural planting that extends along the edges, underneath the billboards, and around to the retaining structure of the hillside in back. This creates a calming environment in an urban context, further reducing the heat of a south-facing exposure. Imagine the difference in sitting and eating during an event with planting and landscape on all sides.

Beyond this, the structure of The Twist serves as a canopy to provide solar shading beneath it, and its construction employs recycled aluminum for the panels and main structure. This environmentally responsive approach is reinforced throughout the project by stormwater strategies, drought-resistant plants, and permeable pavement.

A Good Neighbor

Responding to potential concerns about unwanted effects on the surrounding community, The Twist seeks to maximize its intended visual impact while avoiding any disruption or nuisance to neighbors. The two billboards are angled away from the homes behind the site—ensuring their emitted light is not in alignment with any residential areas—and the structure itself is tucked along the hillside, not perched atop it, mitigating the obstruction of views from houses behind it. Additionally, the art-integrated LED ribbons that run along the length of the canopy are carefully fitted into a recessed channel to provide

Top left and right: *Views of The Twist as seen from the Strip, showing the end display panels, which can be present advertising, promotion, or cultural content.*

Bottom left and right: *Views of the central space of The Twist, showing it used as an art installation and as a community satellite for the 2028 Olympic Games.*

Case Study 1: The Twist

Recycled Aluminum

Integrated LED

Solar Panels

Natural Plantings

Permeable Paver

EV Charging

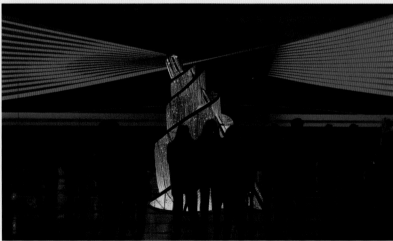

Formed to the Landscape

Top: *Sectional perspective showing energy and environmental features of The Twist. The project's linear LED strips are comprised of individually controlled and synchronized pixels that allow for a dynamic and ever-changing display. Displays are controlled by a master synchronized playlist that allows for multiple content zones to be run at once, or a singular overall display across the form.*

Bottom left: *Art installation at The Twist.* Bottom right: *Diagram showing relationship of The Twist's form to the surrounding topography.*

visibility only from the ground and not from the houses above, allowing for full control over light spillage at night while also maximizing flexibility of the media content.

In fact, the sinuous form of The Twist is intended by its designers to actually mirror the surrounding topography, dipping down in the center and angling up the hillside to the north, responding to the distinctive conditions of this stretch of Sunset Boulevard.

The Magic of Place

Far more than a billboard, Woods Bagot's proposal for The Twist offers a new platform for community gathering and immersive digital storytelling, and an innovative response to twenty-first century opportunities—in which digital experiences once limited to smartphone screens, televisions, and tablets have given way to larger installations, embedded within the built environment.

Building on recent trends—especially evident during and since the Covid-19 pandemic—of transforming parking lots and other vehicular-oriented spaces into outdoor extensions and temporary venues for restaurants, farmers markets, pop-up events, and festivals, The Twist reimagines how an everyday parking lot might be reimagined as a community resource and citywide destination. It holds the potential to become a new landmark for West Hollywood, an invaluable reference point when seeking directions—is it before or after The Twist?—and a powerful magnet for visitors, tourists, art lovers, families, and picture takers of every stripe, from selfie-taking teenagers to professional photographers. Set amidst a world-renowned hub of outdoor media and visual culture, The Twist seeks to transmute the pulsing energy of the Sunset Strip into built form, and so create the kind of environment that, in Kevin Starr's words, might be found "resonating with the magic of place."

Following spread: *Ground-level view of the central space of The Twist, hosting a weekend food-truck festival.*

Renewing the Dream

2 — From Parking

PARI

to
Places

Space Required to Transport Sixty People

Car

Bicycle

Bus

Originally staged in 1991 in Münster, Germany, this well-known image demonstrates the spatial inefficiency of car travel compared to other modes. The same logic can be applied to parking lots, whose sprawling spatial needs might be adapted to other, more productive uses.

Previous spread: Swing Girl, a 2010 street mural by the anonymous artist Banksy, overlooking a parking lot at 908-910 South Broadway in Downtown Los Angeles. Photograph by Veronique Lee.

6

More LA:
Transforming Parking to Places in Southern California
Woods Bagot and ERA-co Los Angeles Studio

PROJECT TEAM
Domenic Alvaro, Meg Bartholomew,
Christian Derix, Fabio Galicia,
Lucy Helme, Luis Jaggy, Dave Towey,
and Lucille Ynosencio

Introduction

Nearly everyone is familiar with the kind of image that compares how much street space is needed to transport the same number of people—sixty, say—in cars, bicycles, and buses. The sea of cars jams up the entire street. The bikes and the bus, by contrast, form compact bundles, leaving almost the entire thoroughfare open for other kinds of life.

In some ways, the MORE LA study, carried out by Woods Bagot in 2018 for the second annual CoMotion LA conference, offers an equivalent of that memorable image—but for parking lots. Just how much of a city's buildable surface is taken up by cars—not when they are in motion, but when they are at rest? How could we imagine using some of that space for other, more beneficial and productive uses, such as housing, commercial, cultural, and retail space, or parks?

The study arises from the singular truth that James Sanders notes in the introduction: while the twenty-first-century advances in mobility transforming Southern California could not be more different from each other—Uber and Lyft car-hailing, Lime and Bird e-scooters, bike-sharing platforms, electric-assist bikes and scooters, the buildout of the Metro system, and, ultimately, the advent of fully autonomous vehicles—they all share one crucial thing in common: *you do not have to park a car.*

What will happen to the region in the coming decades as the impact of this new reality sets in, and the revolution in mobility continues to unfold, and the need for parking begins to decline? How could those miles of existing surface parking be unlocked for more productive urban uses? What if strict required parking minimums for new developments are sharply reduced, or in some cases eliminated altogether? What kind of new projects, and new city, could be imagined?

To explore—and begin to answer—these questions, the MORE LA study looked at three scales, from "macro" to "micro": the scale of the city and region, the scale of typical districts and neighborhoods, and the scale of individual sites within those districts.

At the *macro* scale, the study investigated the essential initial question: just how much buildable surface space of the city and region has been turned over to parking—and what other kinds of uses might occupy that space? Perhaps most crucially—given the city's desperate need for housing—how many new units and residents could fit onto those plots of land, at densities and heights compatible with the character of the neighborhoods in which they are located?

The *middle* scale looked at three distinct districts across the city—selected for their physical, geographic, urbanistic, and social and economic diversity—and explored how alternative scenarios for the reuse and redevelopment of existing parking areas might play out at the neighborhood level, including the provision of new affordable and market-rate housing, green space, and other socially and economically valuable uses.

The *micro* scale looked at individual sites within each selected neighborhood to explore what type of building envelope was in keeping with the reuse scenario proposed for that district, suitable to its transportation accessibility and appropriate to the character of its surroundings. These envelopes were analyzed for the unit yield, zoning uplift, and other characteristics. These site-scale investigations were then developed by Woods Bagot as sketch design vignettes for an appropriate and appealing built solution for each of those locations, taking inspiration from local architecture and common Los Angeles housing precedents.

Macroscale: The City

The first automobile took to the streets of Los Angeles in 1897, yet in 1920, the Los Angeles City Council estimated that still "ninety percent of those who entered the downtown area did so by streetcar." But with the economic boom over the next decade, fueled in part by the region's automobile industry itself (which for decades stood second in size and output only to Detroit's), by 1930 there were two cars for every three people in the city. In today's Los Angeles, fully 78 percent of commutes in the city are by car—and those cars need somewhere to park, at both ends of their journey.

As in many American cities, three main types of parking spaces are found in Los Angeles: off-street residential parking, off-street nonresidential parking, and on-street curb parking. A 2015 study in the *Journal of the American Planning Association* reveals that the overall number of vehicular parking spaces in Los Angeles County *tripled* between 1950 and 2010. Most of this increase was in off-street nonresidential parking, which grew almost five times during this period, to surpass 9.6 million spaces in 2010.

Off-street nonresidential parking has a long legacy in Los Angeles: indeed, one of the earliest city-run parking lots in the world was constructed there in 1922. By 1923, the National Conference of City Planning was "encourag[ing] municipalities to take planned and rational action in allocating sites for off-street parking facilities." These facilities took the form, primarily, of multistory parking structures and at-grade open parking lots. Some of the first dedicated surface parking lots in the United States were built next to early shopping centers, of which the 1929 Chapman Market in Los Angeles was a pioneering (and unusually stylish) example.

Over the following decades, however, most surface parking lots in Los Angeles resulted from the opportunistic repurposing of underdeveloped or derelict land, providing a regular if modest stream of revenue for public or private owners, at minimal cost. They remain in existence today as an urban legacy, a century-old solution to a seemingly pervasive need.

As nearly everyone recognizes, however, surface parking lots represent the *least* productive and socially valuable use of any piece of property they occupy, especially in cities or districts that are otherwise well developed and active. Urbanistically inert, visually unappealing (whether empty or full of cars), deadening to the sidewalks they border (with prisonlike bars, usually, or cyclone fencing), and activated only briefly and intermittently—at best—by people leaving or returning to their vehicles, they offer little in the way of redeeming urban value in themselves, and serve only to enable the use (by drivers) of other, more vibrant activities nearby.

> *Parking lots are not just the handmaiden of traffic congestion, they are temperature-boosting heat islands, as well as festering urban and suburban floodplains whose rapid storm-water runoff dumps motor oil and carcinogenic toxins like polycyclic aromatic hydrocarbon (from shiny black sealcoat) into the surrounding environment and overwhelmed*

Chapman Market in Los Angeles was one of the first nonresidential off-street surface parking lots developed in the city. Many other surface parking lots are vacant lots rather than purpose built.

sewer systems. They represent a depletion of energy and a shockingly inefficient use of land.

TOM VANDERBILT, 2008

MORE LA is hardly the first such attempt to quantify the extraordinary amount of urban space that parking takes up in Southern California; there have been many such efforts in recent decades, including those cited in this book. It is, however, one of the first to take a pragmatic, development-oriented approach to the question, looking at the inventory of existing parking in the city from the standpoint of realistically *repurposing* it for new uses, based on strict guidelines and criteria for its data gathering and calculation. This selectivity distinguishes the MORE LA study from inventories that do not draw the crucial distinction between parking areas that are suitable for redevelopment, and those that are not.

The first of these criteria was to define the kinds of parking space to be studied. Purposefully excluded from the study were above-grade multistory parking structures, underground parking garages beneath buildings, curbside street parking, or surface parking less than 5,000 square feet in size, or sites with an extreme ratio of length to width. Any of these existing conditions make their redevelopment either unrealistic or too expensive. The study also excluded surface parking ancillary to industrial sites. These selective filters accorded with the study's larger goal, which was not to demonstrate how much parking currently exists in Los Angeles, but to determine how much readily developable land could be released by a reduction in parking use. In short, the MORE LA study limited itself to *sizable surface-level parking lots* only—which is to say, sites on which new activities, structures, or green space could, in principle, be built tomorrow.

The next challenge was to identify a meaningful study area. The official boundaries of neither the county nor the city of Los Angeles seemed suitable, thanks to idiosyncrasies in the size and shape of both. Los Angeles County is one of the largest counties in the entire United States, stretching far beyond the borders of the city of Los Angeles to include an area nearly ten times bigger—nearly 5,000 square miles—encompassing immense tracts of near-empty lands (including national forest and recreation areas) across a sizable chunk of Southern California. Unlike the active (and expensive) areas of the urbanized metropolitan Los Angeles, there is little or no need in these vast yet remote areas of the county for parking to be converted to other uses.

The boundary of the City of Los Angeles, on the other hand, presents its own challenges. Unlike the compacted and contiguous boundaries of cities like Chicago and New York, the city of Los Angeles (for historical reasons) is an oddly defined and strangely incomplete municipality, with many large parts of the central urbanized area outside official city limits (especially on its eastern and southwestern sides) and a number of other central districts—including Beverly Hills, Santa Monica, and West Hollywood, all of which are independent municipalities and none of which are legally part of the city of Los Angeles—appearing as missing "holes" in the official map of the city (though in the real world they are obviously fully functioning and integrated parts of the larger urban whole).

Instead, working with local consultants, the MORE LA team developed its own study boundaries, which it referred to as the "Core Metro Area": a large but contiguous area of about 500 square miles, with a population of five million people, roughly corresponding to the Los Angeles basin, and encompassing much of the City of Los Angeles as well as dozens of smaller independent municipalities in the central Los Angeles area. This "metro core" includes most of the higher-density areas of the Los Angeles region, where the transformation of surface parking to other uses is most realistic—and would have the most impact.

The research team relied on data from the US open data site, data.gov, and the LA County open data portal, including the TIGER/Line All Roads County-based Shapefile for Los Angeles County, as well as the US Census and Open Street Map. The road network maps are open source and have clear designation of categories available in the shape files; parking lots are a designated category in this file.

Some initial investigations were carried out by the geospatial team to understand the specific relationship between the data sites' designations and the actual ground conditions, and the files were cleaned and processed accordingly. (An alternative method of identification of this type would be the use of machine-learning image processing on aerial photographs to identify empty land with the characteristics of parking lots. This method would be useful in urban areas where land use and geospatial information is not as available or reliable.)

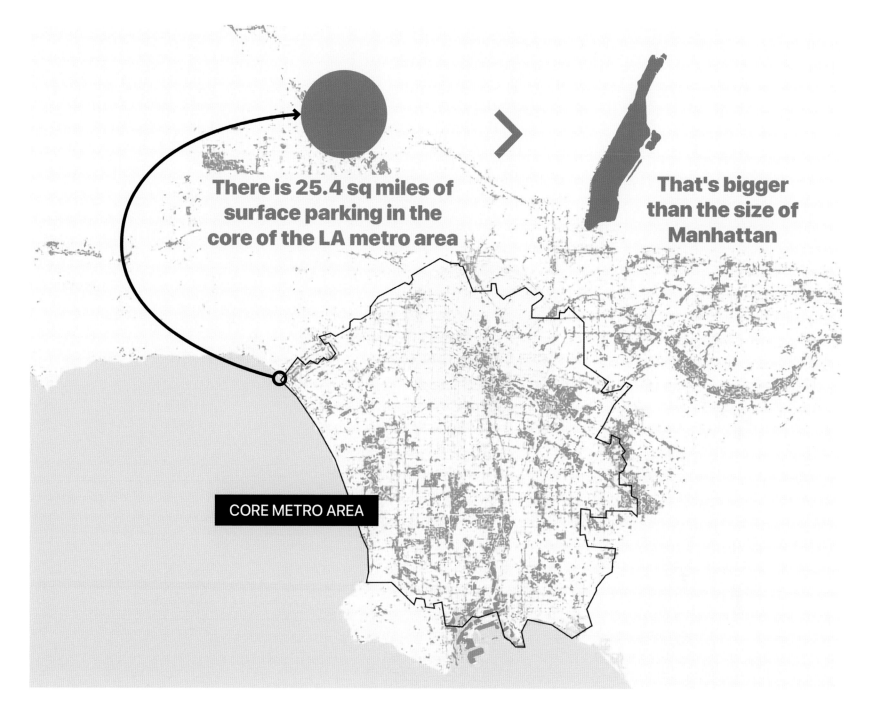

There is 25.4 sq miles of surface parking in the core of the LA metro area

That's bigger than the size of Manhattan

CORE METRO AREA

Map of the MORE LA study area, defined as the "Core Metro Area," showing the total area of surface parking lots greater than 5,000 square feet within the zone: 25.4 square miles, or 16,625 acres.

After processing and mapping this data, the study arrived at its first and perhaps most striking finding: that within the designated Core Metro Area of Los Angeles, *25.4 square miles* were given over to surface parking lots—an area larger than the size of Manhattan. This is the equivalent of 6,578 hectares, 16,256 acres, or over *700 million square feet* of lot area suitable for development.

The next step was to determine how much usable square footage could be built on this vast quantity of surface area. Critically, the MORE LA study used as its guideline (and limit) for increased potential development the average height and density of the *existing buildings surrounding each lot*. This decision was made in clear-eyed aware-ness of the profound sensitivities of many of the city's communities to new development that is out of scale or out of character for their neighborhoods. The MORE LA study was designed to minimize this politically divisive issue by proposing new development that mirrors what exists today—no skyscrapers dropped into single-family districts!

Using the Countywide Building Outlines data set from the LA City Geohub—which includes the building envelope of every building in Los Angeles County—a reasonable FAR (floor area ratio) for each lot was determined. Assuming a standard floor-to-floor height, the FAR of the surrounding blocks for each of the lots was calculated, using the total floor area of the built space-to-site ratio. This could then be applied to the empty lots to outline an acceptable and developable building envelope. Needless to say, in a city as large and diverse as Los Angeles, the prevailing development potential will also differ wildly. In parts of Downtown Los Angeles the average FAR is 3.7, while in more suburban areas it is 0.7 or lower.

Not all of gross floor space is livable, of course, as it includes building structure, services, and ancillary spaces. On the whole, around 85 to 95 percent of the gross floor area of any building is usable space. This was factored into the calculations of the number of units able to be fit into the building envelope and therefore the number of people able to be housed.

To arrive at that final and most important number, the project team also mapped household size, average dwelling unit size, and population density across the investigation area. This provided the figures to attach to the overall net floor area of each of the sites, to determine the overall number of inhabitants who could be housed by developing them.

These calculations resulted in MORE LA's second crucial finding—and one perhaps even more significant to the future of the region. If 100 percent of the total developable capacity of these surface parking lots were built, it would be possible to comfortably house an additional *1.67 million people* in the Core Metro Area of Los Angeles (representing more than a third of the population of the existing four-million-person city). Of course, it is unlikely that every single parking lot in Los Angeles will be developed any time in the near future or be built to its full potential volume. But even a build-out of a *quarter* of those lots' capacity would mean 420,000 additional people could find a new home in the city: enough extra space to sustain Los Angeles's growth for years to come, even under the most optimistic of projections.

The significance for this increased residential capacity is so important that the MORE LA research team calculated it not only for their own Core Metro Area but the county and city boundaries of Los Angeles as well. The equivalent number for the (much larger) LA County is especially startling: housing for over *3.6 million* new people.

Middle Scale: The Neighborhood

The MORE LA study team selected three sample areas of the city for a finer-grained exploration: Downtown Los Angeles, Inglewood, and East Los Angeles. The team based its choices on the factors described above, as well as larger considerations: geographic spread, social and economic diversity, and breadth of scale, density, and character. In these differences, the three selected areas seemed not only to sample the variety of neighborhood types found in contemporary Los Angeles but promised to offer an assortment of ways in which—at the neighborhood and site level—surface parking could be transformed into different kinds of places.

Some key statistics demonstrate those neighborhood differences well. Downtown Los Angeles has a high (for Los Angeles) average FAR at 3.7, while the predominantly low-rise nature of East Los Angeles results in an average FAR lower than 1.0. The jobs/residential profiles reveal the consistent high-density jobs-oriented character found throughout downtown, while jobs in East LA are distributed along key roadway corridors and in Inglewood, are clustered around the historic civic core and south of the new SoFi

Population Infill

More People Housed	3,690 K	1,670 K	830 K
Population uplift	37.8 %	33.0 %	22.0 %

global x 1,000,000 (Millions)

% developed	County	Met	LACity
None (current)	9.76	5.06	3.78
25%	10.68	5.48	4.04
50%	11.61	5.90	4.29
75%	12.53	6.32	4.53
100%	13.45	6.73	4.61

The additional population that could be housed (at various percentages of the developed land) on surface parking lots in Los Angeles County, the Core Metro Area, and the City of Los Angeles.

stadium. Household size and population per square mile also vary significantly; East LA, for example, is home to a high number of people per square mile, roughly equivalent to the urban core of San Francisco, and one of the densest parts of Los Angeles.

MORE LA's district-scale study began with Downtown Los Angeles, which, of course, is a special case. In 2018, the area—whose residential community has been exploding in size in recent years (see chapter 8)—had a population of 48,000 residents in 27,000 dwelling units (totals that have likely increased in the years since, despite the setback of the pandemic). The average site FAR is 3.7, high for Southern California but far lower than most central business districts and lower even than the residential areas of similar-sized cities, such as Singapore, or the transport-oriented suburbs of Sydney. Average dwelling unit size is a relatively modest 1,507 square feet, reflecting the fact that so many homes are apartments and lofts rather than single-family houses. (The relatively high amount of square footage per person, by contrast, reflects the fact that most Downtown LA households are single people and couples rather than large families.) Overall, there are 119,000 surface parking lots in the downtown area, which means 269 square feet of parking exists for each person (while only 29 square feet per person of green space is available). The MORE LA study concluded that the conversion of all of these surface parking lots to the same density as the surrounding properties would result in housing for an additional 117,000 people; a more realistic conversion of half the lots would still result in housing for 83,000 new residents in 46,000 new units—which is to say, nearly twice the number that currently exist in this most booming of urban districts.

East Los Angeles, meanwhile, has a population of 125,000 people in 32,000 dwelling units. The average FAR of 0.7 is typical of residential districts with early twentieth-century subdivisions in proximity to the central business district and several industrial zones. The average dwelling size of 2,066 square feet is relatively large—but because the average household size is also large, almost twice the American average, the square footage of dwelling per person is lower than in both downtown and Inglewood. East Los Angeles does not have as many surface parking lots as downtown, but if the prevailing dwelling and household size is kept consistent, the surface area of just a quarter of those parking lots could be turned into homes for 131,000 people—more than doubling the existing population.

Finally, Inglewood has a population of 112,000, within 39,000 dwellings, with a household size similar to the California average. The average dwelling size is 2,421 square feet, good-sized even by suburban American standards, and evidence of the predominant single-family character of the area. The average FAR here is 0.9, which is reflective of the area's generally low-rise nature, along with several higher-density zones located around the "town centers." There are a remarkable number of surface parking lots in Inglewood, the highest of the study's investigation areas: over 180,000. The overall number of these lots, the prevailing FAR of the area, and the average household size means that transforming one-quarter of the area's parking surface could physically comfortably house an additional 123,000 people—again more than doubling the existing population, although transport accessibility to the southern part of Inglewood would remain of concern.

District Profiles

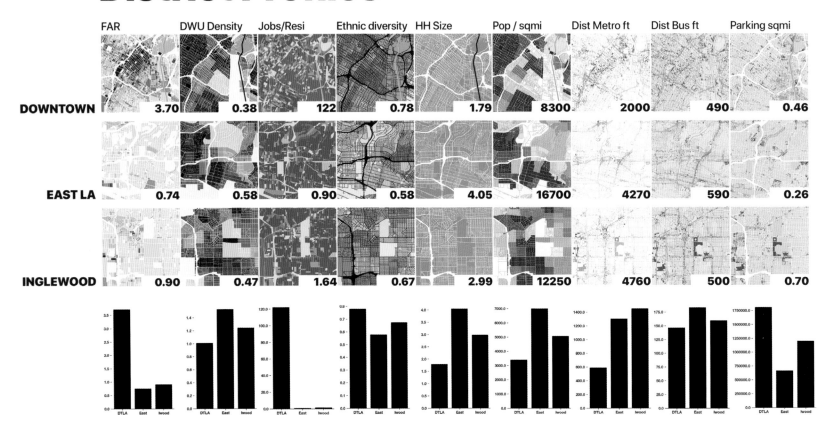

	FAR	DWU Density	Jobs/Resi	Ethnic diversity	HH Size	Pop / sqmi	Dist Metro ft	Dist Bus ft	Parking sqmi
DOWNTOWN	3.70	0.38	122	0.78	1.79	8300	2000	490	0.46
EAST LA	0.74	0.58	0.90	0.58	4.05	16700	4270	590	0.26
INGLEWOOD	0.90	0.47	1.64	0.67	2.99	12250	4760	500	0.70

Renewing the Dream

Opposite: *Color-coded mapping of social, spatial, and economic characteristics of the study's three selected districts of Los Angeles.*

Right: *The potential uplift in population achievable by developing 25 to 100 percent of the capacity of the surface parking lot sites in Downtown Los Angeles (top), East Los Angeles (center), and Inglewood (bottom).*

DOWNTOWN

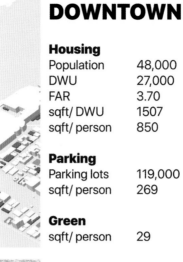

Housing

Population	48,000
DWU	27,000
FAR	3.70
sqft / DWU	1507
sqft / person	850

Parking

Parking lots	119,000
sqft / person	269

Green

sqft / person	29

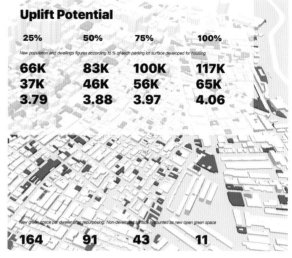

Uplift Potential

25%	50%	75%	100%
New population and dwellings figures according to % of each parking lot surface developed for housing			
66K	83K	100K	117K
37K	46K	56K	65K
3.79	3.88	3.97	4.06

New green space per dweller after repurposing; Non-developed surface is counted as new open green space

164	91	43	11

EAST LA

Housing

Population	125,000
DWU	32,000
FAR	0.74
sqft / DWU	2066
sqft / person	527

Parking

Parking lots	67,000
sqft / person	57

Green

sqft / person	32

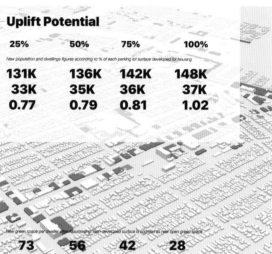

Uplift Potential

25%	50%	75%	100%
New population and dwellings figures according to % of each parking lot surface developed for housing			
131K	136K	142K	148K
33K	35K	36K	37K
0.77	0.79	0.81	1.02

New green space per dweller after repurposing; Non-developed surface is counted as new open green space

73	56	42	28

INGLEWOOD

Housing

Population	112,000
DWU	39,000
FAR	0.90
sqft / DWU	2421
sqft / person	840

Parking

Parking lots	180,000
sqft / person	172

Green

sqft / person	36

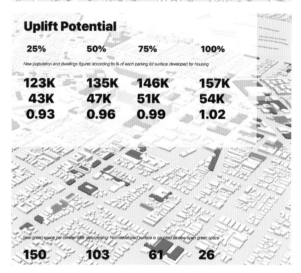

Uplift Potential

25%	50%	75%	100%
New population and dwellings figures according to % of each parking lot surface developed for housing			
123K	135K	146K	157K
43K	47K	51K	54K
0.93	0.96	0.99	1.02

New green space per dweller after repurposing; Non-developed surface is counted as new open green space

150	103	61	26

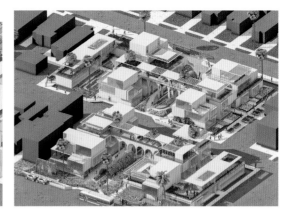

Concept designs for the Downtown Infill (left), *Linear Boulevard* (center), *and Courtyard Proposal* (right).

Microscale: The Site

Thanks largely to its stratospheric housing costs, the state of California—regarded widely (and correctly) as one of the most prosperous and wealth-generating places on earth—has the highest rate of functional poverty in the United States. A recent survey undertaken in Los Angeles showed that an astonishing three out of four households are rent-burdened (meaning that more than 30 percent of their monthly income must go for rent or mortgage payments). A dramatic increase in housing supply would undoubtedly have equally dramatic impacts on the lives of the millions of Angelenos who today struggle with housing costs (as well as those tens of thousands who, having effectively failed at that struggle, are homeless). The MORE LA study demonstrates the extraordinary numbers of new development—and new people—that can be accommodated at a citywide and district scale by converting surface parking lots into livable places, but what would this look like on the ground?

To balance the citywide benefits of unlocking surface parking with local concerns about the impact of new development on existing communities, the MORE LA study (which included architectural designers in Woods Bagot's Los Angeles Studio) continued its investigations at a finer scale, zooming down to a "micro" or site-specific level. Within each of the selected neighborhoods, it was decided, a representative site would be chosen to perform some basic massing and "test-fit" design studies. These studies would not represent formal architectural proposals, but rather "sketch designs" intended as lively provocations for further investigation and conversation. (Among other "provocative" aspects, the sketch designs zeroed out the required parking, to demonstrate how just much additional square footage could be generated, with the elimination of required parking, for needed human uses, whether residential, commercial, retail, community-oriented, or open space.)

The next step was to select the particular sites. As noted above in the district analysis of Inglewood, providing alternative means of transportation is a major barrier in converting many relatively remote parking lots to places. Expanding non-private vehicle transportation is a pressing priority for city-shapers in Los Angeles, but until practical solutions are tested and implemented, the likeliest candidates for conversion are parking lots already with access to multiple forms of transportation. The team thus mapped the transportation catchments (existing and planned) of each potential district, to understand which areas within them might already enjoy good access to transportation networks, particularly the LA Metro, and therefore be used to locate promising sites to investigate in further detail.

The pedestrian catchment area for existing public transportation for bus (left) and LA Metro (center) in Los Angeles, as well as the far more expansive catchment area for the Metro when combined with a $7 to $12 Uber ride (right).

Among other things, the first two citywide catchment maps that resulted—showing areas within a quarter-mile, half-mile, and three-quarter-mile walk of a bus stop and a Metro station—demonstrate how strikingly comprehensive in coverage the region's bus service is, especially when compared to the relatively sparse coverage of the LA Metro (which of course is still expanding).

In the spirit of the overall theme of *Renewing the Dream*—how twenty-first-century mobility can transform movement around the city—the team also prepared a provocative third map demonstrating how new ride-hailing services (like Uber and Lyft) might help to support public transportation (like the LA Metro) by addressing the crucial "last-mile" problem that has long bedeviled transit planners: that compared to denser cities like New York, Chicago, or San Francisco, in low-density Los Angeles relatively few dwellings are within convenient walking distance to a Metro station. The map shows how the LA Metro's walkable catchment area explodes in size with the addition of a $7 Uber or Lyft ride to and from the station, until it covers a majority of residential areas within the Core Metro Area boundaries. Though a $20 daily travel expense ($14 round-trip Uber/Lyft, plus $3.50 for a two-way Metro ticket) is not necessarily affordable to everyone, it might offer an attractive alternative for tens of thousands of middle-class Angelenos, who would be freed forever of long, twice-daily traffic jams on the commute to and from their workplaces. As the map indicates, it is certainly an approach worth further encouragement and promotion by public and private mobility partners.

Any housing proposed in these high-transport accessibility zones would have the needed access to jobs and other opportunities that are essential for sustainable cities. The team therefore plotted reasonably large sites, close to Metro stations and with a large number of bus stops within close range to identify sites with the most potential for investigation for test fit designs.

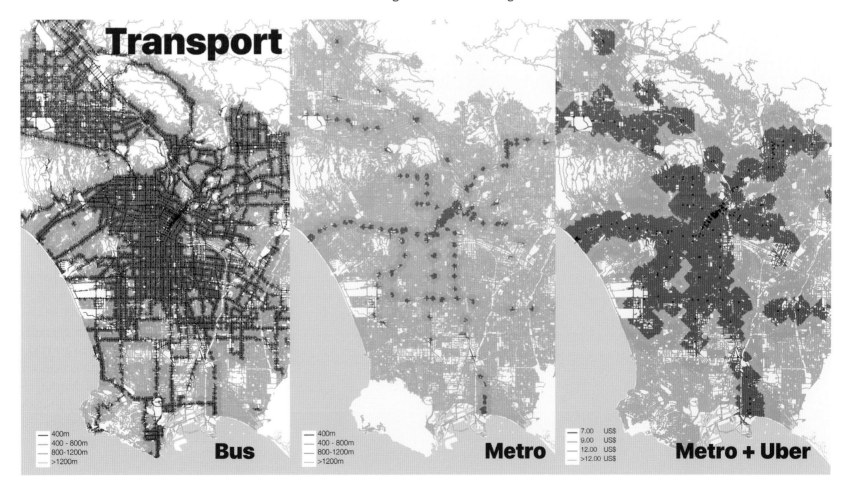

Transport

Bus	Metro	Metro + Uber

400m
400 - 800m
800-1200m
>1200m

400m
400 - 800m
800-1200m
>1200m

7.00 US$
9.00 US$
12.00 US$
>12.00 US$

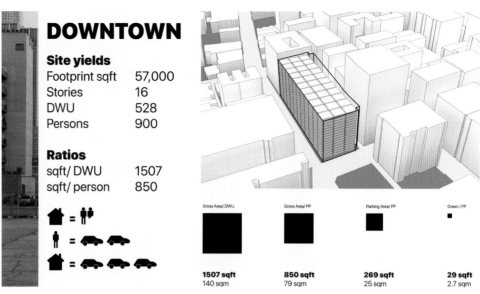

DOWNTOWN

Site yields
Footprint sqft	57,000
Stories	16
DWU	528
Persons	900

Ratios
sqft/ DWU	1507
sqft/ person	850

Gross Area/ DWU	Gross Area/ PP	Parking Area/ PP	Green / PP
1507 sqft 140 sqm	**850 sqft** 79 sqm	**269 sqft** 25 sqm	**29 sqft** 2.7 sqm

The yield in dwelling units and people housed and equivalency in car spaces for the selected site near existing transport for Downtown Los Angeles.

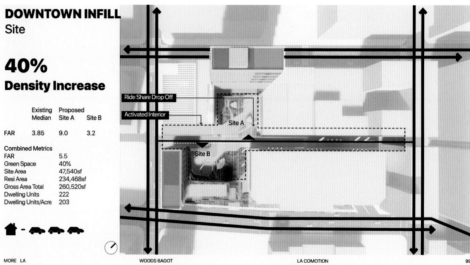

DOWNTOWN INFILL
Site

40%
Density Increase

	Existing Median	Proposed Site A	Site B
FAR	3.85	9.0	3.2

Combined Metrics
FAR	5.5
Green Space	40%
Site Area	47,540sf
Resi Area	234,468sf
Gross Area Total	260,520sf
Dwelling Units	222
Dwelling Units/Acre	203

MORE LA · WOODS BAGOT · LA COMOTION · 99

Ride Share Drop Off
Activated Interior
Site A
Site B

Design test fit for a site in Downtown LA optimized to create open space in an area that is underserved.

In each of the three selected neighborhoods, the MORE LA team chose a single parking lot site within a half-mile Metro walkshed to study more closely. In Downtown LA, they chose a characteristic urban infill site on South Main Street, not particularly distinguishable from any other surface parking lots in the area but particularly close to a Metro station. In East Los Angeles, they chose a more linear site, stretching along one of the wide north-south thoroughfares common to the area, South Atlantic Boulevard. Finally, in Inglewood, they selected a two-block site within a single-family district on South La Brea Avenue, close to transportation, schools, health care, and to the new entertainment district.

To determine the character of the context for each site, the team established a catchment using a radius of 800 meters or 2,635 feet (or approximately one-half mile), within which the average height and the maximum height of the area's buildings, and their estimated gross floor area (GFA) was measured. This helped to determine the likely reasonable envelope and FAR of proposed new development on each lot. The average household and dwelling unit size were drawn from the surrounding census statistical areas and used to determine the full acceptable yield in each location, based on prevailing community densities. The distance to green space was also measured for each site to determine how much of the ground plane should be made available for community access open space.

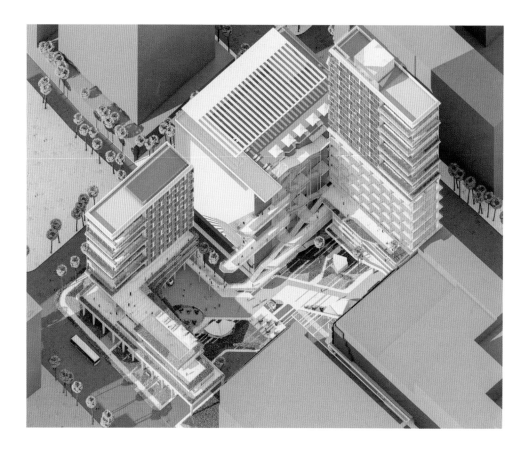

Sketch vignette of the design test fit for the Downtown Infill site.

In Downtown Los Angeles, the chosen site for investigation was 57,000 square feet in size. The average height of the surrounding buildings suggested that approximately sixteen stories would be the appropriate height for a new development fitting the character of the relatively high-rise downtown area. If the entire volume of the site was built out—at an average dwelling unit size of 1,507 square feet and a household size of 1.7 people per dwelling—the structure could potentially house about 900 people. To put it another way, every three parking spaces could be turned into a home for a future Angeleno.

The downtown site borders a service alleyway, a common condition in Los Angeles. Also common is the possibility that local planning processes and community pushback may mean that the entire volume legally allowed for the site is not built out. To transform the initial abstract analysis of the buildable volume of the site into a more realistic development proposal, the team reconfigured the site to comprise two smaller lots straddling the service alley, along with a historic commercial structure typical of the area (see chapter 6). The combined footprint of the three properties is somewhat smaller (by 10,000 square feet) than the lot size of the original study site, but the smaller adjacent sites and the inclusion of an older landmark building made the design proposal more authentic to the kinds of mixed-use development currently occurring downtown.

As developed by the team, the Downtown Infill sketch design proposal was able to achieve a ground coverage of 40 percent green space—vital in a city where, as the County Department of Parks and Recreation, Los Angeles, notes, "there is only 3.3 acres of park space per 1,000 people, well below the median of 6.8 acres per 1,000 people in other high-density U.S. cities." To achieve that generous amount of open space, the site was developed to an FAR of 5.5, higher than the average 3.7 of downtown overall, but not at all unreasonable for the city center of a major metropolis. At a conservative estimate, the design would provide 222 new dwelling units that can house over 350 people based on the average density of a downtown apartment.

The yield in dwelling units and people housed and equivalency in car spaces for the selected site near existing transport for East Los Angeles.

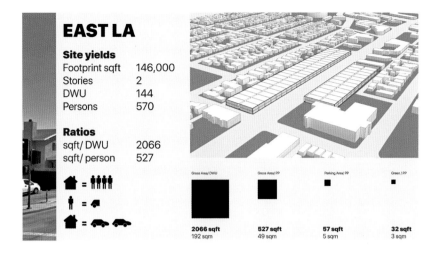

EAST LA

Site yields

Footprint sqft	146,000
Stories	2
DWU	144
Persons	570

Ratios

sqft/ DWU	2066
sqft/ person	527

🏠 = 👥👥
🧍 = 🚚
🏠 = 🚗🚗

Gross Area/ DWU	Gross Area/ PP	Parking Area/ PP	Green / PP
2066 sqft 192 sqm	**527 sqft** 49 sqm	**57 sqft** 5 sqm	**32 sqft** 3 sqm

EAST LA
BOULEVARD | Site

Typical Linear Lot adjacent to the Boulevard contains 262 Existing Parking Spaces to be re-purposed within the conceptual venture of More LA.

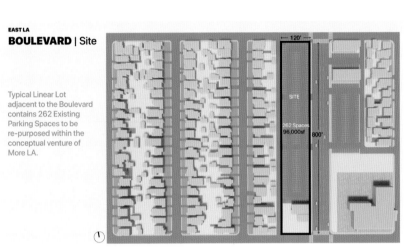

120'
SITE
262 Spaces
96,000sf
800'

Proposal for an underutilized East Los Angeles location, reimagining an activated, pedestrian-friendly street edge that makes more of the potential of the traditional boulevard.

EAST LA
BOULEVARD
Ground

Becoming a vibrant street

RESI LOBBY
Ride Share Pick Up | Drop Off
E-charge
Pedestrian
Micro-Mobility Lane
RETAIL
46' 46'
Restored Boulevard
E-charge

EAST LA
BOULEVARD

100%
Density Increase

	Existing Benchmark	Proposed Boulevard
FAR	.59	1.2
DWU/ACRE	9	18
Green Space	20%	31%
Site Area	96,000sf	
Resi Area	66,000sf	
Retail Area	49,765sf	
Gross Area Total	115,765 sf	
Dwelling Units	39	

🏠 = 🚗🚗

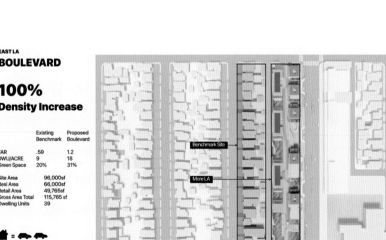

Benchmark Site
More LA

Design test fit for a site in East Los Angeles optimized to activate the culturally crucial boulevard.

Renewing the Dream

BOULEVARD
Features

Establishing the density of a 24 hour community

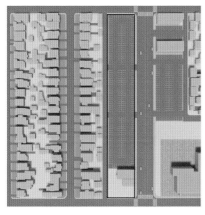

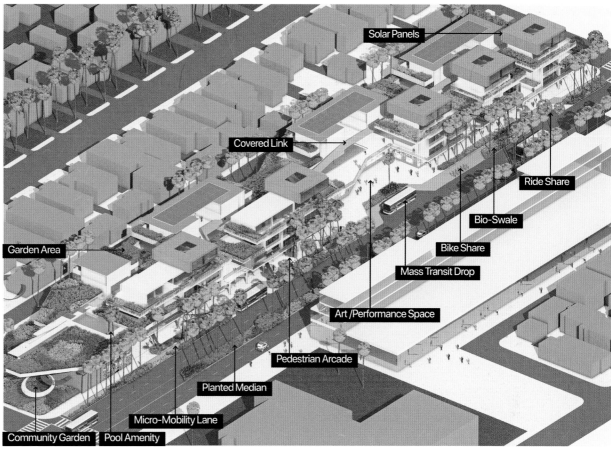

Solar Panels

Covered Link

Ride Share

Bio-Swale

Garden Area

Bike Share

Mass Transit Drop

Art /Performance Space

Pedestrian Arcade

Planted Median

Micro-Mobility Lane

Community Garden | Pool Amenity

Proposed twenty-four-hour community for East Los Angeles with a diversity of uses and users over the course of a day.

The sizable discrepancy between the ideal potential yield and the actual design yield (once all constraints have been taken into account)—which is to say, the difference between housing 900 people and housing 350—reveals the reality of development in any city and begins to demonstrate why the yield figures in previous sections are calculated at 25 percent, 50 percent, 75 percent, and 100 percent of developable capacity. In not all cases is it possible to build out 100 percent of a site's allowable development volume. The complexity and strictures of local planning regulations and livability ambitions put constraints on sites that can be difficult to surmount.

The East Los Angeles study site straddles a broad boulevard, along the commercial strip. The two lots located on either side have a combined footprint of 146,000 square feet, a substantial area to be used as surface parking (though not uncommon in this part of the city). The average height within the catchment zone of the site is two stories. If the whole volume of this development area was built out at the current local average unit and household size, the site would hold 144 dwelling units housing 570 people. In other words, one house could be built for every two parking spaces.

The long boulevards of Los Angeles provide a distinctive urban construct, synonymous in the minds of many with car culture and cruising. But today, as Christopher Hawthorne, the former chief design officer of Los Angeles has observed, many of the city's streets are "being remade to accommodate pedestrians, cyclists and urban street life." Reimagining these sites today thus requires a delicate balance between respecting the old way of life and reinventing it for a new, more sustainable era. One strategy is to retain the traditional vehicular thoroughfare but also elevate it as a place of significance and value for pedestrians and micromobility, as well as cars, a promenade as well as a roadway.

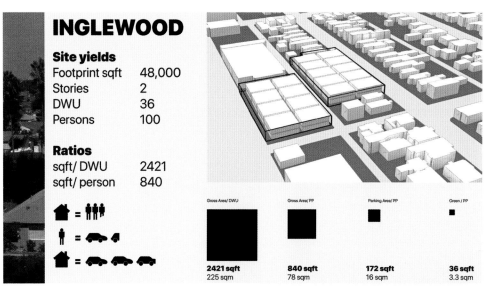

INGLEWOOD

Site yields
Footprint sqft	48,000
Stories	2
DWU	36
Persons	100

Ratios
sqft/ DWU	2421
sqft/ person	840

Gross Area/ DWU	Gross Area/ PP	Parking Area/ PP	Green / PP
2421 sqft 225 sqm	**840 sqft** 78 sqm	**172 sqft** 16 sqm	**36 sqft** 3.3 sqm

The yield in dwelling units and people housed and equivalency in car spaces for the selected site near existing transport for Inglewood.

INGLEWOOD
COURTYARD

70%
Density Increase

	Existing Benchmark	Proposed Combined
FAR	.36	.61
DWU/ACRE	7	17
Green Space	20%	43%

Combined Metrics
Site Area	58,800sf
Resi Area	33,000sf
Gross Area Total	35,500sf
Dwelling Units	23
Dwelling Units/Acre	17

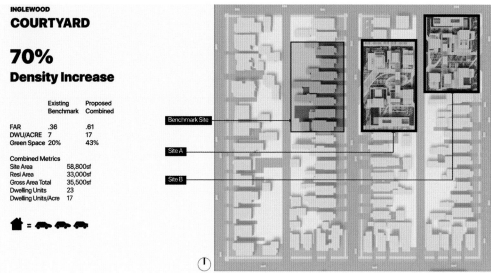

Design test fit for a site in Inglewood optimized to provide socially inclusive multifamily that is respectful of the character and density of the surrounding neighborhood.

The design approach for this site took as a benchmark the strip of residential housing to the west, which provided a clear comparison between what might be achieved and what existed. The team's "Boulevard" sketch design proposal doubled the FAR but also provided activation of the existing boulevard through new retail space, an increase of green space by half again over the current total, and a doubling of the number of dwelling units provided in the same lot area.

East Los Angeles, like other economically challenged parts of the city, is an area that struggles with both long-standing poverty and incipient gentrification. Ensuring that new housing is also affordable is a complex task of development analysis that was beyond the scope of the MORE LA study. That said, if the full potential area suggested by the study was developed, the additional supply would go a long way toward meeting housing demand and helping drive down—or at least stabilize—prices in an otherwise aggressive housing market.

The team's sketch design provides a twenty-four-hour community density and activation, which would likely have a positive effect on safety and would increase the diversity of uses—and users—over the course of a day. In the design sketch, a possible mix of amenities is diagrammatically included as a starting place for discussion, though in practice the elements of this mix would be established in close consultation with the community, in order to create a place of local significance and pride.

INGLEWOOD
COURTYARD
Features

Parking transformed.

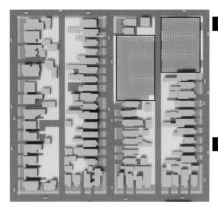

The courtyard model of multifamily housing turning parking to place in Inglewood.

The final site, located in the Inglewood study area, is also a split property, straddling a local street and lining two service alleys. The average height in the surrounding area is 16.5 feet, meaning a mix of one- and two-story structures—mostly single-family houses—though not far away sit some taller buildings of ten and eleven floors. The potential development yield provides for thirty-six new units holding one hundred people, in place of the current parking lots, which hold seventy-nine cars—meaning two or so parking spaces can be transformed into a new house for three people.

Inspiration for the Inglewood sketch design comes from the bungalow court housing that is a true Los Angeles housing typology (and whose significance is explored in detail in chapter 9). Prior to high-rise apartment blocks, as the City of Los Angeles Department of City Planning observes, "the low-rise, high-density courtyard apartment building. . . would eventually become the predominant multifamily housing dwelling type in southern California." Developed in the early twentieth century, the typology has roots in Spanish Colonial architecture as well as the affordable construction of the California bungalow style and was designed to house dozens of people on one or two adjacent single-family parcels of 50 by 150 feet. The economic advantages of the type were complemented by social advantages of communal outdoor space separated from the public space of the street. This layering of privacy through the sequence of open space is said to foster a sense of individual and collective ownership among residents of the courtyard projects.

The sketch design proposal for Inglewood—a free contemporary interpretation of the older courtyard model—can achieve housing for 70 percent more people than the existing single-family dwelling model on the adjacent blocks as well as 43 percent more green space. The two sites can comfortably support twenty-three dwelling units, or about 66 percent of the maximum capacity as calculated by the yield study. For the

Inglewood design, the test fit would house around seventy people, which is fifty people more than the adjacent existing benchmark site.

As well as achieving housing for more people—at a density in keeping with the existing character of the neighborhood—the "Inglewood Courtyard" sketch design provides significantly more amenity through the opportunity to provide shared facilities as well as both shared and private open space. Through-block pedestrian connections run across the site, activating dead spaces such as rear service alleys, that make the area safer and enable pedestrian movement to nearby points of interest. The reinterpretation of the quintessential Los Angeles courtyard model can be part of the solution to moving towards a more sustainable future for the city.

Conclusion

Seen in isolation, a single surface parking lot may not look like much of an opportunity for urban change, but as the MORE LA study demonstrates, when seen on a citywide scale their potential effect can be enormous—and profound. Calculating the numerical impact of that change, the study demonstrates how much can be achieved by taking a "macro" perspective on a simple, ordinary idea. Seeing the parking lots of Los Angeles not as part-time car storage but as potential places for people to live, the city can house from .5 million to more than 1.5 million people *without* increasing current neighborhood densities. This is an extraordinarily tempting possibility—especially in a city where housing is nothing less than a critical concern and where "density" is often a dirty word.

Of course, the macroscale seeks the best outcome for the city as whole, rather than studying the transformational opportunities of "parking to places" on a district-by-district basis. By contrast, development in the real world is almost inevitably a case-by-case undertaking, and local site investigations will reveal the challenges and opportunities of each site by test-fitting designs to its specific conditions. Development is also not a straightforward process, so certain sites may achieve 75 percent or 100 percent of their potential capacity while others might only achieve 25 percent or 50 percent in areas where local opposition to development is strong or other site constraints pose special challenges.

However, density may not always be a dirty word—even in Los Angeles—and the future of the city and region is likely to hold generally higher densities and heights. Among other things, this would mean the "uplift" calculated in this study for housing units and population would be even greater than those shown. Greater density and compactness of development also suggest far more sustainable development models. Examples like the courtyard typology show how this can be achieved in a sensitive way, locally in tune with the identity of Los Angeles.

Certainly, the car itself has long been synonymous with Los Angeles identity and there remains the serious challenge of separating Angelenos—even a little—from the beloved vehicles that have been so deeply embedded for more than a century in every element of their city's culture. But speculation and future gazing aside, the MORE LA study demonstrates strikingly that even while maintaining existing densities and neighborhood character, an immense (indeed, city-shaping) level of transformation could be achieved by converting existing vehicular storage spaces into activated urban places. Much like the ReCharge LA study in chapter 11 of *Renewing the Dream*, which explores alternative uses for the ubiquitous gas station, the findings of the MORE LA study asks us to consider: what other potentially redundant transportation infrastructure might be reimagined for a more livable future?

Street-level view of Boulevard Model for the redevelopment of a parking lot site in East Los Angeles.

Downtown Los Angeles, 2016.

In response to skeptics who say that any vision of Southern California based on a reduction in parking requirements is a fantasy, one can easily point to Downtown Los Angeles (DTLA). Here, a dramatic drop in mandated parking is not wishful thinking but has been a reality for nearly a quarter century—and in that time has shown astonishing results. The widespread elimination of parking minimums by way of the "Adaptive Reuse Ordinance," or ARO—the prosaically named but revolutionary piece of legislation passed in 1999 to allow the conversion of the area's historic office buildings into apartments—has made possible the creation of more than twelve thousand housing units and, with them, one of the most vibrant and exciting mixed-use districts in the country. That signal success has prompted further recommendations, now under review, to extend the same reduction to the area's newly built projects.

No one has looked more closely at the ARO and its role in the rebirth of Downtown Los Angeles than UCLA professor Michael Manville, who has carried out detailed research on the impact of the groundbreaking legislation over the past two decades. In conversation, he describes how the ordinance came to be, why and how it has transformed the character of Downtown Los Angeles, and what its implications are for the future of the larger city.

James Sanders   *To provide some background—before we get to the Adaptive Reuse Ordinance of 1999, which helped to spark the "downtown explosion"—could you first sketch the story of Downtown Los Angeles across the twentieth century?*

Michael Manville   Los Angeles has never been as centralized as the big cities of the East Coast were, or Chicago, or anything like that. But it *did* have, in the early part of the twentieth century, a fairly vibrant downtown. And that downtown had a commercial district, it had a lot of banks, it had what was sometimes called the original Hollywood, with a lot of movie houses and things like that. And it was the terminus of a lot of streetcar lines. So you had a Los Angeles, in the early twentieth century, that did look closer than you might think to a San Francisco or New York or Boston.

In the late 1910s, Los Angeles's downtown started to be overrun with cars, as happened in many American cities. And Los Angeles, to a greater extent than many other cities, decided that it was going to deal with that by physically changing its built environment to accommodate those cars. And this came about, in part, because when the city first tried to resist cars, that plan just blew up. They actually had a downtown parking ban in 1920 that was so unpopular it lasted about seven days. The city rolled it back and then brought in planning experts from around the country to deal with the traffic problem. What they decided they needed was a huge program of street-widening, of reorganizing the streets, and so forth.

Left: *View down Broadway, Downtown Los Angeles, late 1930s.* Right: *Harold Lloyd in* Safety Last *(1923), filmed on the Brockman Building on Seventh Street between Olive and Grand Streets in Downtown Los Angeles.*

And so you started to see a program where—even on streets that had buildings right up to their edges—when those buildings were demolished, the city took portions of the vacant lots and widened the streets, which sounds like something that wouldn't work very well because how often do buildings come down? Except that the Great Depression came. And when the Depression came, a lot of owners knocked their buildings down because they didn't want to have to pay taxes on [economically] nonviable buildings. And so suddenly you had vacant lots, which came to be called taxpayer lots (because the owners had emptied them to reduce their tax burden), and these empty lots not only allowed the streets to be made much wider, but also just put in place a lot of parking, because that's what empty lots get used for. And so wide streets and surface parking became a part of the landscape.

And then after World War II, we had a situation, similar to many parts of the country, where the region started to heavily suburbanize. Development flowed outward; jobs flowed outward. And so Los Angeles did what a lot of cities did, and it launched a program for urban renewal. And the urban renewal program, I think it's fair to say in the downtown, was something of a disaster. The entire section of downtown known as Bunker Hill was taken by eminent domain, it was razed to the ground, and then for decades nothing happened.

And then when finally some buildings were erected—which gave us the modern downtown that you still see, the big, steel-frame high-rises—what it basically did was suck what remaining vitality was in the nice old buildings in the historic part of the city up into the new structures, because any firms that had been in those [older] buildings were basically in Class C office space, and here the redevelopment agency has just built a bunch of government-subsidized Class A office space. So rather than really reinject new life into downtown, the redevelopment just moved activity from the old part of downtown to the new one and created a district in Downtown Los Angeles of very nice old buildings that were economically devalued.

JS *That leads to my next question. These downtown buildings that the Adaptive Reuse Ordinance would transform—what were they at the time?*

Spring Arcade building, a 1924 structure featuring an ornate Spanish Baroque terra-cotta façade, located on Spring Street in Downtown Los Angeles.

MM A lot of them were bank buildings, and others were general commercial buildings of that era. So these were very nice buildings, I think, to most people's eyes. I'm not an architectural expert, but I think that different reasons have been floated for why old bank buildings and other buildings like them are so pleasing aesthetically. In the era before federal deposit insurance, a bank really had to look sort of sturdy and impressive, like it was going to be there forever. And then of course in that era you predominantly have stone and brick construction, and it's hard to make an ugly stone and brick building. Whereas it's pretty easy to make an ugly stucco one.

JS *When you say bank buildings, just to be clear, they weren't little bank branches, they were large office buildings with main bank branches in their first floor.*

MM They often had banks in them, yes, and things like that. And then some of them were factory buildings. On the eastern edge of downtown, especially where the Arts District is today, you had a lot of factories that were there. And so it's a mixture, but

Downtown Explosion

they all declined for different reasons. The office buildings lost a lot of business thanks to the general decentralization of business after the war, as well as the transfer of resources away from these neighborhoods due to urban renewal. The factories, meanwhile, were gradually losing vitality because manufacturing became less and less urban. The era where factories were in the middle of big cities disappeared as we built highways, and you no longer needed your factory to be close to a rail line or big port.

JS *Bring us up to the time just before the ARO takes effect. What had become of Downtown Los Angeles by the late 1990s?*

MM Here's one way to put it. When I first moved to Los Angeles in late 2001, you could walk down the street in Downtown Los Angeles near Pershing Square at 5 p.m., and there was almost no activity. There are some exceptions, of course: this was a place that had a fairly decent-sized daytime population because there were still government buildings, there were still some [corporate] headquarters and so forth, but people really did clear out in the evening. On the weekends, there was an incredibly vibrant shopping district along Broadway, almost entirely Latino, but otherwise almost nothing.

So, the downtown was something of a joke. Nobody went there unless you worked there. Maybe you'd pass through on the way to see a baseball game [in Dodger Stadium], or something like that. And, of course, we had our Skid Row, which has tragically gotten so much larger, but that's always been there. So I think the downtown was associated with some combination of banality and tragedy: it was sort of a boring place, and you would get these difficult reminders of our disadvantaged neighbors and the obstacles they were facing living on the street.

JS *So in 1999 the City of Los Angeles passes the Adaptive Reuse Ordinance. What was it? What were its goals and its provisions?*

MM I think the goals remain somewhat murky; the phrase "success has a thousand fathers and mothers" is borne out by the ARO, because if you talk to people now, about twenty of them will say they wrote the ARO— and they'll all say that what they intended was exactly what happened. I think that if you just look at the language of the law when it was first passed, what's apparent is that there was some idea that a lot of the empty buildings in the downtown were being held back from reuse by just a handful of regulations. And so the law was basically a test of that idea. And some people will tell you that a couple of developers, like Tom Gilmore and Izek Shomof, who owned some of these buildings, really pushed the city to do it. Other people will tell you it was the work of forward-thinking planners and preservationists like Ken Bernstein.

But what the law did—to simplify a bit—was three things. It said that, for commercial or industrial buildings of a certain age or that had been empty for a certain number of years (the law had two different ways of defining buildings as economically underused, basically age and duration of vacancy), it said that you could turn those into housing, and you would not need to do the full seismic retrofit that would normally be required. Now, they were going to be earthquake safe. The city just devised an alternative seismic code to accommodate the fact that these were made of older materials.

The second thing was that the law basically gave what's called the "by-right," or "as-of-right," provision. Normally when you rezone a piece of land from industrial to residential, or commercial to residential, that would trigger a discretionary review. And in the discretionary review process Los Angeles has elsewhere in the city, it's only a slight exaggeration to say that anything can happen. Any number of conditions could be slapped on the project, and that makes it risky for the developer. So what the ARO basically said was that this whole procedure gets skipped. Rather than a situation where you walk in and say, I own this old commercial building, and I want it to be housing—and the city then says, "Okay, four hearings, two years, and you'll be sued three times"—the city just rubber-stamps it.

And then the third—and I think for our purposes the most important—provision was just that there were no minimum parking requirements. The exact wording was that any parking that was on the site had to be preserved, but otherwise none needed to be added. Basically you could deal with parking as you saw fit.

JS   *At that time, if you were going to build a new building, what would have been the parking requirement?*

MM   There's no single answer to that, because for different types of buildings there are different requirements and there are different ways to calculate required guest parking and so forth. But it would have been probably 1.25 spaces per rental unit. For condominiums, the way the city regulates parking has always been kind of ad hoc, determined on a case-by-case basis. But in practice, it was usually somewhere between 2 and 2.5 spaces per unit.

JS   *So really considerable: a condo unit of 1,400 square feet would require something like 700 square feet of parking and aisle access.*

MM   Yes. And when you think about it, that's almost a suburban parking requirement. It's like a driveway and a garage.

JS   *Given that we're now in a situation where there's a lot of goodwill to change things, but we're struck by how difficult it is to change the law, why did the ARO happen? Why did the city do it?*

MM   I've heard different explanations. I think one explanation I've heard is everyone just felt like, what's the harm? There's nothing there, in this part of downtown. There are no neighbors there. And I think probably, in the backs of their minds, a lot of people thought nothing would happen. Maybe they thought [the local developer] Tom Gilmore would go bankrupt and then this would go back to being kind of an empty area, [one] that movie companies occasionally use to film in buildings. I think that's the best explanation I've heard because in many other areas, Los Angeles is so slow to experiment in deregulation. And this was a pretty bold experiment. It wouldn't have happened in Brentwood. I just think when this was passed, in downtown, no one noticed.

JS   *Now let's sketch the broad impact of what the ARO has done. Could you describe what's happened to Downtown Los Angeles in the past twenty years? I wonder if a useful way of sort of thinking about it is the period from 1999 up to 2009 and the Great Recession, and then the period after it.*

MM   Yes. I would say that a very large amount of development occurred in a short period of time and in a small area of space. So, the initial surge of adaptive reuse redevelopment—thousands of units in upward of a hundred buildings—started getting going in the early 2000s, in this handful of neighborhoods that had been profoundly disinvested. And that made it quite noticeable, to have a neighborhood change so

Above: *Pacific Electric Building, about 1919.*
Opposite: *Interior of the Pacific Electric Building,*
converted to residential use, 2006.

Renewing the Dream

quickly and so visibly. Really to go from virtually having no residents to having not just a bunch of residents, but a robust sort of life, because these buildings came in with ground-floor retail and restaurants, clubs, bars, and so forth. And so not overnight, but within a space of a few years, downtown became not just a place where people live but something of a destination. It became a bit of a scene and people would go downtown to go out, which is not something that had been happening before. That people would go downtown to go to dinner and to walk along these streets, and so forth.

The proximity of these buildings to each other wasn't an accident. When you have regulations that hold back the redevelopment of a certain type of building—in this case an older building that parking requirements make very difficult to reuse—it is often the case that those buildings tend to be near each other, which means that through a building-specific regulation you are basically wasting an entire neighborhood. And I think what the ARO showed in that first ten-year span, from 1999 to 2009, is that we had been wrapping an entire neighborhood in red tape.

Now, of course, it helped that you had a real estate boom going at the same time. Because I think some of the first adaptive-reuse buildings would have had trouble getting financing otherwise, and in fact for some of his initial buildings Tom Gilmore scrambled and got financing from a bunch of different places. Barry Shy [another early downtown developer] used almost all private financing. It was hard. You weren't going to be able to go to a big lender, an institutional lender, and say, "I'm redeveloping an old building in Downtown Los Angeles with almost no parking space."

JS *Perhaps not an obvious lending opportunity.*

MM But I suspect that because we were awash in housing capital [at that time], they could more easily get some financing in those early projects. Then what happened is the projects immediately began to be profitable. And when that happens you start seeing some of the bigger institutional lenders peek over the fence. A turning point, I think, was the Pegasus Apartments, which was done by big institutional banks and big development companies. They came in and I think that really put a stamp on a sort of "car-light," "parking-light," urban adaptive reuse in Los Angeles. When the bigger banks got involved it was a sign that this was is something that could work and that people thought was profitable.

JS *In terms of the specific strategies that various developers used, one thing that struck me is that there was already a huge inventory of existing parking in Downtown Los Angeles. So, you might very well have four parking lots or garages within a block of your place, and people weren't going to have to walk far to find a spot, even though it wasn't in their building.*

MM Right. In that way what happened with adaptive reuse really illustrates how confining a conventional parking requirement is, because what the conventional parking requirement says is this: some or all of your tenants are going to have cars and want to park there, and we as the City are giving you one solution to that problem. That one solution is you have this many parking spaces per unit, and they're going to be on the same site as your building.

[Downtown LA's] developers did *not* do what would maybe be some planner's dream and some neighbor's nightmare, which is just to say, "Well, we're just going to build buildings with no parking." What they said was, "actually there are a lot of solutions to this problem. We will try many of them." And the fact that so many buildings and parcels

Lobby of the Ace Hotel in Downtown Los Angeles, 2022.

in Downtown Los Angeles already had available parking spaces, [that] just became another way to solve the problem. The *Los Angeles Times*—unfortunately—has just been hemorrhaging humans for a long time now. And they had a giant parking structure [located downtown]. They didn't have nearly as many staff or reporters [as they once had]. So developers would rent spaces in the *Times* parking garage and make them available to residents. There were also many parking lots that sold spaces during the day to downtown employees. These lots didn't have any business in the evening, and so if you lived in a loft, you could park there at night. And then as some developers got more into really making these buildings upscale, they decided it would be worthwhile to do what they could to put in some on-site parking. And one thing that the Pegasus did was [provide] just a limited number of on-site parking spaces in their mezzanine, to go for the high end of the market. And down the street, they had another lot where they leased the space.

JS   *In other words, they had some kind of dedicated arrangement; it wasn't hit or miss. There was going to be a reserved off-street parking spot for you, you would just have to walk half a block to get there.*

MM   Exactly. I mean, what comes out—which is what most people don't understand intuitively, and which parking requirements have preventing people from seeing—is that parking is like almost any other commodity: it's a market, with market segments. There are some people who really want—and will pay—to have a car right where they live. There are other people who just don't use their car that much and don't mind if it's a half block away. There are still other people that don't mind that it's a full block away. And then there's some people who don't have cars. And developers were able to target different areas of that market by taking advantage of all the different options around their buildings.

JS   *When I first started looking at Downtown LA in the late 1980s, there was a real estate boom going on then, too, but they weren't doing any of these kinds of residential projects then. But by the 2000s, the LA Metro had opened. What impact would you say the arrival of the Metro had on the desirability of these units and the whole feasibility of the premise of living downtown?*

MM   That's a good question....I am not sure. Obviously it can't hurt. But when you think about it, [in 1999] the Metro can get you to Hollywood. It can get you to Long Beach. It can get you to Koreatown. So if you work in Hollywood or in Long Beach or in Koreatown, it made it easier to think about living "car-light," in that way. But honestly, I think a lot of these folks just live downtown *and* work downtown now. I think the thing is that by 1999, the Metro downtown was useful but not so useful that it would suggest that *this* is why [things changed].

JS   *Although presumably, with every passing year, I can imagine that for the downtown restaurants, let's say, it's gotten easier to get there without driving and that makes the area more popular as a place to go.*

MM   Oh, yes. And when you get into the last eight years or so, you just can't underestimate what the presence of [tech-enabled] transportation mobility options has done for people who choose to live downtown in a car-light way. Because the giant question mark hanging over you in 2012 would still be, "What do I do when I want to go see my friend in Palms?" Or for someone like me, "How do I get to UCLA?" Because the Metro didn't solve that, and it still doesn't. But an Uber will. And that's only helped.

JS   *In your studies, you've described the downtown ARO in terms of a "laboratory experiment" about parking regulation. What do you mean by that?*

MM   From a researcher's perspective, what was interesting was two things. One was just you had this "before-and-after" where those buildings had been empty for so long, and someone could look at them and say, "Well, jeez. At least one of the things holding us back is just regulatory barriers." And now we have a test, right? Which is just, "pull the barrier back to reuse the buildings." Now the counterargument there is that a simple "before-and-after" tells you something but not everything, because all sorts of other things were happening as well; you've got a housing boom, capital pouring in, etc.

But the other nice thing is that some of these buildings were heavily clustered, and those clusters aren't big. And so you could also see what was happening as people built *new* construction downtown and compare that to the reuse of the *old* buildings. And in that respect, you've got something close to what we call a "natural experiment" in economics, which is the idea that because of something that just occurred—no one set

Downtown Los Angeles street scene, 2014. "Downtown Los Angeles . . . is enjoying the double whammy of a recent cultural resurgence . . . and the car services that deliver once-reluctant visitors," observed the New York Times *reporter Melena Ryzik in 2014. "The district is drawing comparisons to SoHo in the early 1980s, when former warehouses morphed into galleries and artist lofts."*

it up or designed it—you can look at a phenomenon with both "before-and-after" *and* "with and without." It's almost like the way we do trials for new medicine. We're "treating" some buildings by removing parking requirements, and not "treating" others, and then we could watch what happens, over time, to both of them.

And that's what I did with my study. And what I found is that the parking requirements really *do* constrain developers and play a role in how much gets built and what gets built. Certainly the "treated" buildings became housing, which they had not been before. But on top of that, when you look at those buildings, compared to other buildings that went up in downtown at that time, they had a lot less parking. And they were less expensive as a result. And they had smaller units. These were all the things that we thought would happen if you didn't have these regulations. I think the ARO is a fairly persuasive piece of evidence that the parking requirements don't just hold down the quantity of development in dense urban areas, but they also change the quality of it. By which I mean, what kind of buildings are you offering to people?

JS   *Let's talk a little bit specifically about your study. You studied fifty-six ARO developments. When did you do that? What was your process? And please summarize your findings for us.*

MM   It was around 2011. My initial hope was to go down to the city and pull the records and see how much parking they provided. Of course, none of that's been recorded. One of the things that's been frustrating about parking regulations for such a long time is that they're ubiquitous, but good inventories of parking itself are nonexistent. Every building has to put in parking and the city doesn't usually keep track of what was actually installed. And that's *with* the requirement. Now imagine the process with a bunch of buildings that are *exempt* from requirements; the city is definitely not going to write down how much parking they have. So the data aren't in the building permits.

So I ended up contacting the developers or the building management or both and saying, "What's the deal with parking?" The developer would probably know how many spaces were on-site, but what I needed to know also was just how they dealt with parking for their customers. Because, for instance, if they were just leasing spaces down the street, that wasn't going to be a part of the building record, but it was going to be parking they had provided for their customers.

JS *That's a private deal that they had, that wasn't part of their zoning or anything.*

MM Right. In fact, it could only exist because they'd been *freed* from the zoning. Most of the time a developer or property manager had this information. Fortunately, a lot of these buildings had people who were doing leasing and because customers ask this often, they know that arrangement. One thing they didn't know quite as reliably, so I had a little bit of a tough time figuring out, was how many spaces were initially on-site. Which was important, to figure out how many spaces were added. And I could piece that together for most of them, but that's a little bit of an uncertainty

JS *Did those 1920s and 1930s office buildings generally have any parking at all?*

MM Very few of them had a parking lot originally, but what would sometimes happen with these older buildings is that at some point a building next to it would get knocked over and become an empty lot. The owners of the first building would then buy part of that adjacent lot and now there's twenty parking spaces there. So that becomes a part of their property.

Rooftop hotel bar in Downtown Los Angeles, 2018.

JS Usually not a structure, though.

MM Not a structure. Usually it's an array of surface spaces. Very rarely, someone might have done some [renovation] work once and thrown some spaces in a ground floor.

JS How many roughly ARO projects have there been, in total?

MM I would say upward of one hundred buildings have been converted.

JS Impressive. Your UCLA colleague Donald Shoup has said Downtown Los Angeles has the largest concentration of prewar commercial buildings in the United States. And it's true that there's hardly anywhere, even in Manhattan, that you have long uninterrupted rows of prewar office buildings, because in many cases those structures were torn down after World War II for bigger and more modern buildings. The older parts of Downtown Los Angeles never had a similar postwar building boom, so that many fewer of those buildings got torn down. As Kenneth Jackson, my urban history professor at Columbia, liked to say, "Poverty is preservation's friend."

MM That's exactly right. It's a double-edged sword. They're not worth tearing down because the land isn't very valuable. But then because they don't have value, they're also not worth keeping up. There's a sweet spot there.

JS They were generally dilapidated. I get the feeling that they probably had some marginal ground-floor and perhaps second-floor uses, which probably paid for the rest of the building. In any case, what was the next step in your study?

MM So once we gathered this information about these buildings, from there we have some simple arithmetic, which is first, how much parking did they provide? And second, if we imagine a world where they had been subject to the [conventional] parking requirement, how much would they *have had* to provide? And that's setting aside for a moment the question, could they have even done it, if they had to provide that parking? And what you find is that for condos the difference is huge because the parking requirement is huge. The typical ARO condo building has half as much parking, on average, as the parking requirement would have otherwise called for. For apartments, where the requirement was lower, the total amount of parking is about the same, but— and this is important—much of it wasn't on-site.

When you put that together, the condos and the apartments, what you get is that on average, the ARO buildings provided much less parking than the requirement would have mandated. And the average is a little deceptive here because it conceals the fact that with the ARO buildings you had much more heterogeneity. Los Angeles has an apartment parking requirement that says every building has about one-and-a-half spaces per unit. The ARO apartments had about that average, but where the non-ARO buildings hit that average because they all had 1.5 spaces per unit, the ARO buildings, because they *don't* have a requirement, arrive at that average in a very different way. Some had no parking at all. And then there were some—because there was some preexisting parking or they were shooting for the luxury market—where there was a lot more. So you have the same average but actually very different types of buildings. And some of these buildings you got would have [otherwise] been totally illegal in Los Angeles, because there was no parking provided at all.

JS *Okay. You talk about how the results downtown worked to allay common fears about parking regulations, or more specifically about the lack of parking regulations. Tell us a little bit about that.*

Surface parking lots in Downtown Los Angeles, 2015.

MM Well, I think one of the most common things you hear when you talk about removing parking requirements is—if I had a dollar for every time I heard it, I'd be rich—"Well, people still need to park. You can't ban parking." And I think part of this is just a misunderstanding, which is that *ending a mandate* is not the same as *enacting a ban.* That when you say you're going to remove parking requirements, all you're saying is just that the government does not have the capacity to—and therefore should not—look at every single parcel of land in its city and know exactly how many parking spaces it needs, and where they have to be.

That statement is only controversial because we have flouted it for so long. But there's virtually nothing else about home building where the implied logic of parking requirements holds. Some units have washer-dryers, some don't. Some have pools, and gyms, and some don't. It's at the developer's discretion. We don't require pools, but no one thinks that because we don't require them we've tacitly banned them, or that they'll never ever get built. Parking could be that way too. But I do think one of the concerns that comes up is, "all right, you're not going to ban parking, you're just going to say the developers don't have to build it. Well, they won't build it. And as a result, the new tenants will park on the street, which means I'm not going to be able to park on the street, and it's going to be a burden on me as an existing resident." And I think what we see here is that the developers have an interest in building enough parking. Parking is valuable.

JS *And in many cases necessary.*

MM Right. For some developers, "enough" is going to be something close to zero, because they're actually targeting people who don't drive. But for others, they understand they're going to have a bunch of different types of customers, some of whom, again, are going to want their car right beneath their building, and some of whom are going to want it down the street. But it's important that they offer what their customers want. And then there will be some developers, potentially, who just want to externalize parking onto the community and say, "All my tenants are going to park on the street?" Sure.

But that didn't really become a problem in Los Angeles, for the simple fact that *you can't park overnight on LA's downtown streets.* During the day they're all metered, and during the night there's street cleaning enforced. No other part of Los Angeles is like that. That simple fact solved the problem of "what happens if a developer decides they're just going to let the street do the parking work?"

And so I think two big lessons came out of this. One of them is that you can remove parking requirements and see a flurry of new and more diverse housing in a place that we had previously given up as hopelessly disinvested. But two, that *de*regulated buildings need *regulated* streets. What Los Angeles should be doing is not regulating parking parcel-by-parcel off-street, it should be coming up with a coherent and sensible way to regulate it *on* the street, so that neighbors don't have to worry that new density is going to mean conflicts over the curb. And I think that it was very powerful that all this new development, all this new population, all this new activity came in, and you heard different concerns about it, but none of them were, "I can no longer park on the street," because that just wasn't an issue.

JS *Something we haven't mentioned yet is one of the biggest advantages of not having to build parking, which is that parking is very expensive. In Los Angeles it's now well over $20,000 a spot for structured parking. And if the developer doesn't have to pay for that, they can offer you a condominium, or a rental apartment, at a considerably lower price. Did you study that at all?*

MM We did. I gathered a big sample of unit listings for sale, on both ARO and non-ARO, looking at the buildings that were there that face parking requirements versus the buildings that didn't, and compared how likely a unit was to have one or no parking spaces if it was ARO, or not, and then comparing their prices. Using regression analysis and things like that.

And it was what you might expect. Which is to say the ARO buildings were much more likely not to have parking bundled in with them, and then if you didn't have parking bundled in the price was substantially lower. For a condominium it was on the order of $20,000 to $30,000 less.

I think it's important to emphasize that this is not an artifact of the goodwill of developers. Sometimes people say, "Deregulation makes housing cheaper because developers save money, and they can pass those savings on." But, well, why would they do that? Developers like big profits. Instead the price ends up lower because of competition. Everyone understands that developers will charge as much as they can, but if you don't have a parking space and the building down the street does, you just can't charge as much. And so a different sort of person wants to live in your building, and they're not going to pay as much, and you don't charge as much. From a social perspective that's what we want.

We want this more diverse housing stock that meets the needs of a great diversity of people and especially meets the needs of people who would like to live in Los Angeles and not have a car. We *don't* want to have a situation where those people are implicitly penalized because they rent or buy a parking space for a vehicle they're not going to use. And so freeing up the housing stock in such a way that developers, through the natural process of competition, are offering a savings to people who are traveling in the way we would prefer them to travel is a huge victory.

JS *I would think that making housing cheaper—meaning that a given loan that a developer gets will go further and build more housing, or however you want to define it—is crucial to the future of a city like Los Angeles or New York or any other city that's struggling with a lack of affordable housing. Of course, there are different definitions of affordability. But that same population is going to be competing to find housing— whether it's new housing downtown or if that's not being built, that population is going to go have to find it somewhere else.*

MM Yes. And I think this sort of moves beyond just the ARO, but if you think about a Los Angeles, a New York, a Boston, where the economy's booming, affluent people are moving there, they're coming for the jobs, they're coming regardless of what gets built or not. And if you think about our social goals, our affordability goals, and our environmental goals and say, "Where do we want this influx of people to live?" well, the answer is that vertical living downtown is just about the best. Because otherwise they're in our low-income neighborhoods pushing people out, or they're farther out [at the edge of the region] buying their detached single-family homes and just ramping up the carbon footprint.

And so the more we can do to make it easier to build these mid-rise and high-rise buildings that really encourage a less environmentally stressful, and frankly more human-scaled and human-interaction-driven type of living, the better. And the antithesis of that is a law that says every single housing unit you build has to come with at least one space for a car.

JS *So obviously Downtown Los Angeles was a huge success story for relaxing parking requirements. What are the issues with trying to extend that success story across other parts of the city and the state?*

MM I think that goes back to the question of why this passed to begin with, which is that you had this very unique situation where these buildings were ripe for the redevelopment, and they had no neighbors. And then as it started to get going, you had something that was maybe even more potent, which was that the people first moving into these buildings really *wanted* neighbors. They were lonely. And so they were like, "Yes, please build more. Please build more."

JS *Plus that means more shops and more restaurants and street life.*

MM Right. The first folks in these buildings understood that to have more development follow them would deliver them more amenities, more interaction, and so forth. There aren't that many other places in Los Angeles that fit that bill. And so to go into an existing neighborhood of longtime residents who are accustomed to living the way they are, and then say, "We're going to deregulate. And not just deregulate existing buildings, but maybe deregulate some ground-up construction"—the political dynamic is completely different. Because, if you look at the West Side or a commercial corridor winding out towards the ocean or something like that, you don't have handsome old buildings that are sitting empty. Those really are clustered in the downtown. And I think that's part of the problem.

JS Yeah, and that is a topic that Frances Anderton tackles in our book. Back in Downtown Los Angeles, so successful has the ARO been that the city is talking seriously about applying the same regulation to ground-up construction, new construction.

MM That's right.

JS What's your take on that, and how do you feel that's going to work?

MM Well, it's a great idea. I'm a follower of [my UCLA colleague] Donald Shoup, and I think that parking regulations are affirmatively harmful. That's different from saying parking is bad. It is saying that *mandating* parking is very bad, and the denser the urban environment you're talking about, the greater the social cost, because you are squandering larger opportunities to have a vibrant, vital urban environment. So removing parking requirements, in the downtown or anywhere, makes tons of sense. What will the reaction be? That's hard to say because part of what you always wonder is how quickly developers and their financiers are willing to depart from existing business models. There's part of that business that, for understandable reasons, is very conservative.

JS That's the nature of their business.

Rooftop pool in the Eastern Columbia Building, a 1930 Art Deco office structure adaptively reused into a residential loft, 2016.

MM That's their business. So there's been a model in the downtown, and other parts of Los Angeles of "let's put up a high-rise building with a giant parking podium." Do I think that if we got rid of parking requirements, that overnight that model would be abandoned? No. I wouldn't mind if it was because I think buildings on top of parking podiums are incredibly ugly. If I had to guess I would say it'll play out much the same way the ARO did, where some of your more risk-taking developers will find maybe less advantageous financing and get the go-ahead to do a building without a podium with a lot less parking.

Other people will watch. And if and when it works—and I think it will work, I think there's the appetite for it—then people will start to follow suit. Because no one likes to spend all that money on parking. And so I think if they can be reassured that they won't be at a disadvantage by not doing so, then they won't build parking.

Certainly, there's money involved, and people are cautious about their money. I don't hold that against them. I'm cautious about *my* money. But I do think it'll be huge if we can move to that, because all the development with parking holds the downtown back as an urban place. It reinforces the car orientation of the area for people who want to travel but also it's hard to have a downtown of sidewalks and bicycle lanes with so many curb cuts. Manhattan, for example, has very few curb cuts, and unsurprisingly people like walking there. But if every new building you put up in our downtown has a curb cut, then when you're walking down the street part of you is always wondering if a car is going to slide out and run you over. Which sounds like a small thing, but it's actually a big thing.

JS *In 2019 [just before the pandemic], the Los Angeles Department of City Planning released some rather astonishing numbers for the future growth of Downtown Los Angeles, saying that by 2040—less than twenty years from now—Los Angeles's downtown will see an increase of 125,000 new residents and 55,000 new jobs, representing 20 percent of the city's predicted population growth. The growth over the last two decades has been so dramatic, but do you actually see this continuing at that rate?*

MM I think it's great, but it also has a gray lining too, which is that so much of Los Angeles is so resistant to housing that the city has channeled housing into the one neighborhood that is willing to accept it. And so a lot of construction is happening downtown, and I think that's to the good of downtown. And I think it's good for Los Angeles to have a denser downtown. But at the same time, it is also indicative of how resistant a lot of the city is. And when you look at some of the big high-rise buildings that have gone up, it's hard not to imagine how much more useful some of that housing would have been, and how much less expensive some of that housing would have been, if it was four-story wood frames on the West Side.

But I do think downtown, to its great credit, has been a neighborhood that has been willing to say, "Give us more neighbors." And so the city has—and so it's grown.

JS *What a perfect note to end on. Thank you.*

The Lost and Future LA:
Parking and Housing in Southern California
Mark Vallianatos

Foreword: Losing One's Cool

In 2019, I led a walking tour in the Miracle Mile neighborhood of Los Angeles. The purpose of the walk was to look at old apartment buildings, and to consider if they could still be built today. Participants met in front of the Los Angeles County Museum of Art, next to the popular Urban Light installation. Before we headed out across Wilshire Boulevard to our first stop, I announced three ground rules for the walk. The first was safety: be careful and make room on the sidewalk if anyone else was walking by. The second was respect: whether we loved or hated buildings as architecture, keep in mind that they are all someone's home. The third was participation: ask lots of questions and share your own local knowledge.

I may have violated my own "respect" rule partway through the walk. At least, I lost my cool. We had stopped at a 1926 fourplex on a residential side street off of Olympic Boulevard that had later been downzoned. Near the corner with Olympic, a person was sleeping on the sidewalk. Angelenos have perhaps become too accustomed to the tragic rise in the number of unsheltered homeless residents in Los Angeles City and County. But something about the juxtaposition—a human being forced to sleep on the street (a street where it is illegal to build small apartments), while we were walking to learn about when and how once-popular housing types were banned—suddenly got to me.

The tone of my voice rose a few levels above what might be appropriate—respectful—for an architecture and urbanism tour. Why are the only buildings allowed on that block single-family houses? I asked. Why, in the face of a homelessness and housing crisis, do we ban well-designed multifamily housing for people, but mandate two covered parking places for every home?

This chapter is, in part, an effort to answer these questions.

A demonstration by activists in a homeless encampment in Echo Park, March 24, 2021, in response to a proposed city plan to evict all park encampments in Los Angeles.

Introduction

For all its complexities, the essential argument of this chapter is simple. By elevating homes for cars above homes for humans, parking rules in Los Angeles have contributed to high rents and homelessness. They have also undermined much of what attracts people to Los Angeles in the first place: its beauty, diversity, and openness. Fortunately, removing and shifting these same rules can contribute to a more affordable, welcoming, and sustainable city.

The chapter tells the story of parking policy in Los Angeles, past, present, and future. It begins by exploring LA's "forbidden city": places and buildings that could not be built legally today, largely because of parking regulations. The Los Angeles region boomed during a time when personal vehicle ownership became common, making the city a world leader in figuring out how people should dwell and move in a place with many cars and trucks. Lots of diverse and pleasant low- and mid-rise kinds of housing were built in the city and region, some with parking for cars, some without.

Things began to go wrong when cities started requiring that *all* new homes include parking for vehicles. The chapter's second section, on "forced parking," traces the origins and evolution of these mandatory parking rules. As forced parking was introduced and ratcheted up over time, it methodically eliminated many of LA's most characteristic and beloved housing types and deformed others to become less livable.

The chapter ends with a look at "the city in crisis/future city," a section that proposes several reforms in parking policy to help address LA's twin crises of housing and homelessness. There is a tragedy and irony to the fact that a place which has for so long mandated parking places, now has so many homeless residents living in vehicles. This section reviews recent hopeful changes that point the way to a less parking-dominated approach to urban growth and change. To build on this momentum, the chapter suggests a moratorium on required parking spots until the homelessness rate falls significantly and outlines a number of other key parking reforms.

Forbidden City
Los Angeles before Mandatory Parking Minimums

From time to time a driver crashes their vehicle into a building. Photographs and video from these collisions often go viral online (and indeed did so long before the Internet, in newspapers and on television). These images, one can argue, are also a good symbol of Los Angeles—the place that, more than any other, pioneered the mash-up of cars and buildings.

This is true, above all, because the region grew rapidly just at the moment when private ownership of motor vehicles became common. "A lifestyle based on mass personal automobility [was] first developed in Southern California," observes the scholar James Flink in his 1988 cultural history of cars, *The Automobile Age*, "and nowhere in the world has mass motorization been more pervasive in its impact." As early as 1910, the LA region had the most vehicles per resident in the United States. By 1920, there was one car for every 3.5 people in Southern California, compared to just one per *thirteen* in the country as a whole. In older cities like Chicago, there was just one car per thirty residents at the time.

It is hard to imagine how fast Southern California grew in the 1920s, when the region experienced a quadruple boom. The population of the region more than doubled, from

An out-of-control car embeds itself in the second story of an office building in Santa Ana, Orange County, January 14, 2018.

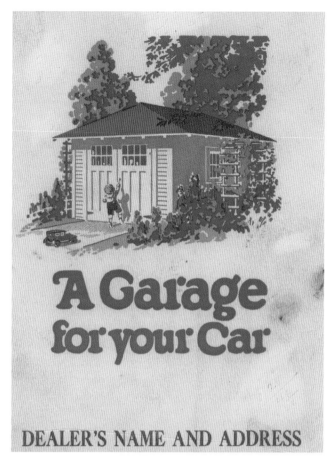

In the 1910s and '20s, Los Angeles pioneered a new kind of structure: a house for cars. Residential garages, large enough for one or two vehicles, typically located near the rear of a single-family house property, and reached by a driveway at the side of the lot, were erected by the tens of thousands across the region.

housing permits issued in City of LA per 1000 residents
*2010 only includes 8 years of data

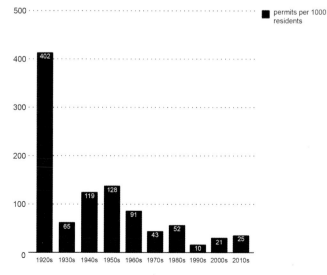

Housing permits issued in the City of Los Angeles per thousand residents, 1920–2020.

approximately 940,000 to two million. Hundreds of thousands of homes were built to accommodate existing residents and the flood of new arrivals. Permits for new homes were issued at a rate that far exceeds even the post–World War II housing boom.

Impressive as this rate of growth was, car ownership rose even faster. The number of registered vehicles in LA County increased nearly *sixfold* from 141,000 to 777,000.

Owners needed someplace to store those autos. Between 1920 and 1929, permits for 106,387 garages were issued by the City of Los Angeles—about half the number of new homes permitted. Many of these were likely single-car garages for single homes, but plenty of others were for commercial garages or multiple-car garages for apartment buildings.

This surge in people, homes, vehicles, and garages meant that mass motorization was now decisively influencing the region's larger patterns of development and the design of its individual buildings.

> From the laying of the first railway down to the port at Wilmington just over a century ago, transport has been an obsession that grew into a way of life. Lines were hardly laid before commuting began along them; scattered communities were joined in a diffuse and unprecedented super-community, whose empty interstices filled up with further townships, vineyards, orchards, health resorts, and the fine tracery of the second generation of railroads—the interurbans.
>
> REYNER BANHAM, 1971

In earlier decades, Southern California had been shaped by rail-based transit. Back in the nineteenth century, and especially during the boom years of the early 1880s, railroads (in collaboration with local real estate interests) had offered special, discounted, one-way "home-seeker" tickets to newcomers interested in relocating to Los Angeles. For a brief time, fares were just a single dollar. Some settlements near rail depots became Los Angeles County's best-known cities, while others never took off and withered into forgotten names. When growth picked up again in the early twentieth century, most land development was clustered near the thirteen hundred miles of the Pacific Electric and Los Angeles Railway streetcar systems. Streetcar companies were themselves active in land development. "Local electric services by street railways and inter-urban lines were to make almost every piece of land in the Los Angeles basin conveniently accessible and thus profitably exploitable," observed Reyner Banham in *Los Angeles: The Architecture of Four Ecologies*. "Not only did the Pacific Electric outline the present form of Los Angeles, it also filled in much of its internal topography, since its activities were everywhere involved—directly or otherwise—with real estate."

Motor vehicles changed this equation. Widespread car ownership allowed developers to build homes and businesses distant from existing streetcar lines, supercharging the region's already sprawling patterns of growth and breaking "the bond between land subdivision and rail transit," in the words of the urban historian Richard Longstreth. Instead, he notes, "[p]atterns of residential development and automobile use acquired a symbiotic relationship by the early 1920s."

Rising car ownership also impacted the design of buildings. With many people now having a personal automobile, the question of whether, where, and how cars could be parked and stored at home (as well as at work, stores, etc.) arose for every developer, architect, builder, renter, and home buyer. In an oral history recorded late in life, the influential Southern California architect Cliff May—perhaps the leading

By the 1930s, builders of multifamily apartment complexes in Los Angeles, including such modernist landmarks as the four-unit 1937 Dunsmuir Apartments by Gregory Ain, routinely included at least one private garage space for each unit in their projects. Photograph by Julius Shulman.

popularizer of the postwar ranch house—described how his parents built a house in San Diego in 1906, and how it was adapted for the auto age. "I think in those days when they built, the streetcar determined where you lived," he recalled.

> *Dad picked out a little side street called Albatross. . . . One day . . . Dad came driving home; I think it was in a Saxon car. So immediately Dad said we were going to build a garage. He had to excavate the whole lawn in front of the house and expose all the foundations, which didn't go down deep enough. . . . They cut one opening into the foundation and formed it so they could dig out underneath the house. Then they put foundation walls all around inside, retaining walls, so they could drive the car in.*

Modern Los Angeles is generally thought of as a place of single-family detached homes, with apartments and renters becoming a majority only relatively recently. But the 1920s housing boom, at least in the city of Los Angeles, was split almost evenly between one-unit homes and multi-unit buildings. Space for vehicle parking was scarcer on these lots than on the single-family houses that May described. As a result, the many small- to medium-sized vernacular apartment buildings built in Los Angeles in the 1920s have varying amounts of parking in different orientations.

The result, as presented in the gallery on the following two pages, was that the housing of this decade offered a wide diversity of ways in which homes and cars could coexist—in an era before cities began mandating vehicle parking:

Forced Parking
The Rise of Mandatory Parking Requirements

Faced with growing numbers of automobiles on city streets, policy makers in Los Angeles in the early twentieth century scrambled to figure out how to regulate cars and trucks. Without any other source of guidance, speed limits and traffic rules were borrowed from those for bicycles and streetcars, while parking regulations for buildings were adapted from those for stables and horses. Los Angeles was a pioneer in city zoning, and in 1908, the city was divided into residential districts—where industry and certain kinds of commercial businesses were banned entirely—and industrial districts, where these more intensive land uses were legal. The residential district ordinance limited horses and stables. "It shall be unlawful . . . to keep or permit to be kept more than four horses, ponies or mules in any barn, stable or covered structure upon any premises within any of the district," the 1908 ordinance declared, "without first having obtained a permit therefore from the Board of Health for the City of Los Angeles."

In 1921, when the City of Los Angeles adopted its first full zoning ordinance, it was one of the first localities in the county to include a zone reserved just for single-family houses. Each house could include a garage limited to a maximum of four motor vehicles—a clear holdover from the earlier four-horse limit. There were no limits on the number of cars that could be parked in a garage on a multifamily residential property that could contain "necessary and convenient space for automobiles." When the city updated the zoning code in 1930, it limited parking spaces to a maximum of two per apartment. The code also banned leasing this parking to nonresidents: "no such garage space shall be rented to anyone not an occupant of such dwelling."

A "zero parking" bungalow court on North Commonwealth Avenue in Los Feliz, with an elaborate front gate and decorative fountain. Built in 1923, it comprises eight homes with very narrow side and rear setbacks. Unlike the fourplexes surrounding it, the court lacks a side driveway to rear carport.

The leftmost and two rightmost of these buildings on South Genesee Avenue just south of Wilshire Boulevard in Mid-City, are all eightplexes, built in early 1931, 1930, and 1929. The blue building has eight parking spots in a ground-floor front garage, the roof of which doubles as patio space for residents. The middle red-roofed building has a rare (for the era) underground garage for eight vehicles. The similar, red-roofed building on the right has zero parking.

This "low-parking" hillside bungalow court on Chickasaw Avenue in Eagle Rock was built in 1929. It has eight homes, plus six garages built facing the street. The court is said to have been built for men working as jockeys at Santa Anita racetrack, several miles away in Arcadia. The apartments are not especially small in scale, but the original bathtubs were, apparently, shorter than usual.

This "zero parking" four-story masonry apartment on Monte Vista Street in Highland Park was built in 1928 with forty-eight apartments and eighteen hotel rooms. The site was downzoned between the 1970s and '90s so that only nine homes could have been rebuilt on the property.

This stretch of Normandie Avenue in Koreatown is one of the most "urban" blocks in the Los Angeles region. Twelve zero-parking apartment buildings of between three and seven stories were built here between 1925 and 1930. Together they contained 644 homes, plus retail space. All of the residential buildings could be built without parking in part because the white building at the top left was originally a three hundred-space commercial garage. Today it is a storage building.

This 1929 four-story, forty-unit masonry apartment building on South Manhattan Place, designed by the prominent local architect Max Maltzman, has a stylish parking lot located next to it—a parking "court," in fact, with two rows of carports (twenty-four spaces total) rather than two rows of homes. The parking court was built in 1931, by a different owner, so it is unclear if it was built for the forty-unit building next door or for another apartment building on the street.

Less than a year later, in 1931, Los Angeles passed a very different type of amendment, adding a parking *minimum* to larger apartment buildings. All new flats, apartments, and apartment-hotels with twenty or more homes were required to include at least one "garage space on the premises" per apartment. With this seemingly subtle shift—from parking *maximums* to parking *minimums*—came the crucial turning point for Los Angeles and perhaps the most formative single regulation in the history of the city's physical landscape.

Why the change? Early zoning rules viewed parking garages as potentially noisy and polluting nuisances that could intrude into residential areas and sought to limit their size and location. However, as car ownership and street congestion grew, planners looked to private developers to provide parking. By the early 1930s, the planning department in the City of Los Angeles was highlighting how residents of a new apartment building "monopolize" the parking on an adjacent street. They proposed requiring all housing with two or more homes to provide on-site vehicle parking, saying it was "absolutely necessary to prevent the unbearable automobile parking situation on streets in multiple residential zones from increasing. An ordinance implementing this one-space-per-unit parking minimum for all multifamily housing was signed into law in January 1935.

These new parking requirements—the first in any large city in the world—radically altered the residential landscape of Los Angeles, making it illegal to build apartments without on-site car garages. Mid-rise apartment houses of the time usually covered nearly all of their lots, leaving little or no room left over for parking. Bungalow courts and courtyard apartments included somewhat more open space, but usually in central landscaped courtyards that were not suited to use as parking, either. A 1931 article in the *Los Angeles Times*, reporting on the impact of the original parking requirement for twenty-plus-unit apartment houses, found that *no* permits for apartment buildings of three or more stories had been issued in the eight months since the parking minimums were imposed. The commentary explained that the required parking "necessitates provisions for the garage in the basement. The increased cost of the structure

An image from a Los Angeles Department of City Planning annual report from the early 1930s, illustrating how residents of zero-parking apartments were "monopolizing" street parking space. Below the image, the report asked, "Question: Can this street adequately serve all abutting lots when similarly developed, or does this ONE building monopolize what rightfully belongs also to its neighbors?"

Renewing the Dream

because of this subterranean garage is declared by builders to prevent financing [or make development unprofitable]."

The recent onset of the Great Depression was, of course, a contributing factor. But when home building picked up again in the second half of the 1930s, entire categories and arrangements of housing typologies had essentially been banned by parking requirements, especially when combined with a 1935 zoning requirement for sizable front, rear, and side yards for all residential properties.

As architects and builders came to realize, these increased parking and yard requirements caused "the tail to wag the dog" in the design of multifamily housing in Los Angeles: builders and architects worked out the parking first, and then laid out the residential units around that. In the 1950s and '60s, Southern California experienced a new apartment boom. Many were what became known as "dingbats": low-rise, wood-frame, stucco-faced apartments often with visually flamboyant front facades, constructed with aboveground parking spaces tucked beneath the building. In some sense a postwar version of the prewar bungalow court or courtyard apartment complexes, the dingbat offered little or none of the graciousness of those older types—mostly because of the need to provide so much parking.

> *Codes have changed radically since the 1920s, and they are the most evident factor for the abandonment of many desirable [prewar] courtyard-housing features....The parking garages that are so discreetly handled in the originals through the use of a lovely tiled forecourt off of the street [or] an entrance from a small garage on the rear alley...have been replaced [in postwar apartments] by a massive concrete garage below grade but open on the side to prevent the necessity for the forced ventilation that would otherwise be required.*
> STEFANOS POLYZOIDES, ROGER SHERWOOD, AND JAMES TICE, 1982

Polyzoides and his colleagues were writing about higher-end courtyard apartments of the late 1920s and early '30s. But the more modest bungalow court—attached or detached homes arranged in two lines or in a U-shape—suffered the same unhappy fate. In projects built before parking requirements, the central courtyard was reserved for pedestrians, and often combined walkways, communal landscaping, and small private entries or front yard space. After the advent of the new parking requirements, traditional bungalow courts were no longer built. Developers did sometimes construct two parallel rows of buildings. But what had been a landscaped central walkway or court became a *driveway*, paved entirely with asphalt and leading to rear parking or to ground-level garages located beneath the residential structures. Due to strict rules for keeping driveways clear at all times, these were inevitably desolate compared to the landscaping of older courts.

In his essay in the 2016 book *Dingbat 2.0*, the architectural historian Steven Treffers writes that dingbat apartment projects were designed to put as many units as possible onto a "standard family lot"—typically 50 by 100 feet, or sometimes a little larger—within the constraints of existing setback and parking rules. A few years after the dingbat boom started, in 1958, parking minimums were increased again to require 1.25 parking spaces for apartments with three or more habitable rooms (including kitchens) in buildings of six or more units. As Treffers explains:

> *Architects would typically work backwards from these regulations, determining how many parking spaces could be provided based on the*

Renewing the Dream

The ubiquitous LA "dingbat," an apartment house whose ground floor has been turned over almost entirely to residents' parking, became a familiar sight in 1950s Los Angeles, its boxy ordinariness attracting the eye of artists such as Ed Ruscha, who included this view of 904 Cynthia Street in West Hollywood in his landmark 1965 photographic survey, Some Los Angeles Apartments (opposite). More recently, the photographer James Black has captured some of the city's surviving dingbats, including The Hauser Apartments in Mid-City, photographed in 2016 (above).

number of automobiles they needed to accommodate. In cases where 1.25 spaces per unit might be required, an architect might exclude a unit....By building seven units instead of eight...a builder would only provide eight parking spaces instead of ten.

In 1964, parking requirements were increased further so that two-bedroom apartments needed 1.5 parking spaces each. But this proved a step too far. Treffers reports that the increase "led to the end of the mass production of dingbat apartments by 1965."

Apartment buildings continued to be built in Los Angeles, of course, but only on much larger lots. After 1965, apartment construction usually meant combining two or more full lots for larger buildings with parking placed fully or partially underground. Ironically, neighbors tended to view these larger buildings as more out of scale with nearby single-family houses. By indirectly banning smaller apartments through higher parking requirements, policy makers ended up contributing to opposition to new, larger apartment structures.

City in Crisis/Future City

Parking Reform and LA's Housing and Homeless Crises

Two higher-parking heirs to bungalow courts, a 1970s apartment (right) *and a circa 2015 small-lot subdivision* (above), *both located on Toland Way in Glassell Park, with a shared driveway rather than shared walkway and landscaped open space.*

Los Angeles's Skid Row, in the downtown area, has long been a symbol of inequality, poverty, and shelter of last resort. The biggest difference between the Skid Row of the first half of the twentieth century and today's Skid Row is that earlier residents mostly rented small rooms, or cots in barracks-style quarters, in single resident occupancy hotels (SROs). These cheap lodgings were, to say the least, not ideal homes. Rooms were tiny, and buildings rarely met fire and safety codes. But as Alice Callaghan, one of the founders of Skid Row Housing Trust of Los Angeles, noted in 1992, "hotels provide the last viable safety net for housing; if people miss this net, they will either become homeless—literally forced to live on the street—or institutionalized."

Los Angeles was fortunate that thousands of rooms in SROs were preserved as part of a policy to redevelop most of the rest of Downtown Los Angeles by concentrating homeless services in Skid Row—but thousands more units from the heyday of SRO hotels were lost. In his 1994 book, *Living Downtown*, the author Paul Groth chronicles "the seemingly irrational destruction of millions of private low-rent housing units that are still desperately needed" in cities throughout the United States. "For the reformers working on the new city [in the early twentieth century]," Groth writes, "single-room dwellings were not a housing resource but a public nuisance." These hotel dwellings were regulated out of existence. In Los Angeles, the development of new SROs around Skid Row was forbidden due to their location within areas zoned for manufacturing as well as for their inability to meet parking requirements; many existing structures were then torn down as it became infeasible (or uneconomical) to bring them up to modern building codes.

With not enough cheap rooms for rent, street homelessness skyrocketed. As homelessness has risen in the Los Angeles region, conditions in Skid Row have gotten dramatically worse. Long lines of tents fill sidewalks. The governor speaks of the return of "medieval" diseases. Homelessness has also exploded outside of Skid Row. According to

While neither the 1962 six-unit dingbat in Silver Lake (below and bottom right) nor the multi-lot 1990 seventy-nine-unit apartments in Glassell Park (top right), promote a great pedestrian experience, at least the dingbat fits in with a range of small apartments and single-family houses and could be developed rapidly by a small property owner using a local contractor.

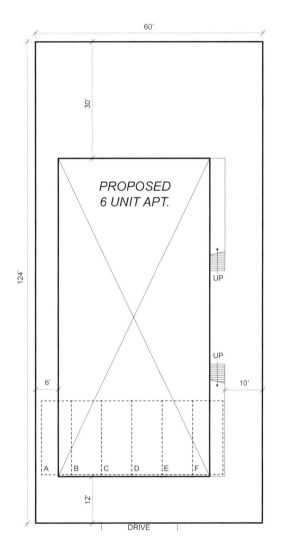

a recent survey, more than 66,000 people in Los Angeles County lack a home; more than 48,000 are entirely unsheltered, sleeping on sidewalks, in tents under freeway overpasses, and, increasingly, in parked vehicles.

This last trend is especially telling, and painfully ironic. Due to housing shortages and high housing costs—caused in no small part by the sheer expense of including parking in every new residential building—vehicles themselves have become the housing of last resort for LA residents otherwise facing life on the streets. During an early 2020 "point-in-time" homelessness census, an estimated 18,924 people in Los Angeles County were counted as living in 11,124 cars, vans, and recreational vehicles. In a further irony, people dwelling in vehicles in the city of Los Angeles are not allowed to park them on streets in residential zones, so they cluster in industrial and commercial districts.

Obscene levels of homelessness, including the perils of living in vehicles, should be the last straw for mandatory parking in Los Angeles. Our eighty-year experience with these requirements can only be judged a failure based on their impact on housing, urban design, and safety.

Plenty of parking was built in Los Angeles before mandatory parking minimums. Plenty can still be built if we eliminate these parking mandates. But by eliminating those minimums, we can legalize better designed homes, for less cost, with less parking for people who can't afford a car or want to be car-free or car-light.

In recent years, happily, there have been some glimmers of hope. Los Angeles and the State of California have at last advanced a number of intelligent policies that reduce or eliminate parking requirements:

— The Adaptive Reuse Ordinance passed in 1999 allowed conversion of underused historic office buildings downtown to residences without requiring additional parking. This led to the creation of nearly twelve thousand new homes and helped to spark downtown LA's comeback as a bustling twenty-four-hour community (chapter 7).

— The city's Transit Oriented Communities density-bonus program allows zero or reduced parking for residential developments close to transit stations that also provide some deed-restricted affordable homes. Between September 2017 and December/March 2021, 28,829 new housing units have been proposed under the program—approximately 20 percent of which are deed-restricted affordable units, the city's planning department has reported. These include some of the first zero-parking housing built in Los Angeles in almost eighty years.

— California state laws passed between 2016 and 2019 have made it easier to legalize and build accessory dwelling units (ADUs), unlocking LA's garages and backyards as a new source of homes. Accessory structures like garages converted to ADUs do not need parking, nor do new ADUs if they are within half mile of transit or in a historic district. With more permissive rules in place, the number of ADUs permitted annually in the city of Los Angeles rose nearly twenty-fold; nearly twelve thousand permits were granted in the first three years after the law's passage, and the numbers continue to rise dramatically year over year.

— A new state law passed in 2022 (AB 2097) eliminated parking requirements within half a mile of all major transit stops, defined as rail stations plus the intersection of two frequent buses. This new rule bars parking minimums in many denser, central locations in Los Angeles.

To reinforce this growing momentum, city and country jurisdictions in the Los Angeles region, together with California's state legislature, should more aggressively reduce and reform existing parking rules through new policies shaped along the following lines:

— An "emergency" moratorium on the enforcement of vehicle parking requirements on new residential buildings or mixed-use buildings in any jurisdiction in Los Angeles County, to remain in place until the homelessness count in the county drops below thirty thousand, and the count of unsheltered homeless residents drops below ten thousand. There is precedent for this kind of emergency legislation. At the end of World War II, the City of Los Angeles temporarily

A 2018 view of one of the dozens of tent cities found across Los Angeles, in which the majority of the city's 42,000 homeless people find shelter—on sidewalks, in parks and plazas, under freeway overpasses, and on boardwalks and beaches. According to planners, the City of Los Angeles must produce 57,000 units of housing per year for the next eight years to meets its needs. In the past several years, however, the city has approved fewer than 17,000 units per year.

waived requirements for covered parking spaces, and at the onset of the Korean War the city reduced parking requirements for apartments. Policy makers and planners imposed these limited-term measures because they understood that wartime material shortages were driving housing shortages—and required an aggressive response. Today's emergency is civil rather than military in nature, but no less dire.

During this emergency moratorium, jurisdictions should revise policies to eliminate, reduce, and improve parking requirements as follows:

— Expand the prohibition on parking requirements near transit to apply to all transit corridors with frequent buses and to zones with on-demand public shuttles, like the Metro Micro program.

— Eliminate vehicle parking requirements for all deed-restricted affordable homes and supportive housing.

— Require no more than one parking space per household for other types of homes and locations.

A Los Angeles homeless man praying over his food, 2013.

— Allow residential parking to be off-site, within 1,500 feet of homes.

— Do not require any additional parking for changes of use (i.e., from commercial to residential, or from one commercial activity to another).

— Lower commercial parking requirements and eliminate them for lots with less than 10,000 square feet and/or for buildings of 2,500 square feet or less.

During this moratorium, jurisdictions should also revise zoning policies to minimize the negative impact of surface and structured parking:

— Ban above-grade parking podiums (ground-level and higher levels of buildings that are reserved for parking garages), or strongly discourage them by treating above-grade parking space as usable floor area (which applies to the building's FAR zoning calculations, determining its allowable size), while allowing underground parking to remain uncounted as usable floor area in those calculations.

— Require that any parking that is built at ground level or above be wrapped by leasable building space, and that parking space have flat floors that can later be converted to non-parking uses.

— Regulate the locations of parking lots and driveways to minimize curb-cut and pedestrian exposure to cars. (For example, require rear parking and access to parking via rear alleys, where such alleys exist.)

Postscript: Towards a Healthy City

The global Covid-19 pandemic of 2020–21 caused cities around the world to rethink streets, public space, transportation, and housing. Some on-street parking was temporarily given over to outdoor dining. Attention to overcrowded dwellings, which disproportionally harm low-income, nonwhite residents, led to calls for more balconies and courtyards for airflow and better quality of life. The lesson of this chapter is that mandatory parking has stolen quality outdoor space from homes and the city at large. The public health priorities of providing safe and pleasant places for people to live, work, and shop during an event like the pandemic only add to the logic that homes for cars should no longer be prioritized.

9

Back to the Garden:
The Courtyard Alternative
James Sanders

Introduction

Much of California is straining under its own success: we have too many people and too few places for them to live, offered at too-high prices, in too many areas touched-by-climate-change-related menaces, like wildfires, all too far from where people work. And the solution is so painfully obvious it feels almost reductive to point it out: Make it legal to build more housing that houses more people.

FARHAD MANJOO, 2020

Planning for a denser, more connected city could begin by acknowledging the durability of prior choices that still shape the built environment.

D. J. WALDIE, 2021

It is no secret that Los Angeles is in the midst of a severe housing crisis, unable to produce enough new residential units to accommodate its existing population, much less the tens of thousands of newcomers attracted each year by Southern California's vibrant economy, extensive educational opportunities, and attractive climate and lifestyle. The resulting shortage, represented by sky-high rents and home prices and the severe lack of affordable options, threatens to choke the region's underlying prosperity and well-being, diminish its ability to attract young people—including those of a creative bent and limited means, so crucial to sustaining its dynamic cultural energies—and has already dramatically worsened long-standing issues of social equity, as is painfully evident in the tragic rise of homelessness on the city's streets and in its parks. "California gained three million jobs between 2010 and 2019, but added fewer than 700,000 housing units," observed *New York Times* columnist Paul Krugman in 2021. "The failure to add housing, no matter how high the demand, has collided with the tech boom, causing soaring home prices, even adjusted for inflation. And these soaring prices are driving less affluent families out of the state."

For many of us in Los Angeles—a metropolitan area that 57 percent of Angelenos can't afford to live in, according to a recent study—this is a city from which we are constantly on the brink of slipping away. Average rent in LA is $2,550 for a two-bedroom apartment. In fact, the disparity between wages and market prices here is the worst in the country, nastier than in New York City or the Bay Area, and it's become the toughest American city in which to buy a house.

SCOTT TIMBERG, 2015

Street view of the proposed California Court project, an eight-unit courtyard complex whose structures—modest in width and height, and set back from the sidewalk with a layer of landscaping—can sit comfortably on a street of single-family houses.

A 1927 courtyard project in Pasadena, designed by Robert Henry Ainsworth, offers an unusually expansive central garden—and one off-street parking space for each of its units. Photograph by Julius Shulman.

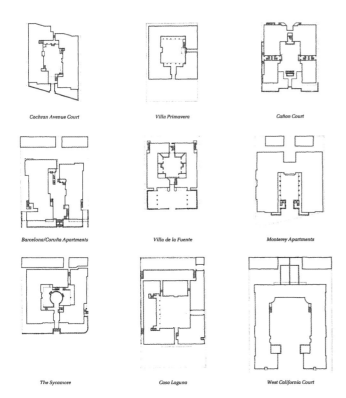

For their 1982 book, Courtyard Housing in Los Angeles, the architects and authors Stefanos Polyzoides, Roger Sherwood, and James Tice prepared comparative site plans of notable courtyard apartment complexes, illustrating how the basic urban pattern (or "typology") of the courtyard model could be readily adapted to the various shapes, sizes, and conditions of sites around the city.

The underlying causes of what Krugman calls California's "housing nightmare" are wide ranging—from overly restrictive zoning rules to the high expense of land acquisition to the prohibitive cost of new construction. But in the context of this book's focus on the relationship of mobility and development in Southern California, two stand out in sharp relief.

The first, as delineated with sharp precision by Mark Vallianatos in the previous chapter, emerges from what in many ways is the heart of *Renewing the Dream*: parking. As Vallianatos argues, the insidious impact of Los Angeles's notoriously strict regulations—generally requiring two off-street parking spaces (or more) for each residential unit—have made it essentially impossible to build any of the "gently denser" alternative housing models that flourished in the region before World War II but have since been made illegal.

The second, related challenge underlies the "battle of Los Angeles" described by Frances Anderton in chapter 1. Essentially forbidden by parking minimums on smaller-sized house lots to build anything larger than a single-family dwelling, developers often shift their sights entirely in the other direction, assembling lots into a site sufficiently expansive for a high-rise apartment building or mixed-use development—big enough to provide a sheltered off-street garage within its walls and thus satisfy the city's strict parking rules. These kinds of large projects certainly serve to expand the city's overall housing inventory, but—as Anderton recounts—their height and scale inevitably become the lightning rods of opposition from the established residents of single-family neighborhoods, who—not entirely without reason—attack these proposals as outsized impositions on the character of their fine-grained communities. Whatever these existing residents' other, less meritorious objections, this simple argument against tall, shadow-casting developments within low-rise residential districts—which so much of Los Angeles remains to this day—has effectively served to outlaw denser development across much of the city, driving the growing shortfall in new units.

But as Vallianatos points out, Los Angeles's urban heritage carries a number of promising solutions to its contemporary housing challenges—and of them, one offers a truly tantalizing opportunity: to draw upon—and adapt for today's needs—one of the most magical and beloved residential models ever to arise in Southern California: the bungalow court and courtyard apartment projects of the 1920s and '30s, in which modestly sized units, laid out in attached or semi-attached arrangements, enclose a central, landscaped open space.

Built in the space of two decades before World War II, these remarkable projects have been deeply woven into the myth and allure of Los Angeles ever since, providing the inspiration for novels, feature films, architectural photography, and, not least, one of the best books ever produced about the built environment of Southern California—the landmark 1982 *Courtyard Housing in Los Angeles*, written by the architects and historians Stefanos Polyzoides, Roger Sherwood, and James Tice—filled with superbly researched plans, elevations, sections, and typological diagrams, and featuring the commissioned photography of the legendary Julius Shulman. No one has ever captured more eloquently the unique appeal of these places—which, the authors make clear, are not only captivating environments in their own right but seem to summarize the magical essence of Southern California itself:

> The courtyard projects continue to embody all that is quintessentially
> Angeleno: the promise of a sublime existence in a sun-drenched
> Garden of Eden filled with orange blossoms and palm trees, the

Detail of central fountain at Casa Laguna, a 1928 courtyard apartment in Los Feliz, designed by Arthur and Nina Zwebell.

mythology of Los Angeles's Spanish origins; the ephemeral flamboyance of Hollywood and the imagery of life as some kind of transitional stage set; the freedom implied in the canonization of the automobile; and the appeal of an undefiled speculative frontier capable of bringing instant wealth and well-being within everybody's reach.

STEFANOS POLYZOIDES, ROGER SHERWOOD, AND JAMES TICE, 1982

Any later effort to understand or draw lessons from these projects—including this writing—must owe a debt of gratitude to the authors of this pioneering work of architectural and urban analysis.

Seen today in the context of the twenty-first-century mobility revolution that is transforming the way many people live and move around the Los Angeles region, it is clear that the prewar courtyard projects offer an unusually promising approach to new residential development in Southern California—and especially to the two major challenges introduced at the outset. For all their lush open space and pedestrian orientation, most of the prewar courtyard projects offered one dedicated off-street parking space for each household—a standard that could now present a reasonable compromise between the needs of a new, less-traditionally car-dependent population and the realities of life in Los Angeles for the foreseeable future.

And as a prime example of what has come to be known as "the missing middle" of housing development—types of dwellings that are denser than single-family homes but less obtrusive than high-rise buildings—they provide one plausible answer to the entrenched antagonism that Frances Anderton frames at the outset of this book. They achieve three or four times the density of conventional suburban-style houses—a site of two or three adjacent house lots, for example, can readily accommodate eight units— with structures no higher than two stories. Arranged so that only narrow ends of their attached or semi-attached units front the street and sidewalk, they present the appearance not of some sort of large, off-putting "project" but of modestly scaled, freestanding, well-separated residential structures, fitting in almost seamlessly with the scale and rhythm of a traditional residential neighborhood.

Most importantly, of course, the courtyard projects reinforce rather than dilute or negate the urbanistic qualities that have long made Los Angeles, at its best, so desirable a place to live. With intimate scale and their generous ratio of greenery to building, they reiterate and extend the mythic imagery of Southern California, of gracious homes and planted terraces tucked within a lush, verdant, sun-washed setting.

Any reinterpretation of the courtyards for contemporary Los Angeles must begin with an understanding of their history, their architectural features and layout, their enduring presence in the city's culture, and most importantly, the lessons they have to offer the present. This background provides the basis for a new design proposal called "California Court," drawing directly on the strengths of the older projects but adapting them in multiple ways to meet the needs and desires of modern American households.

It is a perhaps ironic yet satisfying circumstance that changes in mobility propelling Los Angeles into the future—many based on cutting-edge advances in technology and digital networking—would allow the city to retrieve and interpret, in contemporary terms, some of its most deeply rooted urban models—and most desirable historic precedents.

Our issues are uniquely LA, and our solutions will be uniquely LA. Density does not have to be a dirty word. No one is talking about dropping a ten-story building in the middle of a single-family neighborhood. Thoughtful design can help create a net density increase without

Built across Los Angeles by the hundreds throughout the 1920s, bungalow courts adopted a variety of architectural styles —from Spanish Revival or craftsman—but always included a landscaped central space (right) and frequently featured some type of symbolic "gateway" to the street and larger city (above). Photographs by Julius Shulman.

"A Complete Little Home"

They're a distinctive type of multifamily housing that is really kind of the backbone of Los Angeles's history.

ADRIAN SCOTT FINE, 2018

For more than a quarter of a century—from the years before the First World War to those leading up to the Second—the courtyard projects arising across the Los Angeles region helped to define the special feel and spirit of prewar California.

They arrived in two overlapping waves—the *bungalow court* and the *courtyard apartment*—each associated with a distinct (though related) architectural layout and concept.

The bungalow court came first—emerging as early as 1910, but reaching its peak in the 1920s, when examples could be seen springing up in every corner of the fast-growing city. The process was simple. Working from model plans and builders' guides (licensed architects were only sometimes involved) or copying earlier examples, local builders typically combined two or three single-family house plots into a squarish parcel of land, 100 or 150 feet wide, and then placed six to twelve small cottages around a central courtyard space outfitted with lawn, plantings, and walkways. This central court, usually open to the sidewalk, culminated at the opposite end in one or two cottages (often larger than the others), which neatly enclosed the space and created the distinctive U-shaped plan of the complex as a whole.

The bungalow court consists of a group of individual apartments, each a complete little home, containing a living room, bedroom, bath, kitchen and porch. The houses face upon a central court with a common entrance upon the street. The semiprivate nature of the court makes it unusually delightful.

IDEAL HOMES IN GARDEN COMMUNITIES, 1916

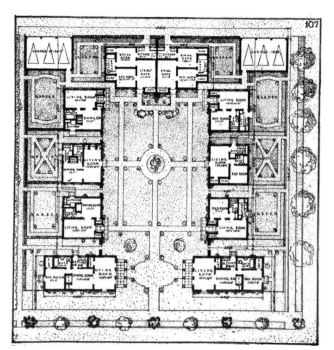

Typical bungalow court site plan by Walter S. Davis, published in California Garden City Homes, *1915.*

Whether freestanding or attached, each bungalow cottage offered its own distinct entrance and backyard area, and each represented, as one builders' guide noted, "a complete little home," with all the appurtenances of a private house. This last was crucial to their success. "The bungalow court cottage," the historian Dennis Sullivan observes, "gave the occupant an affordable home that was much more than an apartment, with the feel of a single-family home."

Though the architectural appearance of the cottages could vary considerably, the most common early choice was the bungalow style, which by then had become wildly popular in Southern California for dwellings of all kinds—from the grand, sprawling Pasadena estates of architects Greene & Greene to tens of thousands of ordinary Craftsman houses for middle-class families seeking a distinctively "California" feel. The bungalow "is 'homey,'" wrote *Radford's Artistic Bungalows* in 1911, seeking to capture its deep psychological lure, "and comes near to that idea you have seen in the dreamy shadows of night when, lying restless on your couch, you have yearned for a haven of rest."

But if its stylistic appeal drew on familiarity with the era's single-family homes, the bungalow court—its very name drawn from the open space at its center—actually "represented a major shift [in]...American dwelling types," argues the preservation architect Bruce D. Judd. "Bungalow courts were the first multifamily prototype to focus more on *space* than *object*, providing residents with the advantages of...shared spaces for communal interaction within a densely urban setting."

Making it all possible was parking—or more precisely, the lack of it. The earliest bungalow courts made no accommodation at all for off-street parking, but by the 1920s, some began offering the provision of a single space for each cottage, located in garages tightly clustered at the rear of the property and reached by a narrow driveway at the side of the lot, or from an alley in the back. This compact car storage still left room for anywhere from eight to twelve cottages on a modest-sized lot.

The decision to add a parking space for each unit arose in part from a growing market for these projects: seasonal visitors from the East or Midwest who motored cross-country—in their own cars—to spend several weeks or more in a small but affordable villa of their own, from which they could enjoy Southern California's temperate climate and visitor attractions.

As the boom of the 1920s took hold, that transient population was supplemented by a larger wave of transplants: retired farmers and shopkeepers from the Midwest, truckloads of "Okies" from the parched stretches of Texas and Oklahoma, Black families hoping to escape the Jim Crow South, and waves of ambitious young people looking to enter the film industry or find work in aviation, oil and gas, or real estate. Builders everywhere saw an opportunity to make a good dollar by providing these newcomers with compact but well-lit and reasonably priced places to live, fitted densely (and thus economically) onto a couple of adjacent lots. It was the bungalow court, in fact, that provided the much of the affordable housing stock crucial to Los Angeles's growth, in these years, into a true metropolis.

Above: *Aerial view of 1920s bungalow court developments in Los Angeles.* Right: *A bungalow court project, photographed by Julius Shulman, late 1970s.*

[The] thousands of bungalow courts in Southern California...may have been a speculator's dream, but they also performed a service. While designed at first for the vacationing Easterner and Midwesterner, the courts could be and were adapted to the use of people with moderate or lower incomes; thus, the bungalow courts extended at least a touch of "casual California living" even to the poor.

ROBERT WINTER, 1980

Though most bungalow courts were constructed in the historic period styles of the time, the instinct behind the type—fitting a number of dwellings onto a compact lot, each with its own entrance and off-street parking space—also had strong appeal to early modernist architects in the region.

As early as 1919, the architect Irving Gill built Horatio Court West, a complex of six attached houses located in Santa Monica, a few blocks from the Pacific, complete with four garage spaces in the rear, all carried out in Gill's distinctive proto-modern style, whose white walls and simple arches subtly evoked (without ever quite mimicking) the region's Spanish-style architecture.

A few years later, in his 1923 Pueblo Ribera beach house project (located down the coastline in La Jolla), the modernist Rudolph Schindler explored the compact assemblage of dwellings in a different way, interlocking twelve U-shaped homes back-to-back, each opening onto its own private landscaped space with window walls that recalled the architect's own 1922 house in West Hollywood. Though the project did not provide a single central courtyard, it provided communal pedestrian paths as well as a garage for every unit, grouped in the manner of a bungalow court.

Street view (above) and courtyard view (right) of Horatio Court West, in Santa Monica, designed by Irving Gill, 1919. In an article published in The Craftsmen *that same year, Gill promoted "the simple cube house with creamy walls, sheer, and plain, rising boldly into the sky, unrelieved by cornices or overhang of roof." Photograph at right by Marvin Rand.*

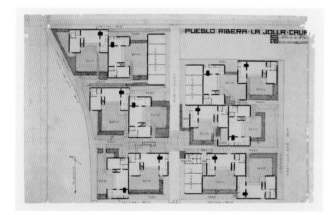

Site plan (above) and garden view (right) of the Pueblo Ribera complex, in La Jolla, designed by Rudolph Schindler, 1925. "I propose to treat the whole in true California style," Schindler wrote to his client, W. L. Lloyd, "the middle of the house being the garden, the rooms opening wide to it, the floors of concrete, close to the ground."

El Cabrillo, a 1928 project in Hollywood designed by Arthur and Nina Zwebell. Developed by the famed Hollywood director Cecil B. DeMille, the project may have been built to comfortably accommodate stage actors from New York, who were being brought to Los Angeles in numbers to appear in the newly invented talking pictures. Photograph by Julius Shulman.

Renewing the Dream

"A Charming Complex"

By the mid-1920s—even as bungalow courts were springing up everywhere to serve people on limited budgets—a new, more sophisticated successor was emerging. "As multifamily housing became a more prevalent option for wealthy clients," writes Bruce D. Judd, "the bungalow court matured into a new prototype of apartment dwelling: the courtyard apartment."

> *This was the courtyard complex, a somewhat fanciful architectural aggregation of apartment units, loosely joined so as to achieve maximum opportunity for patio gardens in the niches and spaces between stuccoed walls. Outlandishly theatrical, featuring every known Moorish architectural device, they quite naturally appealed to cinema people, their friends, and hangers-on. They were also very successfully designed, offering a wide variety of living units to tenants and creating useful gathering places and private parties. Carefully separated from the adjacent streets and sidewalks by walls and bridges, these complexes made efficient use of outdoor spaces no matter how small. They became miniaturized oases, like the Spanish patios that A. E. Hanson so admired in the narrow streets of Córdova.*
> JERE STUART FRENCH, 1993

By common consent, the first courtyard apartment project was the Villa Primavera in West Hollywood, developed in 1923 by the husband-and-wife team Arthur and Nina Zwebell, self-educated designers who had migrated to Southern California from the Midwest. Employing the Spanish Revival style that would become the era's trademark, the Zwebells created a "charming complex," in the author Lindsay Blake's words, "featuring red-tile roofs, white adobe walls, and a central courtyard with a large tiled fountain, an outdoor fireplace, lush foliage, and wandering brick pathways."

Though the newer projects shared a clear resemblance to the bungalow courts before them—a group of compact dwellings with individual entries, fitted around a central open space—the architectural innovations they introduced produced a startlingly different effect.

> *Two-story apartments were wrapped around a richly planted central courtyard, with garages close at hand but unobtrusive. The apartments were attached to each other, but as in the bungalow courts, each one expressed its own personality and enjoyed substantial privacy.*
> CHARLES MOORE, PETER BECKER, AND REGULA CAMPBELL, 1984

In place of the bungalow court's two simple rows, the courtyard projects offered complexly interlocked apartments, fitted into larger, artfully shaped structures. To the visitor, however, those buildings appeared even more tucked away than the bungalow court's cottages, thanks in part to thicker, taller, and more elaborate plantings, but also to the intricate intertwining of greenery with fine-grained elements—steps, fountains, gateways, seating, and artwork—and the design of their residential structures, which offered picturesque compositions of porticoes, balconies, and terraces. "While bungalow courts were modest and restrained," Judd writes, "garden courts tended to be a type of high-style architecture."

Villa Primavera, also known as the Mexican Village, photographed in 1926.

Unlike postwar architects, for whom project garages were often an afterthought or grim and utilitarian affairs, the designers of prewar courtyard apartments considered their parking areas an integral part of the larger architectural composition, sharing the stylistic approach of the overall project. Left: *The garage at Villa Primavera, opening directly onto the street, was intended to evoke Western-style stables.* Right: *A courtyard garage, opening onto a narrow driveway, suggests a picturesque barn. Photograph by Julius Shulman.*

They were often designed by architects inspired by various types of courtyards in the Mediterranean, including patio houses, palaces, markets, and inns. The temperate California climate inspired architects to design spacious patios, verandas and balconies opening into a central courtyard, which was almost always lushly landscaped with spaces designated to both rest and meditation and pedestrian circulation.

BRUCE D. JUDD, ET AL. 2009

Through the 1920s and into the '30s, scores of courtyard apartment projects were built around Southern California. One reason for this popularity was that, like the bungalow courts before them, courtyard projects could be readily built on a couple of adjacent house lots and, despite their higher density, presented to their surroundings a friendly, unthreatening scale (rarely more than two stories) and bounteous landscaping, allowing them to fit comfortably on blocks of single-family houses.

Once again, it was parking—or again, the lack of it—that held the key. Like many bungalow courts, the courtyard apartments provided a single off-street parking space for every unit—located at the side or rear of the property, and usually given the same picturesque treatment as the rest of the project. This accommodation allowed room for residential units *and* a central courtyard, close at hand but visually separated.

Below: *A fountain in the courtyard of Patio Del Moro, a 1925 project in West Hollywood designed by Arthur and Nina Zwebell. The central spaces commonly featured a variety of finely detailed architectural "incidents," which rewarded wandering and exploration.* Right: *The central courtyard of Cochran Avenue Court, a 1928 project in the Wilshire District designed by Charles Gault. The compositional strategy of the courtyard projects often contrasted expanses of stucco-faced wall with artfully placed architectural elements—doors, window bays, balconies, terraces—which added a three-dimensional richness to the otherwise planar surfaces, while also providing a variety of places from which to overlook the shared landscape.*

Another Land

> To have heard the note of water
> in the cistern,
> known the scent of jasmine and
> honeysuckle,
> the silence of the sleeping bird,
> the arch of the entrance, the damp
> —these things, perhaps, are the poem.
>
> JORGE LUIS BORGES (W. S. MERWIN, TRANS.), 1953

Though the bungalow court and courtyard apartment shared the defining feature of the court, it was only in the latter that this central space—and its intimate relationship with the buildings framing it—became something truly magical, an enchanting environment embodying the spirit of relaxed, gracious "California living," though at densities three or four times those of single-family houses. For all this reason and more, it is worth a closer look.

The courtyard, of course, is one of the oldest kinds of residential dwellings, found

Detail of central fountain in the courtyard of El Cabrillo, also known as Casa DeMille.

Renewing the Dream

Details of a 1927 courtyard studio complex on Sunset Boulevard in Hollywood, designed by the architect Henry Gogerty with Warner Bros. art director Carl Jules Weyl. The architectural elements of courtyard projects frequently did double duty—not only enclosing interior spaces within, but, on the exterior, serving as a kind of an "armature" for a rich composition of landscaping.

in cultures all around the world, and all across history. Schoolchildren often encounter it first as the open-air atrium at the heart of the patrician households of ancient Rome—an environmentally sensible response to the warm, dry climate of the Mediterranean. Those Roman courtyards "were true outdoor living rooms, and invariably regarded as such by their inhabitants," the historian Bernard Rudofsky observes. "The wall and floor materials were no less lavish than those used in the interior part of the house . . . [and] established a mood particularly favorable to spiritual composure. As for the ceiling, there was always the sky in its hundred moods." A millennium later, the courtyard tradition flourished again in Arab settlements in the Middle East, before making its way as part of the vast Islamic migration to Spain—a similarly hot and dry environment—where, in the sixteenth and seventeenth centuries, it reached a kind of architectural apogee. Exported to Latin America in the centuries following, the courtyard was eventually adopted by architects and builders as a model in early twentieth-century Southern California, where its suitability for the region's "Mediterranean" climate—and deep-seated Spanish colonial heritage—seemed more appropriate than ever.

Unlike the atrium of a Roman family or the private villas of Spain, however, the courtyard of Southern California's prewar apartment projects was a *shared* environment, a communal vessel that linked the unrelated households surrounding it and onto which their front doors opened. This gave the Los Angeles courtyard a character all its own: neither the private realm of a family house nor the public space of a park or plaza, but something in between, a hybrid environment that sat at a distinct reserve from the public sphere of the city but—as a place of mutuality and casual interactions among neighboring residents—was still somehow urban in character.

> *Once the [outside] borders of the delightful courts are passed, one feels as if they were in another land with beautiful flowers, green lawns, and beautiful little homes to fill the picture and every nook and cranny bathed in golden sunlight, save where the fronds of splendid palms cast their shadows.*
>
> "POLLYANN," *ARROWHEAD MAGAZINE*, 1917

As anyone who has visited these places will confirm, however, there is something else that makes these courtyards so captivating and dreamlike. To step into them is to enter another world. Just a few feet from the street, the visitor is enveloped in a lush landscape, the city's bustle now replaced by an environment not only natural but *primal*—defined by dappled sunlight, by the sway of palms, by the gentle trickle of water in a basin. Time itself seems to slow down. Though the space is framed by manmade walls, it is landscape as much as structure that enswathe the visitor, producing a tranquil, even meditative ambience. "The dwelling and the building are lost," effuse Polyzoides and his colleagues, "and one reads the whole primarily as an urban fragment of the Garden of Eden, expressing the possibilities of individual and communal well-being."

In some ways ageless and prelapsarian, the courtyards were also an embodiment of their own particular place and time: early-twentieth-century Southern California, where, in the space of a few decades, an impossibly verdant landscape had arisen from the semiarid desert environment that was the region's natural state—thanks to the age-old technique that its newcomers had brought with them: irrigation. "Given water to pour on its light and otherwise almost desert soil," observed Reyner Banham in 1971, Los Angeles "can be made to produce a reasonable facsimile of Eden." The result, he wrote, "will carry almost any kind of vegetation that horticultural fantasy might conceive . . . the southern palm will literally grow next to northern conifers." By the 1920s, "cacti and

Top: *Street view of the Monterey Apartments, a 1925 project in Los Feliz designed by C. K. Smithley. This view reveals how successfully the courtyard projects could achieve an unthreatening, houselike presence from the street.* Above: *Casa del Beachwood, a 1920s courtyard project in Hollywood, adjacent to Paramount Studios. Photographs by Julius Shulman.*

roses, palms and wisteria had been brought together in Southern California's domesticating garden," writes the author D. J. Waldie, to create "an abundance of...American-made nature [that] was almost hallucinatory."

It was just this "hallucinatory" profusion that the prewar courtyards sought to condense and re-create, along with the constant reminder—in the trickle of fountains and basins and other water features—of the element that made it possible in the first place. To this day, there are few places that feel as distinctly "LA" as the leafy spaces of the prewar courtyards—where one knows, as Waldie writes, "the scent of dust and jasmine will come in the twilight, as it always does."

Much of this enchantment arose, on closer inspection, from the courtyard's meticulous composition of landscape elements, deployed at a variety of heights and scales. Towering palm fronds, combined with olive and cypress trees, created a porous ceiling to filter the region's sometimes harsh sunlight, while leaving plenty of blue sky visible. At eye level, flowering bushes—roses, azaleas, jacaranda, bougainvillea, camellias, and hibiscus—provided gorgeous bursts of color set against a wider field of greenery: shrubs, trumpet vines, philodendrons, and cushiony plots of lawn. Other accents came from overflowing plants and flowers in clay and terra-cotta pots—themselves surfaced with a brightly colored glaze—placed on the courtyard's textured flooring, or atop red-tiled staircases or low stucco walls.

> *Plants stand in organic and dynamic contrast to the geometric, static architecture of the courtyard...almost subversive in their willful asymmetry, sprawling, hanging, and swaying. Even the most elegant and graceful arch has a hard, fixed, edge. A vine softens this edge, changes with the seasons, grows with the years. The hard, geometric order of the courtyard is still there, but partly masked by the...organic order that moves over it. This softening of hard edges and surfaces also changes the acoustics in courtyards, making them less reverberant. Plants also reduce glare, partly by shading...and partly by softening the contrast between bright blue sky and starkly white walls.*
>
> JOHN S. REYNOLDS, 2002

This complementary mix of structure and landscape achieved the larger "architectural ambition," as Polyzoides and his coauthors put it, "to make or suggest 'place' by controlling the ground, the walls, and the canopy of the courtyard with plant materials, thereby modifying the temperature, the sounds, the smells, the view, and the physical extensions of each dwelling." Indeed, this emphasis on landscaping often overflowed the courtyard and spilled onto the front yard, bringing the same character—of buildings tucked into greenery, not the other way around—to the street and sidewalk.

To be sure, this unusual approach—structure dominated by landscape—owed its existence to a larger philosophy of residential development, so pervasive that it was shared by those most unromantic of individuals, real estate owners: *landscape first, building second.* The essential precondition of these projects, this concept stood directly opposed to most modern development practice. Contemporary builders, it is understood, often regard landscaping as a frill, added after the "real" construction—rentable or salable space—is complete. If budgets run tight—as they so often do—the landscape allocation is the first line item to be trimmed or eliminated. The prewar courtyards, by contrast, were shaped by a contrary belief: that their commercial viability—their essential marketability—relied on their landscaping as much as their buildings. Landscaping,

An early travelogue called Hollywood the Unusual *(1927), includes scenes of the newly built Andalusia (top) and Patio del Moro (bottom), revealing that the lush planting of the prewar courtyard projects was essentially in place from the time of their construction.*

to this way of thinking, was no less crucial to success than power, water, or sewer service—and would be no less likely to be skimped on or omitted.

But that special time—and philosophy—did not last. By the 1940s, with the coming of World War II, the era of the courtyard projects came to an abrupt end.

> *The elaborate Mediterranean-inspired garden court apartments of the 1920s and '30s gave way to more stripped-down, vernacular versions of courtyard housing in the World War II and postwar years. This can be attributed both to the need to quickly build housing for war industry workers and returning veterans as well as the shift in taste toward Modern styles.*
>
> BRUCE D. JUDD ET AL., 2009

In the 1940s, several forces converged to transform the courtyard beyond recognition. The fierce pressure—both during and just after World War II—to produce large amounts of housing in short order left little room for the intricate compositions, extensive landscaping, and stylistic flourishes that had characterized the prewar projects. Other factors came into play, including the adoption of a modernist aesthetic, an increasing concern for privacy, and a turning away from the street (itself increasingly filled with auto traffic), which discouraged the traditional U-shaped court plan, open to the sidewalk.

But the coup de grâce, as Mark Vallianatos makes clear in the previous chapter, was the restrictive parking and zoning regulations imposed in the late 1940s by city officials, eager to make the single-family house the standard by which all else would be judged. Wider minimum setbacks at the side and rear of the lots and the increase in mandated off-street parking made it geometrically impossible to fit eight or ten residential units, along with twice that number of parking spaces *and* a landscaped courtyard, on the kind of modestly scaled urban properties—usually the size of two or three house lots—commonly available in the developed parts of the city.

Thus arose the "dingbat," the ubiquitous walk-up apartment building of the postwar era, which turned over nearly all of its ground surface to parking, and placed the project's units (and sometimes, a patch of concrete deck) *above* that level. Unable to accommodate substantive planting, the hard-surfaced deck was often given over to a smallish communal swimming pool. From sidewalk level, the dingbat presented the distinctly unappetizing sight of a small sea of parked cars, oil-stained driveways, and concrete columns. From the interior, it offered a stripped-down landscape of concrete decking and the smell of chlorine. Eventually, as Vallianatos notes, increasingly strict regulations made even the parking-friendly, modest-sized dingbats impermissible, and only much larger, taller—and more controversial—residential projects could proceed, at least in areas where they were allowed. By then, the prewar courtyard projects—now literally illegal—had become a fondly remembered but historically remote piece of the city's history, lost irretrievably in the past.

Except in the public imagination and on-screen—where their allure continued, as vibrant as ever.

The Mythic Courtyard

During the twenties and into the thirties, with what was doubtless an enormous assist from the Hollywood vision in the days of its greatest splendor, an architectural image of California developed that was exotic but specific, derivative but exhilaratingly free. It had something to do with...the benign climate, with...floral luxuriance, with the general availability of wood and stucco, and with the assurance provided by Hollywood that appearances did matter, along with the assumption (for which Hollywood was not necessary but to which it gave a boost), that we, the inheritors of a hundred traditions, had our pick. What came of this was an architecture that owed something to Spain, very little to the people who were introducing the International Style, and a great deal to the movie camera's moving eye.

CHARLES W. MOORE, 1965

Across the twentieth century—and beyond—the bungalow court and the courtyard apartment would carve an outsized place in the culture of Los Angeles, mostly by way of the city's primary cultural product: feature films and television series.

Even the modest bungalow court attracted filmmakers—in part for its picturesque character but even more for the opportunities it offered for plausible connection among strangers, otherwise difficult to come by in a city of single-family houses. A related source of appeal was the diversity of its residents, a by-product of its affordability, which encompassed the kind of societally "marginal" characters—the door-to-door salesman and onetime vaudevillian Harry Greener (Burgess Meredith) in *The Day of the Locust* (1975), for example, or the pot dealer and amateur philosopher "The Dude" (Jeff Bridges) in 1998's *The Big Lebowski*—that spark a dramatist's imagination and, despite their limited means, bring variety to the city's life: aspiring actors, aging retirees, industry craftspeople, writers, artists, musicians, freethinkers, eccentrics of every kind.

But it was the apartment courtyard—whose fanciful architecture was compared right from the start to Hollywood film sets—which burned most brightly on the screen, transformed over the years into a mythic presence, one that has endured nearly a century after the projects themselves were built.

This arose in part from the same storytelling opportunities—built on the casual intermingling of diverse strangers—as the bungalow court. *In a Lonely Place*, a 1950 film noir set in an invented courtyard called the Beverly Patio Apartments (based on the Villa Primavera in West Hollywood, where the director Nicholas Ray had lived for a time) draws much of its narrative energy from the interactions of two neighbors, Humphrey Bogart and Gloria Grahame, who might otherwise have no opportunity to meet at all, let alone become entangled in complex web of romance and intrigue.

Other films located different resonance in the courtyard apartment projects, which were at once more isolated *and* sociable than the bungalow courts before them. In *Chinatown* (1974), Roman Polanski and Robert Towne's portrait of 1930s Los Angeles, powerfully evokes the courtyard's sense of intimacy—and utter seclusion from the larger world—in a scene in which the detective Jake Gittes (Jack Nicholson) uncovers what seems to be an affair between a powerful city official and his mistress, discreetly hidden in the secluded confines of a 1920s courtyard.

By contrast, newer films and television series—including FOX's long-running "Melrose Place," of course —have been drawn to the courtyard's *sociability* among its residents, who can assemble in ways large and small in its shared central space. Indeed,

Based on the 1939 novella by Nathanael West, The Day of the Locust *(1975),* set in a bungalow court called the San Bernardino Arms, Tod (William Atherton), a newcomer to Hollywood, crosses paths with a motley collection of residents, including film hopeful Faye Greener (Karen Black).

Filmed on an elaborate stage set at Columbia Studios re-creating the Villa Primavera—where the director Nicholas Ray had lived in his early days in Hollywood—In a Lonely Place *(1950),* featuring Gloria Grahame and Humphrey Bogart as neighbors whose lives become intertwined with romance and intrigue, transfigures the courtyard into a filmic setting, one critic wrote, of "cloistered, dreamlike spaces."

Left: In 'Til There Was You *(1997), written by Winnie Holzman, Gwen (Jeanne Tripplehorn) is mesmerized by the courtyard of an apartment complex called "La Fortuna"—a Paramount set replicating the actual El Cabrillo. Above: In* Chinatown *(1974), filmed in The Ronda in West Hollywood, the detective J. J. Gittes (Jack Nicholson) obtains evidence of an official's secret affair.*

In La La Land *(2016) Mia, an aspiring actress played by Emma Stone, shares an apartment with three housemates in a bungalow court in Hollywood (filmed at the Rose Towers in Long Beach).*

In Monster-in-Law *(2005), Charlie (Jennifer Lopez) lives in El Cadiz, a 1936 project by Milton J. Black, the city's last courtyard apartment complex built in the Spanish Revival style.*

San Vicente Bungalows, 2019, recently renovated into a chic, clublike hotel.

in recent decades an entire courtyard way of life has arisen on-screen—perhaps only rarely matched in the real world—driven by the unmistakable sense of human connection woven into the design of the courtyard.

> *The point is that legendary people lived in La Fortuna, that...La Fortuna has a story irrevocably intertwined with the very history of this city. This building has value, it holds precious secrets—about what this city once was, and what it aspired to be—and it's held on through change, and against incredible odds, against earthquakes, and indifference, and we need to hear that story, we need to tell it, because this city can be a cold, cruel place, and that's the awful truth.*
> GWEN MOSS (JEANNE TRIPPLEHORN) IN *'TIL THERE WAS YOU* (1997)

The 1997 film *'Til There Was You* offers nothing less than a feature-length paean to the courtyard and its threatened place in the contemporary city. Early on in the film, a writer named Gwen Moss (Jeanne Tripplehorn) stumbles into the magical precincts of "La Fortuna"—based on the actual El Cabrillo apartments—and is enchanted not only by its fanciful architecture but its wide-ranging cast of characters. The film follows Gwen's quixotic struggle to save the complex from demolition—a story that reflects real-world battles in which many surviving bungalow courts, and even a few apartment courtyards, have been razed to make way for larger projects.

Like most newer films, however, *'Til There Was You* ignores the greatest source of divergence between the on-screen courtyards and those of the real Los Angeles—which is simply that in the twenty-first century, no younger, "ordinary" LA character like Gwen could likely afford to move into one of the city's classic prewar courtyards, most of which have grown so desirable that, on a square-foot basis, they are among the most expensive places to buy or rent in the entire city. Those prewar projects that have been converted to hotel use, meanwhile—the double row of "cottages" of the Chateau Marmont or the renovated bungalow units of the San Vicente Club, both in West Hollywood—are today some of the most selective accommodations in the city, their astronomical nightly rack rates a testament to the still-vibrant allure of these dwellings.

Now recognized officially for their architectural distinction (The Andalusia, El Cabrillo, El Cadiz, and the cottages of the Chateau Marmont have all been designated as national or local landmarks), most apartment courtyards—and many surviving bungalow courts—have endured as places admired enviously by visitors and treasured zealously by residents—most of whom would not think of living anywhere else, despite their old-fashioned apartment layouts, often cramped kitchens and bathrooms, typical lack of private outdoor space, and overall age and wear.

Given this remarkable level of devotion, it is natural to wonder if—given proposed reductions in parking minimums now in play in Los Angeles—it might be possible to recapture in modern terms some of the magical appeal of these prewar complexes. Could a new project, designed around the prewar standard of one off-street parking space per unit, combine contemporary layouts and construction with the gracious landscaping, house-like appeal, and sense of allure provided so often by older courtyard projects in such abundant and tantalizing fashion?

> *In a very real sense the entire society was a stage set, a visualization of dream and illusion which was, like film, at once true and not true.*
> KEVIN STARR, 1990

California Court:
A Courtyard Project for the Twenty-First Century

If apartment buildings are to be viable alternatives to single-family houses, they must offer some of the presumed amenities of suburban living: quiet, privacy, security, adequate outdoor space, easy accommodation of the automobile, and the miscellaneous equipment of today's recreation-oriented family.
STEFANOS POLYZOIDES, ROGER SHERWOOD, AND JAMES TICE, 1982

A recent visitor [to West Hollywood's courtyards] from Canada was heard to say, "Why don't all the people in Los Angeles live this way?"
DAVID GEBHARD AND ROBERT WINTER, 2004

While contemporary in design and amenities, the California Court project offers several of the features of its prewar precedents. Its residential units at once gather to frame the central landscaped space while offering the feel of an individual "houses," each with its own entrance area, front door, and house number. The richly planted central garden, while more elaborate than many single-family houses (and the essence of the project's allure), remains environmentally efficient and drought-sustainable by virtue of being a communal space, shared by eight households, whose individual portion amounts to a plot of land 26 feet square.

Reimagining the city's beloved prewar projects for modern-day Los Angeles, the proposed California Court project adapts the bungalow court and the courtyard apartment into a contemporary design suitable to the needs and expectations of twenty-first century urban households. Accommodating eight two- or three-bedroom homes of 1,800-2,400 square feet each on a modest-sized, half-acre site, the project is intended as a provocation, demonstrating that an appealing form of housing can be provided at substantially increased densities—sixteen dwelling units per acre, or three to four times that of conventional detached houses—while sitting entirely comfortably within the scale and character of a single-family neighborhood. Importantly, this level of density exceeds the threshold—about twelve to fifteen households per acre—needed to sustain successful public transit.

The key to the project is its provision of a single dedicated off-street parking space per household, rather than the two (or more) spaces typically required in Los Angeles.

This recognizes realistically that even as the mobility revolution takes hold, most households in Los Angeles will sometimes require a private automobile to conveniently reach many parts of the city for work, school, or pleasure—even if one or more family members uses alternative transportation for their daily commute (Metro or bus, ride-hailing or ride-sharing, e-bikes or e-scooters, bicycles or walking), or, as is increasingly the case since the 2020–21 pandemic, chooses to work remotely from home. In a sense, the California Court project represents a return to the common parking standard of Los Angeles households before World War II, one accepted readily to this day by the residents of the city's existing prewar courtyard projects, which provide—at most—only one garage space for their tenants.

From this seemingly simple compromise on the amount of off-street parking arises the opportunity to create a modern-day version of the prewar courtyards, one that combines the rich landscaping and intimate scale that made those older projects so alluring with modern residential layouts that offer more interior space, more private outdoor space, and more contemporary layouts and fittings than are found in the older structures.

In essence, California Court combines the *layout* of the bungalow court—two facing rows of houses around a central open space—with the *spirit* of the courtyard apartment project: a complexly shaped, richly planted communal garden, intertwined tightly with its surrounding structures. At one side of the property, a landscaped "parking court" accommodates the eight off-street vehicular spaces beneath a lightweight roof structure inspired by mid-century modernist carports, while also providing such twenty-first-century elements as micro-vehicle parking, solar-panel arrays, individual EV charging stations, and a water-retention and redistribution system.

In terms of its urban (or, one might say, political) impact, California Court relies on the same intrinsic neighborliness as prewar bungalow courts, which met the street only at their narrow ends. Staggered so that one side is further set back than the other,

Fitted into half of the depth of a standard Los Angeles block of 320 feet, and the rough equivalent in width of three 50-foot-wide or two 75-foot-wide house lots, the eight-family project offers an increase in density of 300 percent or 400 percent over typical single-family houses—but in meeting the street with two modestly scaled structures set back with planting from the sidewalk, it maintains the character of a low-rise block. A landscaped parking "court" includes eight carports, roofed areas for micromobility vehicles, and recycling bins, and at each parking space, an outdoor closet for household utility storage (as is often found on the walls of suburban garages). Residential units in the rear of the project can readily accommodate a setback third floor, providing a home office/studio or third bedroom and additional outdoor space.

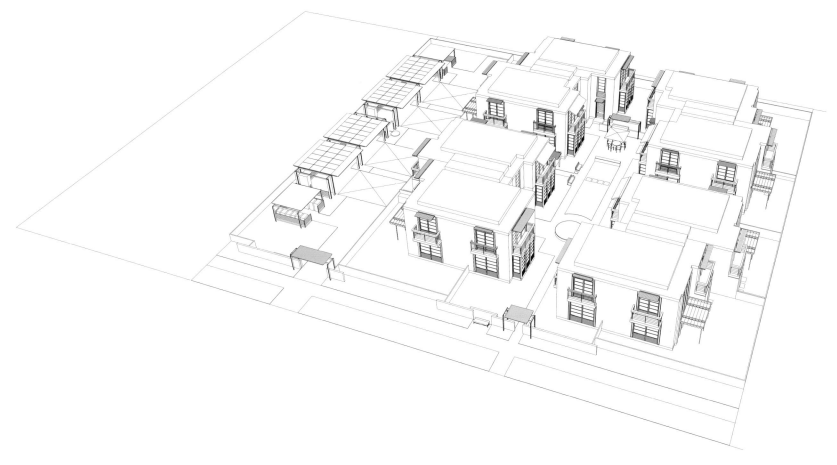

The site plan shows first-floor interiors at right and second-floor interiors at left. Laid out in two standardized plans—in a "corner" and "central" configuration—the residential units slide forward and back to enclose the courtyard. Though the units are clustered into pairs, each is a self-contained "fee-simple" structure with one wet wall adjoining its neighbor and natural light on three sides, offering the bright and airy feel of a freestanding house. While recalling prewar precedent, the project also combines solar, EV charging, and water-retention capacities into an integrated twenty-first-century environmental system. Each parking stall includes a Level 2 EV charging station, while the solar panels of the carport roofs generate a total of 300 kWh per day, providing power for EVs and the households. Water-retention systems on the carport and the houses' green roofs collect and channel runoff into cisterns, to be recirculated for irrigation and gray-water use.

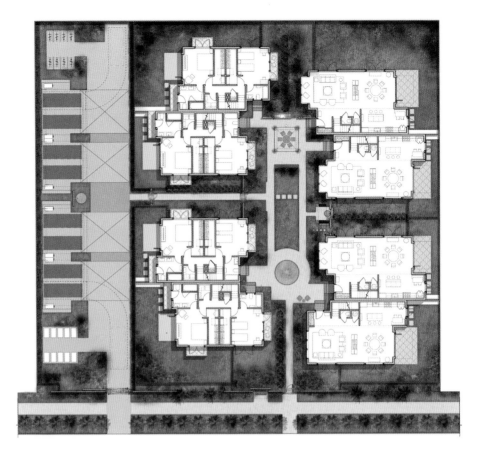

the modest-looking ends of the new project—each structure just two stories tall and thirty-five feet wide, separated by nearly twenty feet, and placed twenty to fifty feet from the property lines to either side—appear from the street as two adjacent houses, and so readily maintain the scale, rhythm, and character of a single-family block. Even in the 1930s this advantage eased the arrival of courtyard projects in established residential neighborhoods; today, the ability to disguise the project's density when seen from the sidewalk—thus allowing it to comfortably "fit in" on a block otherwise filled with free-standing houses—is crucial to its acceptance by single-family communities (page 162).

As in prewar layouts, the visitor's or resident's procession from the city street to the sheltered heart of California Court has been conceived as a kind of narrative journey: commencing with the entrance, which deploys a flowering trellis to create a distinctive gateway, and continuing along a landscaped pathway leading to the open space at its core—which, opening up on all sides, is intended to suggest the visitor has entered not simply a residential complex but a *secret garden*, one whose enchantment lies not only in its own appeal but its startling proximity to the outside world (still to be glimpsed nearby, of course, with a glance backward).

> [Bungalow courts] shared the integration of garden and house. The gardens and courtyards helped, along with patios and porches, to bring the outdoors closer and to provide some seclusion in what was a cluster of homes.
>
> DENNIS SULLIVAN, 2011

Like its prewar precedent, much of the allure of this space rests on its landscaping, shaped in collaboration with the California-based garden designer Wade Graham, which offers a lush, gardenlike ambience in place of the dry "xeriscape" character common to

The project draws on distinctive Southern California precedent in its provision of a prewar-style, pedestrian-friendly parking "court" with patterned paving, a perimeter of planting, and a landscaped water feature (much like the Los Feliz courtyard project shown at bottom), and open-sided carports, inspired by mid-century Case Study projects such as House 21, in Laurel Canyon, designed in 1958 by Pierre Koenig (top).

new Southern California landscape in recent decades. Despite this apparent fecundity, California Court achieves a high level of environmental and drought sustainability, thanks largely to its shared, communal nature. Because the common landscape serves eight homes, each household's portion represents an almost postage-stamp-sized area, twenty-six feet square, limiting the amount of irrigation required per unit. Nearly all plant species have been selected with an eye to drought resistance, and the project as a whole includes advanced rainwater retention systems and other drought-responsive elements.

> *Most courtyards...feature some object at or near their center; fountain, well, pond, tree, statue, large potted plant, table with chairs, hammock, something which draws the eye, and that may invite you to stay.*
>
> JOHN S. REYNOLDS, 2002

In its layout, California Court offers a contemporary interpretation of the prewar courtyards, one centered, much as they were, on a focal point where the court's pathways come together to form a small "piazza" centered on a water feature: here a wide, shallow basin filled with koi, upon which lily pads calmly float. Complemented by two other small fountains tucked away elsewhere in the courtyard, this feature brings the refreshing element of water into the heart of the project. As was true in the older courtyards, its quiet burble reveals how tranquil this inner space is—especially in contrast with the larger city—and provides an object of elemental, even meditative awareness, even as it reflects the natural and man-made elements around it.

> *Water has a particularly important role [in the courtyard]: it represents life and coolness, freshness and purity. It collects in the lowest place (emphasizing the courtyard as a resting place), and while its surface catches light and reflects the sky, its depth symbolizes the earthly zone below the courtyard floor. . . . When sunlight strikes water, it is reflected in a constantly shimmering pattern, even from a surface that appears to be absolutely calm. . . . Despite its brightness, it represents coolness, because if is a product of both water and breeze; the stronger the breeze, the faster the dance.*
>
> JOHN S. REYNOLDS, 2002

Passing deeper into this space, the visitor discovers an extra layer of texture and detail: a series of architectural "incidents" or "moments"—trellises, flowering pots, seating areas, statuary, tilework, additional water features, and places for meditative enjoyment—which, as in the original courtyard projects, reveal themselves only upon wandering, offering a sense of unfolding that encourages and rewards exploration. Responding to the more contemporary desire for group entertaining, these spaces include a fully equipped outdoor kitchen and umbrella-shaded dining area.

Drawing from prewar examples, the central space of California Court performs a crucial balancing act: establishing a collective identity even as it ensures a distinctly individualized feel for each unit—closer in spirit to a single-family home than an anonymous apartment. Each dwelling enjoys its own well-marked, house-like front entrance, opening onto the communal greenery of the courtyard but placed at a small, crucial remove—thus providing a sense of layered entry, moving in graduated steps from public to private. As in the older projects, grace notes around the entrance area—outdoor furniture, planter pots, an individual street address, and an enframed front door—offer a ceremonial air to the simple act of entering the home, and reinforce the feeling that, while part of a larger

whole, each residence is the distinctive vessel of a single household. In providing this "house-like" character for each dwelling—encouraging the domestic pride and pleasure typically associated with a freestanding home—the project seeks to emulate the prewar courtyards' success in attracting to a multi-dwelling project a clientele who might otherwise have considered only a single-family way of life.

The emphasis on offering an individualized feel extends to the interiors. Attached along one wall only, each unit offers exterior exposures on the other three sides, ensuring expansive daylighting but also, even more importantly, a distinctly "house-like" sense of being surrounded on all sides by nature. (The one attached service wall gathers the unit's stairs, closets, utility room, and bath and kitchen wet walls.) Recognizing that contemporary Los Angeles households commonly desire (or expect) a certain amount of private exterior space, each dwelling offers a landscaped yard with plantings and flower beds, dining terrace, sundeck, outdoor kitchen, and outdoor storage unit for garden equipment, etc.

> *Like all myths, "casual California living" has elements of reality, as both admirers and scoffers have noticed. Moreover, the myth has given identity to large numbers of Californians.*
>
> ROBERT WINTER, 1980

In the end, it was the singular achievement of the prewar courtyards to bring to relatively high-density housing the unmistakable character and pleasures of what the historian

Robert Winter and others have described as "casual California living": an informal, indoor/outdoor way of life that, taking advantage of the region's dry and generally temperate climate, created an almost seamless continuity from the interiors of a house to its open-air surroundings.

At California Court, that larger aspiration has driven every aspect of the project's design. In its units, every habitable room opens with large glazed doors and windows onto a terrace, balcony, or deck (often shaded by canvas awnings or wood-and-metal trellises) and each room offers at least two exterior exposures, not only assuring that its interiors remain bright and airy but allowing the sights and sensations of nature—the scent of plants and vines, the wafting breeze, morning birdsong and evening cicadas—to permeate its interior. These elements are also designed to encourage foliage to drape thickly over the facades, while planter trays bring still more greenery up to the roofs—all to positive visual, environmental, and energy effect.

Indeed, the built construction of the project, mixing simple wood frame-and-stucco walls with intricate metal-and-glass door and window bays (to be prefabricated off-site), might accurately be considered a kind of "armature" for its greenery, reasserting the primal rule—*landscape first, buildings second*—that lay behind the abiding appeal of the original courtyard projects.

In the end, the goal of the project is to reenergize for the twenty-first century one of the oldest and most abiding promises of the "California dream"—joining the timeless pleasures of nature to the comforts of modern society—even while charting a new, more sustainable trajectory for the future.

> *A Chinese elm is swaying beneficently in a cool breeze. The grass and ficus and boxwood and lemon trees are green with a kind of sparkling purity that seems to promise honesty and freshness and present pleasure. [The] windows reflect the fluttering, descending leaves and light. It's a dream, birds are singing, a mourning dove gurgles in the lattice of the rose arbor. This is where I live, a dream.*
>
> AMY WILENTZ, 2006

Above: *Interior of The Ronda, a 1927 project in West Hollywood designed by Arthur and Nina Zwebell.*
Right: *Interior and garden of the Schindler house, in West Hollywood, designed by Rudolph Schindler for his family and another couple in 1922. Photographs by Julius Schulman.*

Opposite top: *Rendering of the California Court project, showing its central garden and outdoor dining area.*
Opposite page, bottom: *Detail of the courtyard facades, showing the terraces, balconies, awnings and trellises that encourage the indoor/outdoor way of life distinctive to Southern California, while providing numerous places of overlook onto the communal landscape.*

Charge

LA

10

ReCharge LA, Part 1:
The Future of the Gas Station
Woods Bagot and ERA-co Los Angeles Studio

PROJECT TEAM

Meg Bartholomew

Alicen Coddington

Matt Ducharme

Russell Fortmeyer

Gözde Uyar

Kevin Wu

Introduction

As everyone knows, the electric-vehicle (EV) revolution is coming—fast. All new passenger vehicles sold in the state of California—the single largest automobile market in the United States, and one whose decisions set the standards for nearly a dozen other states—will be required by law to be electrically powered by 2035. By that date, General Motors will be producing only electric vehicles, worldwide. Ford plans to reach the same goal even sooner, by 2030. Hertz, the country's largest rental car company, recently announced the purchase from Tesla of a hundred thousand new electric vehicles, intended to make up nearly a quarter of its rental fleet within a few years.

This EV revolution is already propelling another dramatic development: the rapid growth of charging stations. The United States already contains more than a hundred thousand such stations, but President Biden's $1.75 trillion recently approved infrastructure package will increase that number fivefold, to half a million—even as private companies, including Tesla, expand their own search for partners and property owners to enlarge their existing charging networks.

Though internal combustion engines still power the great majority of cars on the road—about 18 percent of new vehicle sales in California in 2022 were plug-in EVs or hybrids—those numbers are quickly changing, and a little more than a decade from now, gas-powered vehicles will represent an absolute minority of cars on the road, their numbers dwindling fast. A decade after that, when no new gas-driven vehicles will have been manufactured or sold in the United States for years, they will represent just a small fraction of the total—and be on their way out entirely.

For cities, this turnover to EVs—and to charging stations—carries with it a transformative opportunity. As the number of gas-powered cars diminishes steadily, so will the demand for gas stations, which currently occupy an extraordinary number of prime sites in urban areas, including 550 within the borders of the City of Los Angeles alone (and far more in the metropolitan region). On the whole, these gas stations will not be replaced entirely with EV stations. Unlike gas stations—centralized in large, well-isolated sites, with underground storage tanks and intrinsically high risks of flammability and explosion—electric-charging stations require a tiny footprint and present no unusual danger, so can be safely located almost anywhere that a car can park, including inside commercial buildings, apartment houses, and household garages.

So how might these hundreds of sizable, well-located gas station sites, typically placed on major boulevards and avenues—or, often enough, at "100 percent" corner sites at the intersection of *two* major thoroughfares—be repurposed for more socially and economically valuable uses?

In late 2020, seeking to explore the opportunities afforded by this transformative shift, Christopher Hawthorne, chief design officer of the City of Los Angeles—a longtime leader in urban mobility, intent now on being the first American city to reach 100 percent clean energy by 2035—invited Woods Bagot and its experience consultancy ERA-co,

Above: *A former gas station site reimagined as an EV charging–enabled urban park.*

Previous spread: *rendering of ReCharge LA project, designed by Woods Bagot Los Angeles Studio.*

Overleaf: *Stephen Shore's classic photograph,* Beverly Boulevard and La Brea Avenue, Los Angeles, California, June 21, 1975, *captured one of the commonplace realities of twentieth-century Los Angeles: that gas stations occupied not only many prime corner sites, but, often enough, two or even three adjacent corners of the same intersection.*

along with five other noted design teams (Abalos+Sentkiewicz AS+, Inaba Williams Architects, MOS Architects, Perkins + Will, and Spiegel Aihara Workshop/SAW), to participate in an online symposium called Pump to Plug. Held in collaboration with the 3rd LA public-affairs series at USC's Academy in the Public Square and in partnership with the Los Angeles Cleantech Incubator, the symposium invited teams to produce forward-looking proposals in three categories: the design of charging stations, the future of gas station sites across Los Angeles, and facilities for an electrified long-haul trucking fleet.

Woods Bagot and ERA-co chose to produce studies for the first two of these categories. Their proposal for a prototypical charging station, located on the symposium's selected site at 749 Los Angeles Street in Downtown Los Angeles, envisions electric mobility that reenergizes future infrastructure (Case Study 2). In response to the symposium's second category, ERA-co's global data team has prepared ReCharge LA, a citywide study of the future of the 550 gas station sites within Los Angeles.

The team's approach employed machine learning to determine each site's most beneficial use—based on its social, economic, and spatial characteristics—and to test these as development proposals. Through this data-driven approach the team could propose a comprehensive citywide strategy that also considered alternative funding models.

Overall, the team's findings determined that the 550 existing gas station sites could be transformed into 20,000 new dwellings (home to about 40,000 residents), create 43,000 new jobs, *and* provide an additional seven acres of green space.

The average area for each site was approximately 22,000 square feet, leaving a substantial development opportunity on many sites to offset the cost of remediation and the provision of affordable housing and other public components. This chapter begins by presenting the study's methodology, proposes four development typologies, and finally outlines potential implementation strategies.

Renewing the Dream

Inevitably, the study should be regarded as a thought experiment: a means to test an approach, not to provide a final or definitive answer. Further analysis of the data and the introduction of additional data sets, such as site valuation, as well as updated data, would be required to undertake this study on a commercial scale.

Part 1: Analysis of Existing Sites

Proposing an individual design strategy for each and every one of LA's 550 gas station sites would obviously require an immensely complex process, with engagement with multiple stakeholders over a long period of time. Over such a large and diverse array of sites, a data-led approach can help simplify and potentially quicken the process by providing a framework for decision-making that groups together sites with similar spatial, social, and economic opportunities. This allows design strategies to be developed group by group, and then tailored for individual sites after further consultation and detailed investigation.

To carry out this approach, the team employed an "unsupervised" machine-learning clustering algorithm. (Unsupervised, in this context, means that no training data has been employed to consider a particular outcome; instead, the data is treated without preexisting hypotheses that may bias the outcome.) The clustering grouped the sites by characteristics based on metrics from public data sets and the spatial analysis of their urban form. This approach provides an evidence-based, data-driven methodology to create a broad design strategy that informs proposed future uses and building types.

Initial Mapping

As a glance at the map on the following page will confirm, the 550 gas stations are spread across nearly the entire 502-square-mile breadth of the City of Los Angeles. Each can offer a unique opportunity for potential future development that supports and strengthens its surrounding neighborhood.

In our study, the existing context of these sites provides the key for informed design decisions. Our initial investigations began by mapping the stations over such background information as the existing street network, land uses, and site ownership. Furthermore, the study looked at the proximity of each gas station to the venues of the 2028 Olympic Games to capture uses they might offer visitors to the Games or to serve as Olympic legacy opportunities. These investigations provided crucial background on each site's surrounding districts.

Metrics

Moving beyond background data, additional metrics were explored in detail and grouped in three broad categories: spatial, social, and economic. Data sources included the US Census and American Community Survey, Open Street Map, and publicly available data from the City of Los Angeles. Certain sources were used in their raw form, others were normalized as required, and on occasion new metrics were calculated to measure spatial characteristics.

Calculated metrics included proximity to freeways and LA Metro transit stations (both existing and those scheduled to open by 2026) as well as the proximity of the sites

Above: *Map of existing gas stations sites in the city of Los Angeles, 2020.* Opposite page, top left: *Initial investigations showed the extensive coverage within a fifteen-minute pedestrian catchment from each gas station site. When repurposed for different uses, the sites play a critical role in advancing an equitable housing future of Los Angeles, as well as the "15-Minute City" vision for its future, since one or more gas stations can be reached within fifteen minutes' walk from most existing housing and workplaces.*

Top right: *A site-ownership map shows the variety and distribution of the various owners of the gas station sites. The diversity of owners—both larger corporate owners and private individuals— adds to the complexity of funding and development models.*
Bottom left: *A land-use map presents several targeted areas whose predominant uses match the future potential uses of the sites.*
Bottom right: *A map of the 2028 Olympic Games identifies sites in the vicinity of each venue, which can be repurposed to serve Olympic-related activities or support legacy value for the Games through complementary long-term development.*

Renewing the Dream

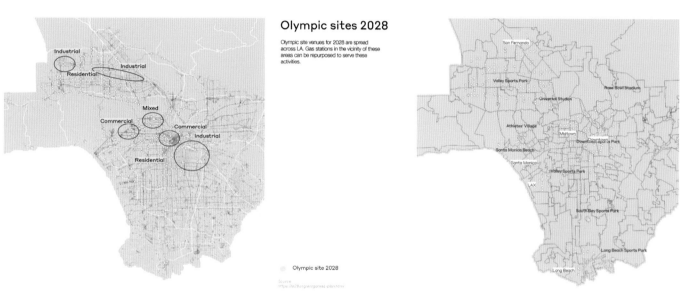

Walking distance to gas stations

550 gas stations have an extensive catchment coverage in the city. When repurposed for different uses in the long term, at least one or more gas stations can be reached within 15 minutes walk from the majority of neighbourhoods.

Walking distance in minutes

15'   10'   5'

Ownership - Gas Stations

26% 76 (Phillips 66)
21% Chevron
17% Arco
12% Shell
9%   Mobil
4%   Valero
10% other

- 76 (145)
- ARCO (91)
- AUTOBAHN (1)
- AVE 64 FUEL (1)
- CHEVRON (118)
- CLEAN ENERGY (2)
- CONSERV (2)
- COSTCO (5)
- GAS DEPOT (1)
- MOBIL (49)
- PALISADES GAS AND WASH (1)
- RALPHS (1)
- SAN PEDRO GAS N MORE (1)
- SC FUELS (5)
- SHELL (69)
- SINCLAIR (12)
- UNICO (1)
- UNITED OIL (10)
- USA GASOLINE (15)
- VALERO (23)

Existing land use

- Commercial
- Government
- Industrial
- Institutional
- Recreational
- Residential

Olympic sites 2028

Olympic site venues for 2028 are spread across LA. Gas stations in the vicinity of these areas can be repurposed to serve these activities.

○ Olympic site 2028

Source:
https://la28.org/engames-plan.html

to each other, their total automobile parking area, their open space ratios, and their street intersection density, which was calculated as a proxy for walkability. Raw and normalized data were mostly socioeconomic data sets such as dwelling counts, ethnic and racial diversity, amenity density, population density, annual gross income per household, tenure types, and dwelling values. All provided valuable information about the people that lived near the gas station locations, but some can bias algorithmic results, as discussed later. (Further development of the study could include additional data sets, such as site valuation and transaction data, useful in categorizing sites with development potential versus sites that will likely be cost prohibitive, depending on the intended use.)

With the data collected and processed, all data sets were mapped over an area divided into grid cells with a size of 800 by 800 feet, within the boundaries of Los Angeles County. Each gas station site was then intersected and joined with the cell in which it was located. Each site could thus be tagged with key attributes of the larger urban area in which it sits.

Spatial

Proximity to highway
Proximity to Metro 2026
Proximity to transit lines
Parking area
Intersection density
Open Space Ratio
Proximity to other gas stations

Proximity to highway

Proximity to Metro 2026

Intersection density

Parking area

Social

Dwelling count
Ethnic diversity
Amenity density
Population per sqm

Dwelling count

Ethnic group - White percentage

Ethnic group - Hispanic percentage

Amenity density

Economic

Annual gross income per household
Dwelling tenure - rented or owned
Dwelling value

Annual gross income

Dwelling tenure - Rented

Dwelling tenure - Owned

Dwelling Value

A matrix of maps of Los Angeles County presents the range of metrics investigated in the study, generated from the underlying spatial, social, and economic data and associated, in the study, with the point location of each gas station site.

Methodology

Once this base layer of information had been gathered, an analytical framework was produced to contextualize and classify each gas station within its quantified spatial, social, and economic conditions. The analysis was carried out using a widely accepted machine-learning clustering algorithm, which groups the sites according to similar characteristics. These characteristics are based on the attribute tags of the metrics described above, such as proximity to transport nodes, walkability, population, and amenity densities, as well as ethnic diversity, income, and tenure types.

Various combinations of these metrics were included in twelve different runs of the clustering model, until a result was produced that spread the different uses—affordable housing in particular—across the city relatively equitably. Future study will permit the permutations to loop through *all* possible combinations of metrics, to find the optimal solution based on generally agreed-upon objective outcomes for the city and additional paid or private data sets.

The resulting twelve options included sets of four, five, and six clusters of sites. The team determined that the option with six clusters, formed with seven metric variables, resulted in the most equitable distribution on the map, while retaining the distinctive characteristics of context within each cluster. (While this step could be automated in a more extensive study, in our work we often find that this qualitative overlay to the interpretation of quantitative results provides a useful step to harness the industry experience of our resident experts.)

Spatial

Proximity to highway
Proximity to metro 2026
Proximity to transit lines
Parking area
Intersection density
Open Space Ratio
Proximity to other gas stations

Social

Dwelling count
Ethnic diversity
Amenity density
Population density

Economic

Annual gross income per household
Dwelling tenure - rented or owned
Dwelling value

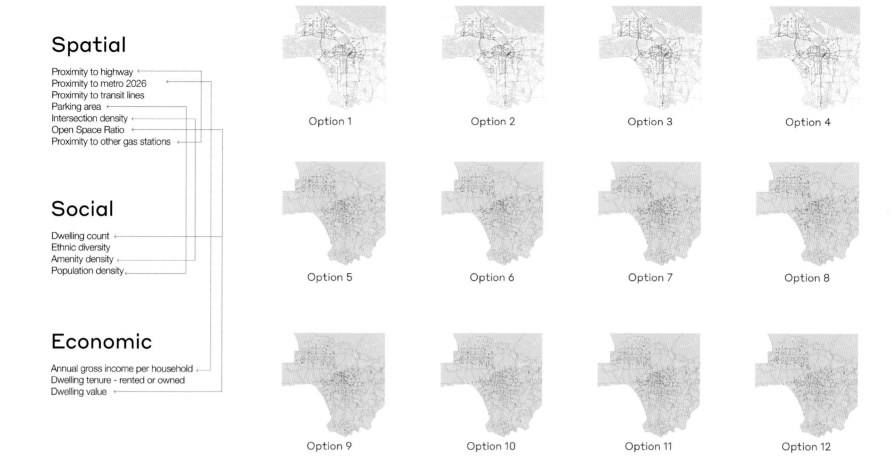

Option 1	Option 2	Option 3	Option 4
Option 5	Option 6	Option 7	Option 8
Option 9	Option 10	Option 11	Option 12

A matrix of the various cluster options, analyzed though fourteen spatial, social, and economic metric variables.

Six-Cluster Model

The most successful study model, which demonstrated a good spread of uses and clear delineation among each grouping, was based on six clusters and seven metric variables. These metric variables included proximity to the LA Metro and freeways, income, amenity density, proximity to other gas stations, open space ratio of the property, and population density.

For simplicity, each of the seven selected metrics can be considered part of four broad categories: built density, accessibility, equity, and amenity.

The first category, built density, was determined by two metrics: open space ratio and population density. The former was calculated by dividing open space area by parcel area, and the latter was calculated by dividing residential population per parcel area.

Each gas station site was also explored in respect to accessibility by private vehicles and public transportation, determined by its proximity to freeways and 2026 LA Metro stations. Each of these metrics was measured by creating catchments from the sites, using the roadway network provided through Open Street Map.

The single economic metric used in this cluster was annual income per household, gathered from the US Census. This informed a metric of distributional equity for the populations most in need. (The reasoning behind selecting this as the only social or economic metric is elucidated below.)

The density of the sites and the proximity of gas stations to each other (based on the number of gas stations within 2500 feet of each other) formed the activity-levels criteria. Amenity density considers the number of everyday amenities within walking distance from a location, including parks, shops, and services.

6 clusters

The most successful clustering model, showing a good spread of uses and clear delineation between types, found 6 clusters from 7 variables.

Proximity to highway
Proximity to metro 2026
Annual gross income per household
Amenity density
Proximity to other gas stations
Open Space Ratio (inverted to calculate built area ratio)
Population density per sqkm

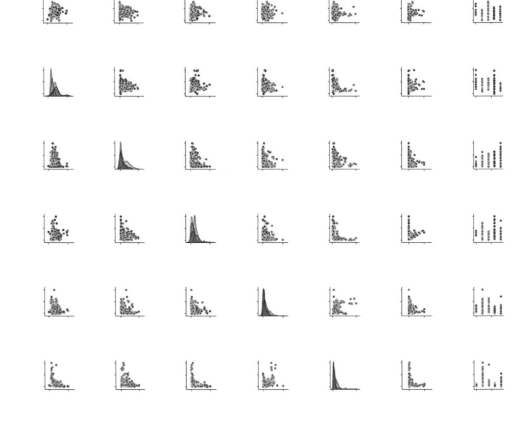

A pair plot of the selected metrics from the final clustering model, presenting how each metric relates to the others.

Most of the metrics used in the selected clustering model are spatial in nature. The driving ambition of this study was to provide an equitable spread of uses across the city, in particular for affordable housing. It is important that these uses are placed according to appropriate spatial opportunity. The residents of affordable housing need easy and convenient access to jobs and education through a mix of uses and good transportation links, as well as ready access to other urban amenities such as parks and local shops. These are objectively spatial criteria.

The team's decision to focus mostly on these spatial metrics to the relative exclusion of social and economic metrics also arises from the reality that Los Angeles—like many expanding cities around America and across the world—is heavily segregated and unequal, with distinct clusters of ethnic and racial groups and widely varying levels of economic opportunity across the larger urban landscape. In the models that used values associated with these social and economic characteristics —such as ethnicity, tenure, or property value—a clear bias was evident, with the results heavily skewed, creating geographically contained clusters around these dominant metrics. This would imply a geographic concentration of uses, such as affordable housing, in single zones, an approach that has been considered by many as undermining equal opportunity. The ultimate selected model did not include these metrics, in order to reduce bias in the outcome, and create an equitable spread of amenities and affordable housing possibilities across the city with access to real opportunity.

The result of the unsupervised machine-learning grouped all the sites in six clusters, creating a kind of patchwork across Los Angeles. The six clusters can be further grouped based on their built densities. The different types included:

— One cluster with a higher level of population and built density;

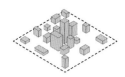

Built Density
Open space ratio

Calculated by dividing open space area by parcel area.

Residential population

Calculated by dividing census residential population data per sq miles.

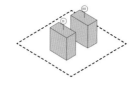

Equity
Annual income per household

Data from the census on average annual income distributed in a grid.

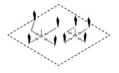

Accessibility
Proximity to highway

Calculated by creating a catchment from highways on road network from Open Street Map.

Proximity to Metro 2026

Calculated by creating a catchment from existing and proposed metro and transit stations 2026 on road network from Open Street Map.

Activity
Amenity density

Calculated by dividing number of amenity point data per sq miles.

Proximity to other gas stations

Counting the number of gas stations within 0.5 miles (10 minute-walk) buffer from each station.

The metrics used in the final selected model, grouped into categories.

— Three clusters with a medium level of built density, but differing in population density, accessibility, income, and amenities in the area;

— Two clusters with a lower level of population and built density, both high income but differing in the amount of other activity in the area, as measured by amenity density.

These site characteristics were then reviewed to determine the most suitable potential future uses for each site, as presented in part 2 of this chapter.

Part 2: Proposed New Uses and Building Types

The team's analysis produced six clusters of gas station sites around Los Angeles, grouping each site with others that shared similar urban conditions, according to selected metrics. Examining the qualities of these clusters, the team then proposed new potential uses for the sites, based on a set of rules outlined below.

In collaboration with Matt Ducharme, Woods Bagot's West Coast design leader, his colleagues in the firm's San Francisco and Los Angeles studios, and the production staff at ERA-co, the team tested the redevelopment potential of each type of use by looking at a generic test site from the study in order to visualize what each option might look like in real life.

Clusters

Clusters are summarised under four
categories with the seven metrics below:

Built density
Built area ratio
Residential population

Accessibility
Proximitiy to highway
Proximity to metro 2026

Value
Annual income per household

Activity
Amenity density
Proximity to other gas stations

Cluster

1 Higher built and population density, Accessible, Lower income, Active, Spread

2 Medium built and population density, Accessible (metro only), Lower income, Less active,

3 Lower built and population density, Accessible (car only), Higher income, Less active, Spread gas stations

4 Lower built and population density, Accessible, Higher income, Less active, Spread gas

5 Medium built, higher population density, Accessible, Lower income, Very active, Dense

6 Medium built and population density, Accessible, Medium income, Moderately active, Dense gas stations

*The six selected clusters of gas station sites,
mapped onto Los Angeles County.*

Use 1: Affordable Housing

The gas station sites in highly accessible, low-income, active locations—those in Cluster 1—were tagged for potential reuse as locations for affordable housing. This was considered a suitable development option given the intense need of the overall Los Angeles region for additional affordable units, and the abundant opportunities for residents in these particular sites to access jobs and services through proximity to both uses and multiple modes of transportation. This proved to be one of the largest and most widely spread clusters of all studied, suggesting a genuine opportunity to use former gas station sites to address—at an appropriately sweeping scale—the region's critical shortage of affordable housing.

The existing levels of density in these clusters increases the possibility of providing higher levels of building density—and thus higher numbers of overall units—due to the higher floor area ratios (FAR) that would be deemed appropriate for the rezoning and redevelopment of these sites, which are currently zoned primarily for commercial use.

To illustrate these reuse opportunities, Woods Bagot and ERA-co's teams developed a concept design for affordable housing situated on a generic Los Angeles site. The design achieves necessary density while remaining sensitive to the surrounding context and providing as much urban amenity—through green roofs, public space and surface treatment, landscaping, and shade—as possible.

These affordable housing sites from Cluster 1 are distributed across Los Angeles in many different neighborhoods, including one known as Vermont-Slauson, in South Los Angeles. This area is typical of this cluster in that it already supports what is, by LA standards, a relatively high density of development. The combination of a young

Clusters to Proposed Uses

Cluster

1. Higher built and population density, Accessible, Lower income, Active, Spread gas stations
2. Medium built and population density, Accessible (metro only), Lower income, Less active, Spread gas stations
3. Lower built and population density, Accessible (car only), Higher income, Less active, Spread gas stations
4. Lower built and population density, Accessible, Higher income, Less active, Spread gas stations
5. Medium built, higher population density, Accessible, Lower income, Very active, Dense gas stations
6. Medium built and population density, Accessible, Medium income, Moderately active, Dense gas stations

Proposed

Affordable housing with optional plug station at base

Mixed use with optional plug station at base

Plug station only

Corner store with plug station

Park and plug

Mixed use

Proposed Uses to Typologies

1. Affordable housing with optional plug station at base
2. Mixed use with optional plug station at base
3. Plug station only
4. Corner store with plug station
5. Park and plug
6. Mixed use

Plug & Play
plug station with optional small retail / leisure facility

Plug & Park
Urban park with plug charging facilities

Affordable Housing
with optional plug station at base

Mixed-Use
with optional plug station at base

WOODS BAGOT + ERA-CO

In a two-step procedure, sites in the six selected clusters were assigned appropriate proposed new uses, which were then translated into four proposed building types or "typologies."

population and single-family households in this district, with the prospect of gentrification from the surrounding region, suggests that affordable housing is a likely need for the area. The transport accessibility to Downtown Los Angeles and other nearby economic zones will allow future residents convenient access to job opportunities.

Use 2: Mixed-Use Development

Sites in the study that are low to moderately active in their surrounding uses but offer a population density sufficient to support retail and commercial activity, have been tagged for mixed-use redevelopment (or Clusters 2 and 6 from the selected model). The mix of uses on these sites could include an affordable residential component, but most of the site area would likely be needed as commercial development opportunities to offset the cost of site remediation—a crucial factor in their redevelopment, as explored in detail below—and the development of lower income-producing assets.

The building types for this use offer slightly higher density to maximize development return. The mixed-use typology provides the best opportunity to build up the revenue stream needed to subsidize other, less-profitable uses—in particular, affordable housing. The ground floor activated along the street edge and a green roof provide amenity for users of the building as well as the wider neighborhood.

A good example of a district with a number of sites tagged for mixed-use is Larchmont, a desirable prewar middle-class neighborhood that is close to downtown and

The affordable housing option can scale to its neighborhood setting, and if implemented on a sufficient number of former gas station sites, can represent a new equitable and inclusive vision of twenty-first-century Los Angeles.

that offers a walkable, main-street-centered urban layout. Its existing diversity of uses and retail-oriented, pedestrian-friendly character would support additional mixed-use development, and recent approvals of higher density mark it as a potential development opportunity, one whose economic attractiveness might help to offset the cost of building affordable housing on sites nearby or in other parts of the city.

Use 3: "Plug and Play" Conveniences

For sites in low-density areas with less active surrounding uses—Clusters 3 and 4—the team proposed a more limited redevelopment approach, as small-scale "plug-and-play" conveniences that might combine EV charging stations with a small corner store or local gym. These sites' lack of surrounding clustered activity and their low density suggest that they would not have enough catchment population or attraction potential to support major commercial and retail uses. Also, because of the low-density surroundings—and their consequent low-density zoning—the option to build affordable housing at a sufficiently high FAR for economic viability would most likely not be achievable. This does not exclude these sites from being future affordable housing options, in cases where they are also located in highly accessible parts of the city, with good public transportation links, and might be rezoned at a later date to afford a suitable density.

A prototypical area of the city with sites of this type is Canoga Park, in the San Fernando Valley. The surrounding development is single-story, low-rise, and predominantly residential. For the majority of the gas station sites in this part of the city, high- or medium-density development for affordable housing or mixed-use is either unlikely

The mixed-use typology can seamlessly blend office, retail, housing, and community space with a focus on a high level of amenity.

to get planning approval or may only be considered in the future with other catalysts, for example transportation hubs. These sites were tagged by the team for low-density uses such as electric charging stations only, especially in areas with little transportation options, or small-scale conveniences, such as corner stores or local gyms. Alternative uses, such as affordable housing, can be considered in the future if surrounding conditions change.

Use 4: Parks and Green Space

The last of the clusters, unlike the others, is comprised of relatively geographically contained sites that are located in an area close to the city's center. While interspersed with sites in other clusters, Cluster 5 forms a distinct, spatially close group of a small number of sites. Although the team's principle was originally to avoid this degree of tight geographic proximity in any of the clusters, on closer inspection this area contained significantly higher population density, mostly lower income residents, with high activity density—but a notable dearth of public parks and green space generally. Providing

A "plug-and-play" typology could be a place to charge one's car and go to the gym, quickly get some groceries, and or relax in landscaped shade off the street.

shaded play space and access to greenery in these denser, central city areas was considered a use that would benefit both local residents and the city's working population.

Balancing Priorities

In attempting to balance priorities among these various reuse and redevelopment options, it would seem at first glance that the overwhelming crisis of housing and homelessness in today's Los Angeles demands that affordable housing remains the clear first choice. However, the cost of environmental remediation of these sites will likely be high, adding to the already daunting subsidies required to develop affordable and supportive housing projects. The cost of development may need to be offset by development opportunities elsewhere, particularly through the mixed-use development sites. As such the affordable housing and mixed-use sites would run concurrently in the short-term staging.

Parks and green space, however, are also a clear priority for Los Angeles. A Parks Needs Assessment undertaken in 2016 by the Los Angeles County Department of Parks and Recreation "shows that there are many areas in the County with high park need and a lack of vacant land for new traditional parks." The need for parks in the area around the study's selected cluster is designated as "very high" by the needs assessment. The opportunity to convert the gas stations in this study to parks can have enormous impact considering the shortage of available land, especially in this area of the city. This should be considered a medium-term priority.

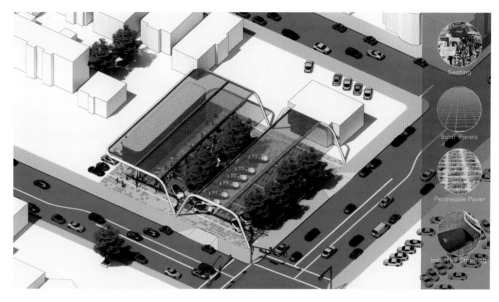

Data from the Los Angeles Countywide Parks and Recreation Needs Assessment showing limited access to green space in the downtown and inner-city region.

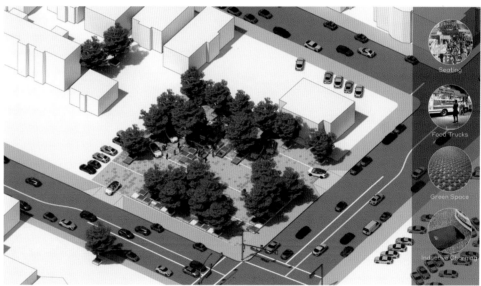

The longer-term priorities lie with the single-use plug-and-play stations, considered as low priority development opportunities. As time passes, these sites can be reviewed for possible alternative uses, such as affordable housing or mixed use, as planning rules evolve, additional growth occurs, and the market shifts to allow higher density on these sites.

Implementing Change

The common lot size of gas station sites across Los Angeles (which are commonly a square of roughly 150 feet by 150 feet) is approximately 20,000 to 22,000 square feet, which is a reasonably attractive lot size for many residential or mixed-use developments.

The ubiquitous presence of gas stations throughout Los Angeles, and the fact that they are often located on wide, major boulevards—and indeed, located not infrequently on prominent corner sites where two large thoroughfares meet—offers a remarkable opportunity for a high level of economic *and* social value to be unlocked by the redevelopment of these sites. Like many major cities in the United States and elsewhere, Los

Citizen Investment Trust Model

New Dwellings	**20,000**
People Housed	**40,000**
Green Space	**300,000**_{sqft}
New Jobs	**43,000**

Possible outcomes for responsible development investment through a governance model that prioritizes impact.

Angeles has a housing affordability crisis and also lacks green space essential to livability and quality of life. With coordinated effort, the opportunity presented by the city's five-hundred-plus gas stations could have an extraordinary impact on the future health and prosperity of Los Angeles.

The sizable 20,000-plus square feet average footprint of these sites, their desirable proportions and ease of access and, not least, their equitable distribution across the city, creates favorable conditions to reuse them for desperately needed affordable housing and other kinds of mixed-use developments. What is not at all favorable about these sites is the contamination effort required to clean them up. The soil beneath these sites is often saturated with PCBs and other harmful chemicals that have infiltrated over the decades of their use as gas stations, all of which must be removed before any redevelopment, along with the large steel underground tanks used for storing the fuel supply, which are subject to their own issues of seepage and leaking.

Due to the large number of variable factors, there is no standard pricing for environmental remediation of gas stations, which is generally budgeted on a site-by-site basis. Except in cases where the land value is exceptionally high, the full cost to remediate will likely outweigh the development value of the new use. Where the previous owner is a major oil company, the developer will likely be indemnified for any contamination removal. Without this indemnity, it may be difficult to access capital required for redevelopment. Many of the gas stations in this study are in areas where the land value is still low. If redevelopment is approached on a site-by-site basis it will simply not be feasible, in all likelihood, to change their use, due to the cost of remediation outweighing the alternative highest and best use value. Which would leave most of them, within a few decades, as the empty, unappealing ruins of the late Petroleum Era—hardly a desirable outcome for the city or the region.

Priorities

The priorities for each typology are indicated below from short-term focus to long-term end state.

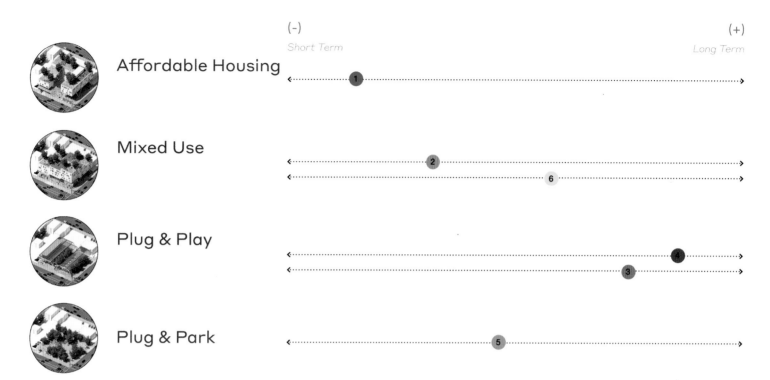

Affordable Housing

Mixed Use

Plug & Play

Plug & Park

(-) Short Term

(+) Long Term

Priorities for the study's four reuse and redevelopment options, over the shorter to longer term.

Approaching a large fraction of the city's 550 gas station sites *together*, as a consolidated package, could enable the unbalanced costs incurred on some sites to be offset by sites with higher market value. Though inevitably preliminary in nature, the ReCharge LA study points to a remarkably promising opportunity—one at the heart of the "Pump to Plug" initiative as originally conceived by the City of Los Angeles and its partners. The enormous shift unfolding in the coming years—as the cumbersome, century-old gas station gradually but steadily makes way for the more technologically advanced, environmentally sensitive, smaller and more agile EV charging station—will do far more than change the way people drive their cars, and more, even, than accelerate the shift away from the oil-dominated paradigm that has defined surface transportation since the start of the twentieth century. It holds the promise of transformative change for cities everywhere, as hundreds of acres of valuable, centrally located urban sites become available to help address the most pressing challenges of the modern metropolis—above all the lack of affordable housing.

Beginning the process by which the city of Los Angeles's 550 existing gas station sites could be transformed into 20,000 new dwellings for 40,000 residents, commercial complexes with 43,000 new jobs, and large swaths of green space for the city's underserved citizens, the study hopes to serve as a crucial step forward in turning the promise of the city's forward-thinking mobility initiatives into the reality of a more prosperous, more just, and more equitable Los Angeles.

ReCharge LA, Part 2:
A Prototype EV Station for
Downtown Los Angeles
Matt Ducharme and
Woods Bagot Los Angeles Studio

PROJECT TEAM
Matt Ducharme
Rick Gunter
Christiana Kyrillou
Kent Wu

Rendering of ReCharge LA Prototype EV Station, showing the community gathering around food trucks. The billboard provides shade for the seating area adjacent to the nearby building.

Introduction

Across most of the twentieth century, the American gas station—like the automobile itself—held a special place in the public imagination.

It was a commonplace yet crucial piece of infrastructure, a fixture of the modern landscape, the essential enabling component of the complex system of cars, roads, and freeways that arose in the twentieth century's first decades and reached a kind of apotheosis in its middle years. Though itself fixed in place, the gas station spoke to a sense of freedom of movement, and, as a key part of the cultural currency of American life, was represented, re-created, and interpreted in countless ways, from fine-art paintings and photographs to popular Hollywood films.

But change is coming for this ubiquitous if humble icon. The dramatic rise of electric vehicles, underway for several years but now accelerating dramatically, will see the venerable gas station supplanted by different uses, among them a new kind of multifaceted urban resource—and amenity—for Los Angeles and other cities: the EV charging station.

In late 2020, as part of a "Pump to Plug" symposium held in partnership with the 3rd LA public-affairs series at the University of Southern California's Academy in the Public Square and the Los Angeles Cleantech Incubator, LA chief design officer Christopher Hawthorne asked several leading architecture firms to imagine the future of the EV charging station, by developing a concept proposal for a prototypical facility on a city-owned surface parking lot (and adjoining privately owned lot) at 749 Los Angeles Street in Downtown Los Angeles.

Responding to the city's forward-thinking challenge, Woods Bagot's design studio, working in close collaboration with its experience consultancy, ERA-co, sought to develop an innovative design concept, ReCharge LA, which reimagined the EV charging station as a flexible, exciting, and community-oriented hub: one that would satisfy the needs of the project's program, extend the cultural heritage of Los Angeles—above all its longtime love affair with the automobile—explore cutting-edge building technologies, and, it was hoped, offer a new platform for neighborhood expression.

In the largest sense, the ReCharge LA prototype sought to find in electrified mobility an opportunity to reinvigorate and reenergize the entire city—to look again to Los Angeles for inspiration, and to locate in the project a new and meaningful "cultural currency" for the future of Southern California.

Part 1: Design Inspiration

As they undertook their design effort, the Woods Bagot team sought to address three large questions.

How can the EV charging station provide a new kind of automobile-related space, adapted to twenty-first-century needs, and representative of local communities? How do we continue—and expand—the century-long heritage of cultural expression associated with the gas station and the automobile, which has been so formative in establishing the identity of Southern California itself? And, given the changing daily needs of a complex urban culture and the rapid rate of change associated with EV technology, how do we provide an adaptable and embedded infrastructure that can enjoy different lives throughout the day and week, and evolve over time?

To develop a prototypical design that would begin to address these questions, the team explored a range of inspirational sources, starting with the deeply rooted place of the car and gas station in the heritage of

Ed Ruscha, Standard
Station, *1963.*

twentieth-century Southern California and moving on
to twenty-first-century technologies and urban strategies that could be mobilized for the project. In a play on
the symposium's name, "Pump to Plug," the ReCharge LA
effort would reenvision the site at 749 South Los Angeles
Street by "pumping up" sustainable mobility and "plug-
ging into" the auto culture of Los Angeles.

The project can be seen as part of the Los Angeles
studio's broader exploration of the distinctive mobil-
ity-based urbanism of Southern California, also
represented in Case Study 1 of this book—the proposal for The Twist, an experiential community hub on
Sunset Boulevard in West Hollywood that interprets in
a contemporary design the famed billboard culture and
auto-oriented experience of the Sunset Strip.

Pump Up the Green and Plug into Culture

In developing the project, the team was inspired initially by the powerful place that gas stations have long
held in the American imagination, and above all in

Southern California: from the iconic mid-century paintings and photographic series by Ed Ruscha to memorable
film scenes in *Back to the Future* and countless other
Hollywood features to the design and spirit of innovative
mid-century modern gas stations around the Southern
California, from Beverly Hills to Palm Springs.

Iconic Car Culture and Neighborhood
and Ethnic Identity

Since the postwar years, the automobile has served not
only as the primary means of transportation in Southern
California but also as a startlingly protean form of cultural expression—sometimes carrying with it charged and
deep meaning for particular geographic areas and ethnic
groups.

In the 1950s and early '60s, for example, Los
Angeles gave rise in the same years to the sleek and
whimsical "Kustom Kars" created by George Barris
and others on the far West Side (subject of Tom Wolfe's
classic 1965 essay, *The Kandy-Kolored Tangerine-Flake*

Above: *Frame enlargement from Back to the Future (1985),
whose most evocative re-creation of the Southern California
of the mid-1950s (to which its leading character has traveled
through time) is its scene of a Texaco station's uniformed
attendants energetically servicing a customer's car.*
Right: *The floating modernist roof of an actual 1950s Mobil
station in Anaheim, photographed by Julius Shulman.*

Streamline Baby), and to the "Lowrider" movement that swept through working-class communities of East Los Angeles, which transformed the '58 Chevy Impala into a popular expression of Chicano identity (and, by way of backlash, brought forth Section 24008 of the California Vehicle Code, which banned any car part lower than the wheel rims).

In the 1990s and 2000s, this deep-rooted cultural tradition would continue to expand in new ways—and with new groups—as that same 1958 Chevrolet Impala was adopted by the fast-growing Black hip-hop culture of South Los Angeles, as a wave of obsession with "JDM"—Japanese Domestic Market—vehicles swept through the largely Asian American reaches of the San Gabriel Valley, and as the region's long-standing fascination with cars of all kinds would find their landmark in the Petersen Automotive Museum, rising proudly on Wilshire Boulevard directly across from LACMA, and unabashedly elevating the history and culture of the automobile to the status of fine art.

How might the EV station of tomorrow harness this extraordinary cultural heritage and provide a setting by which it might continue to grow and expand in the future?

Gas Station Iconography

By mid-century, not only the automobile itself but the ubiquitous structure that enabled its movement—the gas station—could sometimes be elevated to the highest echelon of modern design. The multiple pump islands and the simple, functional structure—featuring conveniences and sundries, inspection station and garage, along with that humblest yet most valued amenity, a public restroom—were typically sheltered under a wide, floating roof that kept rain and sun away from the staff, the customers, and their vehicles.

A variety of noted modernist architects from Beverly Hills to Palm Springs saw in that floating plane the opportunity to bring exciting structural and formal expression to a highly visible and exceedingly democratic building type.

Community Gathering

In Los Angeles as perhaps nowhere else on earth, the car and truck have become the armature of new kinds of urban gatherings and activities. Over the past twenty years, for example, the LA food truck has risen in significance from a little-noticed working-person's amenity—typically found near factories and in less-advantaged communities—to become a centerpiece of LA's rise to global culinary greatness, driven by the diversity and excellence of its ethnic food traditions. Ranks of food trucks serving just about every kind of cuisine can now be found almost everywhere in the city, from poor and working communities to the plazas of elite museums, universities, and shopping areas.

The car has also emerged in Los Angeles in recent decades as the *theme* of distinctive kinds of urban assembly, in the region's popular "auto meets" where families come together on weekends to show off and admire customized cars and other vehicles.

In developing their concept for the EV station of the future, the design team surveyed a variety of ways in which vehicles serve as the basis for new ways of coming together in a city and enjoying the common public realm:

— *Food trucks* offer cuisine from a number of different cultures and are emblematic of a creativity that recombines these traditional cuisines to create something new.

— *Cars and Coffee* is a weekly event held at Griffith Park's Merry-Go-Round no. 1 that brings together local automobile, photography, and design enthusiasts.

— *Donut Derelicts* takes place every Saturday morning, when the parking lot outside an unassuming doughnut shop in Los Angeles floods with some of the most impressive vintage and late-model cars imaginable.

— *Sideshow Takeovers* is a meeting of powerful and heavily "modded" cars and sideshow audiences, occurring most of the time illegally, on a public road or lot where drivers perform "donuts" and other elaborate and sometimes risky car maneuvers.

Urban Gathering Places

Though Los Angeles enjoys its share of traditional public spaces, many of its most distinctive gathering places are the product of a very different approach to urban assembly and should be explored and understood on their own terms, not as lesser versions of East Coast or European models, such as Piazza Navona in Rome or Bryant Park in New York—formal, pedestrian-oriented gardens or piazzas, firmly defined by their surrounding architecture. In

Top: *The Tramway Gas Station, a 1965 Palm Springs landmark designed by Albert Frey and Robson C. Chambers, features a cantilevered hyperbolic paraboloid canopy visible for miles. Its striking wedge-shaped form now serves as the city's welcome center.*

Bottom left: *A weekend auto meet in Los Angeles draws hundreds of families and specialty cars.*
Bottom right: *Crowds gather in front of food trucks in Grand Park on New Year's Eve, 2018.*

Plug and Play - Infrastructure Modules

Canopy Surface *(Hackable Billboard)*

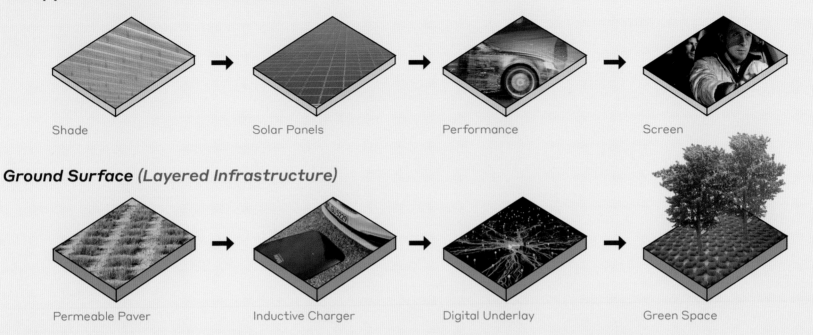

Shade → Solar Panels → Performance → Screen

Ground Surface *(Layered Infrastructure)*

Permeable Paver → Inductive Charger → Digital Underlay → Green Space

recent decades, Los Angeles has pioneered new kinds of "town squares," often transitory and flexible, informal, and opportunistic in spirit, and often integrating the automobile as an essential element. They can be something as simple as a car meet and races on the black asphalt surface of a weekend parking lot—but as much a source of community pride, family enjoyment, and urban spectacle as any older civic environment.

Which is not to say there still isn't a great deal also to be learned from more traditional models such as Piazza Navona or Bryant Park, both of which, for all their richness and complexity, can be understood in large part as richly textured surfaces below people's feet, and shade canopies above their heads. This notion, too, played an important role in the design team's thinking for their EV charging station of the future.

Part 2: Design Concepts

The basic design concept for the team's prototype was based on turning the essential challenge of the EV charging station—the reality that, using current technology, a full charge requires the vehicle to remain connected for thirty minutes or more—into a boundless urban opportunity. By its very nature, the current EV charging station wants (and needs) to be one element among other adjacent amenities and attractions, allowing users to enjoy and entertain themselves in various ways while charging is in progress. (By the same token, of course, the absence of nearly all of the problems of the traditional gas station—from the high risk of flammability and explosion to the unpleasant smell of gas fumes—means that a wide range of urban activities can occur in immediate proximity to an EV charging station, as they could not in a conventional station.)

The design team began with the essential elements of the program, as established by the city's symposium: DC fast-charging facilities for twenty vehicles, a thousand square feet for infrastructure elements, food and beverage service, and public open space. From there, they began to imagine an entirely new kind of facility, one that would build on the rich base of Los Angeles culture and tradition even as it pioneered advanced kinds of urban construction. The team began to envision a host of design concepts. A flexible, embedded infrastructure that could accommodate different "shifts" throughout the day and night, from weekday to weekend, and over the years. A grid of modular floor pavers that could evolve with changing technologies. A hackable, multipurpose digital LED screen, supported by a slender-shaped frame, to serve as a shading device, a movie screen, or a video backdrop. Beneath the frame structure and shade screen, food trucks might gather by day, for coffee in the morning, and lunch at midday. In the evening, reconfigured, the screen could become a modern-day drive-in theater or serve as a video backdrop for performance for on-site events or, on weekends, a souped-up car meet or urban park.

Flexible Floor and Canopy Surfaces

Recognizing that the site of the EV prototype would need to remain largely free of permanent structures, the design team focuses intervention on two primary surfaces, above and below eye level: a canopy, conceived as a "hackable billboard," and the ground, conceived as a layered infrastructure.

Opposite page, top: *Covered with multiple layers, the surface of ReCharge LA's canopy and ground serve multiple purposes. The canopy simultaneously provides shade, collects energy with solar panels during the day, and adjusts into alternate positions that reveal LED screens for performance in the evening. The ground is layered with infrastructural elements that blur the lines of traditional parking lots: permeable pavers with embedded inductive chargers, digital information to help safely guide pedestrians, and a green layer provides an opportunity to create public park space with trees and plantings. Bottom: Traditional concepts of urban gathering, from Piazza Navona in Rome (left) to Bryant Park in New York (center), have evolved to encompass car culture in Los Angeles (right).*

Plug and Play - Vignette

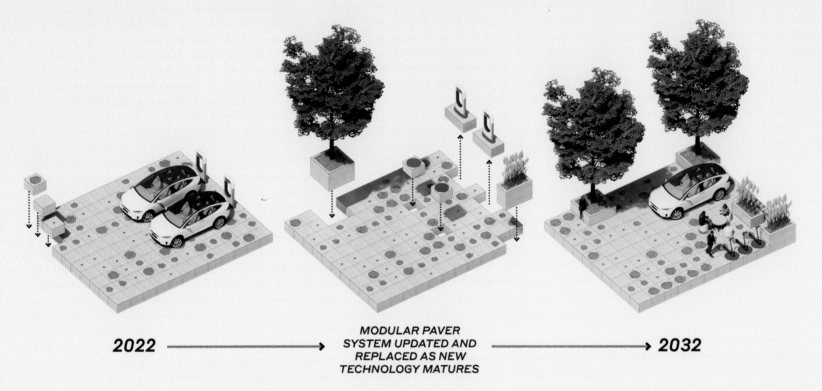

2022 ⟶ MODULAR PAVER SYSTEM UPDATED AND REPLACED AS NEW TECHNOLOGY MATURES ⟶ 2032

The team saw a canopy structure as the essential means of combining extensive shade—always an advantage in Southern California—with a minimal footprint, allowing maximum flexibility of uses at ground level. But for the team, the canopy's large flat screen, its surface layered in solar cells and LEDs and given the ability to pivot and rotate, could be useful in a wide variety of ways, from collecting energy from the sun positioned more-or-less horizontally during the day, then adjusted in orientation to become a delivery device of information in the evening, via LED technology.

The notion of a flexible armature, capable of supporting screens and other equipment, draws directly on an obvious precedent—one deeply intertwined with Los Angeles: the rigging grid of a Hollywood soundstage, which serves as a basic scaffolding to allow for a multitude of different environments. "It is more than a blank canvas," team leader Matt Ducharme suggested, "it is a dare...an invitation to release your creativity to define a sense of place. If this rigging can allow for a screen to move into different positions, for instance, one can create an immersive environment with just a few screen elements."

Likewise, the team suggested that the ground surface could become more than just a surface to walk or drive one's car on. Using rain-permeable pavers, it can be an active participant in sustainable strategies. As the technology progresses, inductive EV charging of the cars can be employed, so that the entire ground plane is providing charging. Eventually this allows for a much more fluid relationship between park surface, flexible infrastructure, and potential activations of the site.

To allow for flexibility over time, the Plug-and-Play surfaces are conceived as modules that can be swapped as technology changes, or as the uses for the site shift over time. As elements accumulate, they can create an entirely different kind of ground surface with embedded technology, sustainable strategies, and plantings.

Part 3: Proposed Design

Initial Layout (2022)

In its initial configuration—designed to be readily approved and installed—the proposed installation is concentrated in the portion of the overall site that is already owned by the city, facing Los Angeles Street. In this area, twenty DC fast-charging points are located on a new ground surface, placed underneath a new canopy-and-screen structure. The adjoining area remains in its current use as parking but can become an open-air food market on weekends.

The ReCharge LA design addresses changes in technology over time, using modular pavers that can be swapped out and rearranged. In 2023, charging points are discretely located on portions of the site and functionally operate like a traditional parking lot. As the technology progresses, inductive charging in 2032 allows for a much more fluid and nuanced relationship between infrastructure, public space, and gathering.

Top: *Rigging on a Hollywood soundstage.* Center: *Hanging screen with embedded LEDs in a project by Diller, Scofidio + Renfro.* Bottom: *Large-scale LED screen serving as event backdrop.*

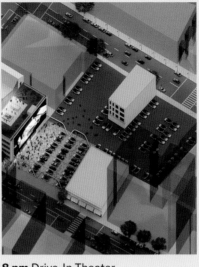

7 am Charging & Coffee

1 pm Lunchtime Food Trucks

8 pm Drive-In Theater

Weekend 11 pm Car Meet

As the day passes and turns into evening, and then as the weekend comes, the structural frame and canopy system can flexibly adapt to a wide variety of uses and activities, suitable for the hour and day of the week.

Food Truck Alley 2032

Drive-In Theater 2032

Car Showcase 2032

Urban Park 2032

Daily and Weekly Transformation

In its initial configuration, the ReCharge LA installation is designed to shift its shape and use across the day and week, to allow for different types of activation. The new canopies play a key role in this transformation. On weekday mornings, the canopies provide welcome shade for a charging area and coffee stand, which shifts to a series of food trucks at lunchtime and throughout the afternoon, all the while collecting significant solar energy in their embedded solar cells. In the evening, the canopies rotate into a vertical position against on the adjacent building's parting wall, and the embedded LEDs become a screen for a drive-in theater.

Over the weekend, the two canopies shift into an entirely different orientation to serve as a background screen for regular car meets, projecting livestream imagery of the specialty vehicles and community members who are in attendance, along with programmed content and music.

Evolution after 2028

Anticipating advances in vehicle-charging technology that will make the charging process shorter and more efficient within the coming years, the ReCharge LA installation is designed to expand its activities and amenities over time, as more space becomes available for uses other than charging. The design also anticipates the expansion of the site through the public acquisition of the privately owned property along Main Street, which will allow for a valuable through-block connection for pedestrians and slow-moving vehicles as well as additional areas for programming and events.

By the early 2030s, new uses for the expanded and interconnected site could include a "food-truck alley" with landscaped seating areas, a larger and more permanent car show and drive-in theater, and a permanent landscaped park for the underserved downtown area.

A final gallery of renderings offers a glimpse at a potential future for Los Angeles, in which the mobility revolution allows the ubiquitous service station to be transformed from its traditional role as an enabler of gas-powered automobility into a forward-looking, multipurpose amenity—one that not only powers a new era of urban movement but encourages new forms of community, gathering, and delight.

Opposite, upper left: *A "food-truck alley" serving Downtown Los Angeles and including EV charging areas and up to ten food trucks and adjoining café seating areas shaded by plantings and canopy structures.*
Upper right: *The drive-in theater occupies the southern portion of the site along Los Angeles Street while food trucks are to the north along Main Street.*
Bottom left: *The car meet becomes a true event with both a main stage for the community to show off their "ride," and smaller breakaway spaces for cars to be lined up in a gallery.*
Bottom right: *The true potential of an embedded infrastructure is realized where the distinction between park space and charging is blurred.*

Oriented vertically, the canopy screen becomes vertical and provides a showcase for art in a social setting, surrounded by cars.

Opposite and overleaf: *Beyond feature film screenings, the large-scale LED screens can provide the energized, dynamic backdrop for a wide variety of uses and activities, from community gatherings to product launch events to opening night parties to weeknight "hang-outs" bringing together residents and visitors from across Downtown Los Angeles and beyond.*

Renewing the Dream

Case Study 2: ReCharge LA, Part 2

Contributors

James Sanders, FAIA, is an internationally recognized architect, author, and filmmaker, whose work has garnered him a Guggenheim Fellowship, an Emmy Award, and elevation to the College of Fellows of the American Institute of Architects. With Ric Burns, Sanders wrote and produced the PBS series, *New York: A Documentary Film*, and its companion volume, *New York: An Illustrated History* (Knopf, 1999, 2021). His landmark study of the city and film, *Celluloid Skyline* (Knopf, 2001), was hailed by Jane Jacobs as a "marvelous—miraculous—book," and in 2007 became an exhibition in Grand Central Terminal. His book *Scenes from the City* (Rizzoli, 2007, 2014), produced with the Mayor's Office of Media and Entertainment, includes contributions by Martin Scorsese and Nora Ephron. His firm, James Sanders Studio, has developed projects for New York University, Regional Plan Association, André Balazs Properties, Ian Schrager Company, and the Museum of the City of New York, among other clients. His articles about Los Angeles and New York have appeared since the 1980s in the *Los Angeles Times*, *New Yorker*, the *New York Times*, and elsewhere. He sits on the board of the Skyscraper Museum, is a Fellow of the Urban Design Forum, and since 2016 has served as Global Design Council Chair for Woods Bagot.

Nik Karalis, Chief Executive Officer of Woods Bagot, possesses a diverse portfolio of civic, architectural, and interior projects. His work has received international acclaim and he has won a number of prominent international design awards, including the Australian Institute of Architects national and state awards, IDEA national award, FX international award, and WAF shortlists. Karalis believes that the guiding principle of architecture should be the ability to address human context and is taking on the major challenges faced by cities and city dwellers globally through a holistic approach to the built environment that focuses on the user experience, integrating architecture, technology, interior design and urbanism.

Frances Anderton is an author, curator, and radio producer and host, known for her weekly radio show, *DnA: Design and Architecture*, broadcast for many years on KCRW, NPR's station in Los Angeles. She also produced KCRW's acclaimed current affairs shows, *To the Point* and *Which Way, LA?* Anderton curates events and exhibitions, including *Action/Reaction* at the Pasadena Museum of California Art and *Sink or Swim: Designing for a Sea Change*, at the Annenberg Space for Photography. She has written for the *New York Times* and *Dwell* magazine and her books include *Grand Illusion: A Story of Ambition, and Its Limits* (2011) and *Common Ground: Multifamily Housing in Los Angeles* (2022). Born in Bath, England, Anderton studied architecture at the Bartlett at University College London.

Eric Avila is an urban cultural historian, studying the intersections of racial identity, urban space, and cultural representation in twentieth-century America. Since 1997, he has taught Chicano Studies and History at UCLA. and holds an affiliation with the Department of Urban Planning. He is the author of *Popular Culture in the Age of White Flight: Fear and Fantasy in Suburban Los Angeles*, (University of California Press, 2004), and *The Folklore of the Freeway: Race and Revolt in the Modernist City* (University of Minnesota Press, 2014). He received his undergraduate and graduate education at the University of California, Berkeley.

Meg Bartholomew, former Head of Impact and Analytics at ERA-co, is an expert in urbanism with a background in development, urban sociology, and economics. Bartholomew specializes in understanding place and people through quantitative analysis using these metrics to inform design with purposeful impact. Bartholomew received a Master's in Cities degree from the London School of Economics, has been a researcher at the LSE Cities group, and has worked at all scales of settlement, from remote Indigenous communities to the world's largest cities, to gather a deep understanding of both economic drivers and human behavior and their spatial effects.

Francesca Birks specializes in understanding how emerging drivers will impact and shape the future of the built environment. As a trained futurist, she develops future scenarios by researching trends and providing actionable insights to shape that preferred future. As a certified facilitator and experienced design strategist, she has planned and facilitated strategic design engagement processes and visioning workshops to help clients co-create aspirational futures.

Steven Cornwell is the CEO and Global Director of ERA-co. Over the course of twenty years, Cornwell has garnered an international reputation for developing leading brands from a broad range of sectors including real estate, place, culture, consumer retail, media, transit and infrastructure, and professional services. Prior to establishing ERA-co in the United States, he was CMO of the publicly traded real estate and development company Howard Hughes Corporation and CEO and Executive Creative Director of Cornwell Brand & Communications in Australia, which he started in 1994 with his wife, Jane Sinclair.

Matt Ducharme, Woods Bagot's West Coast Design Leader, heads a diverse group of collaborators that combine global expertise with engagement, empathy, and creative problem-solving. With degrees in structural engineering as well as architecture, he has led award-winning projects in the US and Australia that include civic, mixed-use, skyscrapers, performing arts facilities, stadiums, and master planning, including 447 Collins Street, Australia's first true mixed-use tower. He received his M Arch from the University of Michigan and his BS from the University of Wisconsin.

Russell Fortmeyer is the Chief Sustainability Officer of Woods Bagot. Trained in both engineering and architecture, he has focused on progressing sustainability in the built environment to address climate change and the natural environment, social equity and human health, and the application of green technologies to architecture. His professional interests include sustainable buildings and certification, climate action and resilience planning, decarbonization and energy strategy, urban microclimates and human comfort, and materials and circular economy research.

Greg Lindsay is the senior fellow for applied research and foresight at NewCities, a senior fellow of MIT's Future Urban Collectives Lab, and a nonresident senior fellow of the Atlantic Council's Scowcroft Strategy Initiative. He was the urbanist-in-residence at URBAN-X—BMW MINI's start-up accelerator—and is founding director of strategy at CoMotion, a media-and-events platform devoted to the future of transportation.

Michael Manville is Associate Professor of Urban Planning at the UCLA Luskin School of Public Affairs. His research focuses on transportation, housing and land use regulations. He holds an MA and a PhD in Urban Planning, both from UCLA, and his writing has been published in the *Washington Post,* the *Los Angeles Times,* the *Atlantic,* and most major journals of urban planning and transportation.

Donald Shoup, FAICP, is Distinguished Research Professor in the Department of Urban Planning at the University of California, Los Angeles, where he has taught for more than fifty years. His landmark books, *The High Cost of Free Parking* (2005) and *Parking and the City* (2018), examine how parking reforms offer the simplest, cheapest, and fastest way to improve cities, protect the environment, and promote social justice. Shoup is a Fellow of the American Institute of Certified Planners and an Honorary Professor at the Beijing Transportation Research Center, and has received the American Planning Association's National Excellence Award for a Planning Pioneer, and the American Collegiate Schools of Planning's Distinguished Educator Award.

Mark Vallianatos serves as Executive Officer, Innovation, at LA Metro, where he helps oversee strategic planning and special projects. Vallianatos previously worked on and taught urban and environmental policy at Occidental College. He also cofounded Abundant Housing LA and has advocated for more homes of all types and for policies to prevent and reduce homelessness. He is the coauthor of *The Next Los Angeles: The Struggle for a Livable City* (2006), and received his Bachelor of Arts and Juris Doctor degrees from the University of Virginia.

About Woods Bagot

Woods Bagot is a global studio spanning design, research, data, and performance to create *People Architecture*, placing human experience at the center of the design process to deliver engaging, future-oriented projects that respond to the way people actually use space. Founded more than a century and a half ago as the first architecture practice in Australia, Woods Bagot has grown over the decades into one of the world's largest global design firms, with seventeen studios in cities across North America, Europe, the Middle East, Asia, and Australia.

A multi-authorship practice whose more than one thousand design professionals specializing in architecture, interiors, and master planning, Woods Bagot does not adhere to a single signature style, but instead seeks to develop projects in creative collaboration with clients, communities, and other partners. The studio places a special emphasis on the gathering and exploration of data, in order to predict and design for changing human behavior.

About ERA-co

ERA-co is a global experience consultancy that harnesses the power of data and analytics to unlock the true potential of neighborhoods, towns, and cities. Operating in the space between creativity, business, and urbanism, it explores the dynamic interactions between people and place to design human-centric experiences.

ERA-co's proprietary place intelligence tools and processes bring meaningful insight and clarity to the most complex of urban challenges. The consultancy seeks to create visionary strategies that catalyze our client's long-term economic goals, while ensuring the transformative growth, health, happiness, and well-being of the communities it helps serve.

Acknowledgments

The production of *Renewing the Dream*—and of the studies that initiated it—has inevitably been a long and complex process, so we are especially grateful to have the opportunity to express our appreciation in print for the many individuals—inside and outside Woods Bagot and ERA-co—who have contributed to making this "dream" a reality. It has been a deeply rewarding experience working with all of them.

Our deepest thanks go:

To our distinguished guest contributors: Frances Anderton, Eric Avila, Greg Lindsay, Michael Manville, Donald Shoup, and Mark Vallianatos.

To our superb graphic designers, Paul Carlos and Urshula Barbour of Pure+Applied, and their talented and hardworking team, including Emily Force.

To our publisher Charles Miers, our editor, Ellen R. Cohen, and to the entire production and publicity team at our distinguished publishing partner, Rizzoli Electa.

To John Rossant, the founder and CEO of CoMotion LA, who first invited Woods Bagot to prepare its MORE LA study at its 2018 annual conference, setting the project in motion, and to Christopher Hawthorne, former Chief Design Officer of the City of Los Angeles, who invited Woods Bagot to join his office's "Pump to Plug" ideas competition in 2020, and whose larger ideas on the "Third L.A." have proved inspirational to our own approach.

To Jason Foster, president and COO of Destination Crenshaw, and to Los Angeles Councilmember Marqueece Harris-Dawson, for their generous time and assistance.

To Matt Ducharme, Rick Gunter, and Christiana Kyrillos and their talented teams at the Woods Bagot Los Angeles Studio, who helped produce so much of the design work in this book.

To Steven Cornwell, Tarran Kundi, and Anthony Nelson at ERA-co, who, along with Meg Bartholomew, Francesca Birks, Alicen Coddington, Christian Derix, Russell Fortmeyer, Lucy Helme, Fabio Galicia, Luis Jaggy, Dave Towey, and Gözde Uyar, helped prepare our data studies.

To Susan G. Johnson, for her work securing the rights and reproductions of our images—for her invaluable help in bringing Woods Bagot and Rizzoli together to produce this book.

To Linnea Soli for her extensive assistance in the editorial content and graphics of this book. For the California Court project, to design associate Kelsey Sellenraad, to landscape design collaborator Wade Graham, to technical consultant P.B. Turgeon, and to digital visualization consultants Cristian Farinella and Lorena Greco at Atelier Crilo.

To the production designers David Wasco and Sandy Reynolds-Wasco, the producer Marc Platt, the director Damien Chazelle, and the photographer Dale Robinette for making possible the reproduction of the production still from *La La Land*.

To Aliya Kalla at the Getty Research Institute Library, Carley Hildebrand at the LA Conservancy, Vicki Rand of the Marvin Rand Estate, and David Brodsly for so energetically assisting our illustration research, and to all our photographers and sources for helping us assemble the constellation of images that help bring to this volume alive.

Finally, we would like to express our special appreciation to the board leadership of Woods Bagot, for supporting this effort in myriad ways over the years it has taken to bring to fruition.

James Sanders and Nik Karalis
January 2023

Selected Bibliography

Anderton, Frances. *Common Ground: Multifamily Housing in Los Angeles*. Santa Monica, CA: Angel City Press, 2022.

Avila, Eric. *Popular Culture in the Age of White Flight: Fear and Fantasy in Suburban Los Angeles*. Berkeley, CA: University of California Press, 2004.

———. *The Folklore of the Freeway: Race and Revolt in the Modernist City*. Minneapolis: University of Minnesota Press, 2014.

Banham, Reyner. *Los Angeles: The Architecture of Four Ecologies* (rev. ed.). Berkeley, CA: University of California Press, 2001.

Ben-Joseph, Eran. *Re-thinking a Lot: The Design and Culture of Parking*. Cambridge, MA: MIT Press, 2015.

Brodsly, David. *L.A. Freeway: An Appreciative Essay*. Berkeley, CA: University of California Press, 1981.

Chester, Mikhail, Andre Fraser, Juan Matute, Carolyn Flower, and Ram Pendyala. "Parking Infrastructure: A Constraint on or Opportunity for Urban Redevelopment? A Study of Los Angeles County Parking Supply and Growth," *Journal of the American Planning Association*, Volume 81, Issue 4, November 23, 2015: 268-286.

Davis, Walter S., et. al. *Ideal Homes in Garden Communities*. Los Angeles: The Garden City Company of California, 1919.

Dawes, Amy. *Sunset Boulevard: Cruising the Heart of Los Angeles*. Los Angeles: Los Angeles Times Books, 2002.

Easter, Makeda, and Deborah Vankin, "Top Artists Sign on for Destination Crenshaw, a 1.3-mile Monument to Black L.A.," *Los Angeles Times,* September 1, 2022.

French, Jere Stuart. *The California Garden and the Landscape Architects Who Shaped It*. Washington, DC: Landscape Architecture Foundation, 1993.

Gebhard, David. *Schindler*. San Francisco: William Stout, 1997.

Gebhard, David and Robert Winter. *Los Angeles: An Architectural Guide*. Salt Lake City: Gibbs-Smith, 2004.

Grabar, Henry, ed. *SOM Thinkers: The Future of Transportation*. New York: Metropolis Books, 2019.

Grant, Thurman, and Joshua G. Stein. *Dingbat 2.0: The Iconic Los Angeles Apartment as Projection of a Metropolis*. Los Angeles: Doppelhouse Press, 2016.

Heckert, Virginia. *Ed Ruscha and Some Los Angeles Apartments*. Los Angeles: Getty Publications, 2013.

Manville, Michael. "How Parking Destroys Cities." *The Atlantic*, May 18, 2021.

Marx, Paris. *Road to Nowhere: What Silicon Valley Gets Wrong About the Future of Transportation*. New York: Verso, 2022.

Moore, Charles, Peter Becker, and Regula Campbell. *History Observed: Los Angeles: A Guide to Its Architecture and Landscapes*. New York: Vintage, 1984.

Norton, Peter. *Autonorama: The Illusory Promise of High-Tech Driving*. Washington, DC: Island Press, 2021.

Polyzoides, Stefanos, Roger Sherwood, and James Tice. *Courtyard Housing in Los Angeles: A Typological Analysis*. New York: Princeton Architectural Press, 1982.

Parolek, Daniel, with Arthur C. Nelson. *Missing Middle Housing: Thinking Big and Building Small to Respond to Today's Housing Crisis*. Washington, DC: Island Press, 2020.

Reynolds, John S. *Courtyards: Aesthetic, Social, and Thermal Delight*. New York: John Wiley & Sons, 2002.

Rossant, John, and Stephen Baker. *Hop Skip Go: How the Transport Revolution Is Transforming Our Lives*. New York: HarperCollins, 2019.

Shoup, Donald. "Pricing the Curb," *Parking & Mobility,* April 2020.

———. *The High Cost of Free Parking.* New York: Routledge, 2011.

Shoup, Donald (editor). *Parking and the City.* New York: Routledge, 2018.

Schwartz, Samuel I. *No One at the Wheel: Driverless Cars and the Road of the Future.* New York: Hachette, 2018.

Suisman, Doug. *Los Angeles Boulevard: Eight X-Rays of the Body Public* (rev. ed.). San Francisco: ORO Editions, 2014.

Stephens, Josh. *The Urban Mystique: Notes on California, Los Angeles, and Beyond*. Ventura, CA: Solimar Books, 2020.

Townsend, Anthony M. *Ghost Road: Beyond the Driverless Car*. New York: Norton, 2020.

Vanderbilt, Tom. *Traffic: Why We Drive the Way We Do (and What It Says About Us)*. New York: Alfred A. Knopf, 2008.

Waldie, D. J. *Becoming Los Angeles: Myth, Memory, and a Sense of Place*. Santa Monica, CA: Angel City Press, 2020.

———. *Where We Are Now: Notes from Los Angeles*. Santa Monica, CA: Angel City Press, 2004.

Winter, Robert. *The California Bungalow*. California Architecture and Architects, No. 1. Los Angeles: Hennessey & Ingalls, 1980.

Image Credits

© 2023 Wayne Thiebaud Foundation/ Licensed by VAGA at Artists Rights Society (ARS), NY: 51
ADAM AMENGUAL/The New York Times/Redux: 180
Architecture and Design Collection. Art, Design & Architecture Museum, University of California, Santa Barbara: 169 bottom left
Atelier Crilo: 162, 182, 186 all

bpk Bildagentur/Sammlung Moderne Kunst/Pinakothek der Moderne/ Bayerische Staatsgemäldesammlungen/ Munich/Germany/Stephen Shore/Art Resource, NY: 192
Brian Kellogg/Kerrie Kelly Design Lab: 39
Bridgeman Images: 128 right

© Catherine Opie, Courtesy Regen Projects, Los Angeles and Lehmann Maupin, New York, Hong Kong, London, and Seoul: 33
Cavan Images via Getty Images: 73 top
Chon Kit Leong/Alamy Stock Photo: 139
City of Münster, press office.: 106
Collection Center for Creative Photography, University of Arizona © The Ansel Adams Publishing Rights Trust: 44
Courtesy CicLAvia: 36 all
Courtesy City of Los Angeles: 152
Courtesy of Petersen Automotive Museum: 213 bottom left, 214 bottom right
Courtesy Orange County Fire Authority: 146
Courtesy Stephanos Polyzoides: 164 bottom, 168 left
Creatista/Bigstock: 213 top
Crenshaw Line Aerial, August 6th '22, Los Angeles County Metropolitan Transportation Authority. Public Domain.: 85

David Brodsly: 24 top
© David Hockney, Tate, London/Art Resource, NY: 20
© Dennis M. Keeley: cover, 30
Digital Image © The Museum of Modern Art/Licensed by SCALA/Art Resource, NY. Courtesy the estate of the artist and Maxwell Graham Gallery, New York: 76
Digital Image @ 2021 Museum Associates/LACMA. Licensed by Art Resource, NY: 53
DogoraSun/Alamy Stock Photo: 73 bottom
Downey McDonalds, Bryan Hong: 95 top left

© Ed Ruscha: 29 all, 154, 210
Emily Berl/The New York Times/Redux: 10, 136
Essco Lumber Products via archive.org: 147 top

Frank Romero, Courtesy of the artist: 56, 59

Gina Power/Shutterstock.com: 41
Google Earth V 9.181.0.1 (January 18th, 2023): 150 top 4th from left, 150 bottom 2nd and 3rd from left,, 151 top left
Gordon Dean, Valley Times Collection/ Los Angeles Public Library: 28 left

Hayk_Shalunts/Shutterstock.com: 141
Huntington Library, San Marino, California: 48

Ilja Masík/EyeEm via Getty Images: 18
Image by Plomp for Mithun: 67
Image Professionals GmbH/Alamy Stock Photo: 137
Image provided by Automotus: 80
iStock.com/adamkaz: 13 top
iStock.com/anouchka: 213 bottom right
iStock.com/egdigital: 9 top
iStock.com/imagean: 96 bottom right
iStock.com/peeterv: 8 top

James Black: 155
James Sanders: 150 top 1st, 2nd, and 3rd from left, 150 bottom 1st and 4th from left, 151 2nd, 3rd, and 4th from left, 156 all, 157 top and bottom right, 172 left, 173 right, 175 all, 185 all
James Sanders Studio: 183, 184
Jim Newberry/Alamy Stock Photo: 60
© J. Paul Getty Trust. Getty Research Institute, Los Angeles (2004.R.10): 148, 165, 166 all, 168 right, 170, 172 right, 173 left, 174, 176 all, 187 all, 211 right
Julius Shulman: 15b, 164 top

© LA ART: 37 top
LA LA LAND courtesy of Lions Gate Films Inc.: 17 bottom, 34
Laurin Rinder/Shutterstock.com: 160
Leonard Nadel, Housing Authority Collection/Los Angeles Public Library: 28 right
LHB Photo/Alamy Stock Photo: 93
Library of Congress: 169 top left and bottom right
Linnea Soli: 64, 79
© logoboom/Adobe Stock: 16 top
Los Angeles Conservancy: 129 left, 143

Mario Tama/Getty Images News via Getty Images: 62 all
Marvin Rand Archive: 169 top right
Matt Gush/Shutterstock.com: 159
Mel Melcon via Getty Images: 11, 70
© metamorworks/Adobe Stock: 12 top, 66
Michael Wells: 133
MikeDotta/Shutterstock.com: 75
MSPhotographic/Shutterstock.com: 129 right
Musings on a Glass Box, designed by Diller Scofidio + Renfro in collaboration with David Lang and Jody Elff and presented at Fondation Cartier pour l'art contemporain from October 24, 2014, to February 22, 2015. Photo by Luc Boegly. Courtesy of Diller Scofidio + Renfro.: 217 middle

Old Visuals/Alamy Stock Photo: 21

Peter Ptschelinzew/Alamy Stock Photo: 214 middle
Photo © Museum Associates/LACMA, by Robert Wedemeyer/© Carlos Almaraz Estate: 54
Photo 75650036 © trekandshoot | Dreamstime.com: 126
Photo by Luis Inzunza/Metro: 69
Photo by Rob Grabowski/Invision/AP: 217 bottom
Photofest: 177 all, 179 all, 211 left
Photograph courtesy of the City of Lakewood Historical Archive: 22 top
Planet Observer UIG/Alamy Stock Photo: Endpapers

rarrarorro/Adobe Stock: 214 bottom left
REUTERS/Mario Anzuoni: 17 bottom
Ringo Chiu/Shutterstock.com: 144
© Robert Ginder, Courtesy of Craig Krull Gallery: 23
Robert Landau/Rock and Roll Billboards: 95 top and bottom right
Robyn Beck/AFP via Getty Images: 68
© scharfsinn86/Adobe Stock: 12b, 65 bottom

Security Pacific National Bank Collection/Los Angeles Public Library: 46, 171 all

The Architectural Archives, University of Pennsylvania by the gift of Robert Venturi and Denise Scott Brown: 95 bottom left
Tierney/Adobe Stock: Endpapers, 26
treckandshoot/Shutterstock.com: 42

University of Southern California Libraries and California Historical Society: 22 bottom, 25, 49, 50, 84, 109, 128 left, 132
University of Southern California via Getty Images: 8 bottom
Unwind/Shutterstock.com: 38
Urban Rail, Robert Schwandl: 24 bottom

Veronique Lee: 13 bottom, 104

Walter Cicchetti/Shutterstock.com: 37 bottom
Walter S. Davis: 167
Woods Bagot: 6, 7, 14 all, 15 top, 16 bottom, 82, 87 all, 88, 89, 91, 92, 96 top left, 96 top right, 96 bottom left, 99 all, 100 all, 102, 111, 113, 114, 115 all, 116 all, 117, 118 all, 119, 120 all, 121, 122 all, 123, 125, 134, 147, 157 left, 188, 191, 194-208, 214 top, 216, 218-223

Xinhua/Alamy Stock Photo: 9 bottom

Youst via Getty Images: 65 top

Index

Opposite: *Evening view of The Twist, a 2020
design proposal by Woods Bagot's Los Angeles
Studio for the Sunset Strip.*

Cover Image: *Detail of Blue Bus photographed
by Dennis Keeley as part of his series:* Freeway:
A Survey of the Quotidian Landscape *(2018).*

Endpapers: *Satellite image of Los Angeles,
taken by Landsat from an altitude of 438 miles
on October 23, 2014.*

Aerial view of Los Angeles, 2018